AMERICAN ZEALOTS

Columbia Studies in Terrorism and Irregular Warfare

Columbia Studies in Terrorism and Irregular Warfare

Bruce Hoffman, Series Editor

This series seeks to fill a conspicuous gap in the burgeoning literature on terrorism, guerrilla warfare, and insurgency. The series adheres to the highest standards of scholarship and discourse and publishes books that elucidate the strategy, operations, means, motivations, and effects posed by terrorist, guerrilla, and insurgent organizations and movements. It thereby provides a solid and increasingly expanding foundation of knowledge on these subjects for students, established scholars, and informed reading audiences alike.

For a complete list of titles, see page 219.

AMERICAN ZEALOTS

Inside Right-Wing Domestic Terrorism

ARIE PERLIGER

Columbia University Press / New York

Columbia University Press
Publishers Since 1893
New York   Chichester, West Sussex
cup.columbia.edu
Copyright © 2020 Columbia University Press

Library of Congress Cataloging-in-Publication Data
Names: Perliger, Arie, author.
Title: American zealots : inside right-wing domestic terrorism / Arie Perliger.
Description: New York : Columbia University Press, 2020. | Series:
Columbia studies in terrorism and irregular warfare | Includes
bibliographical references and index.
Identifiers: LCCN 2019059874 (print) | LCCN 2019059875 (ebook) |
ISBN 9780231167109 (hardback) | ISBN 9780231167116 (paperback) |
ISBN 9780231552097 (ebook)
Subjects: LCSH: Domestic terrorism—United States. | Terrorism—Political
aspects—United States. | Right and left (Political science)—United States.
Classification: LCC HV6432 .P4725 2020 (print) | LCC HV6432 (ebook) |
DDC 363.3250973—dc23
LC record available at https://lccn.loc.gov/2019059874
LC ebook record available at https://lccn.loc.gov/2019059875

Cover design: Lisa Hamm
Cover image: Davis S. Holloway / Reportage Archive / Getty Images

Contents

Acknowledgments *vii*

1 The Challenges of Comprehending and Responding to
Domestic Terrorism 1

2 An Ideological Typology of the Violent Far Right 9

3 Historical Pillars of the Violent American Far Right 30

4 Tactics of the American Far Right 70

5 The Rise and Decline of Far-Right Violence
in the United States 90

6 Perpetrators of Far-Right Violence 113

7 Contemporary Discourse of the American Far Right 128

8 The Future of the Violent American Far Right 151

Appendix: Methodology and Statistical Results *163*
Notes *167*
Bibliography *193*
Index *207*

Acknowledgments

The journey that culminated in the publication of this book began almost a decade ago, when I started my collection of data on far-right violence in the United States. In the early 2010s, the threat from the far right seemed to many to be secondary to other, more imminent terrorist threats. Some even contended that there was no such a threat at all. Others provided important encouragement, support, and assistance for my project. Hence, it is a pleasure to have the opportunity to thank those with whom I have had the privilege to discuss the nature of the violent American far right and learn from their experience and knowledge.

The initial stages of the data collection and analysis were supported by the Combating Terrorism Center (CTC) and the Department of Social Sciences at West Point. I would like to thank Nelly Lahoud, Gabriel Kohler-Derrick, Liam Collins, Cindy Jebb, Daniel Milton, and my other colleagues at the CTC for their ongoing support, even when the CTC was under fire for allowing me to study domestic terrorism. My immense gratitude also goes to my research assistants over the years: Limor Yungman, Matthew Sweeney, Matthew Wolfenden, Matthew Fabels, and Victoria Gouveia, whose help with building the far-right attacks dataset was critical to this book.

I owe a great debt to those colleagues who spent considerable time and effort reading and commenting on drafts of this study; their critical assessments were invaluable. My gratitude goes to the anonymous reviewers who provided constructive feedback and to Eitan Alimi and Leonard

Weinberg, who reviewed earlier versions of the text. I have also benefited from my conversations with dear colleagues who provided important insights during my work on this project, including Assaf Moghadam, James Forest, Mia Bloom, Victor Asal, and Brinton Milward.

Throughout my academic career, I have enjoyed the support of two generous mentors and friends: Ami Pedahzur and Bruce Hoffman. I would like to thank them for all their support. I would not be the same scholar without them.

I would also like to thank the dedicated team at Columbia University Press. I'm grateful for their patience and support while the book was being written. Caelyn Cobb and Michael Haskell were instrumental in leading this project to publication, and Robert Fellman's meticulous editing greatly enhanced the quality of the text.

Lastly, but most importantly, I would like to thank Lilya Perliger for being an incredible and supportive partner all these years and for inspiring me to become better, both academically and as a human being.

This book is dedicated to my mom, Elsa Perliger, and my children, Naama, Yotam, and Eithan, who I hope can live in a world with less hatred.

AMERICAN ZEALOTS

1

The Challenges of Comprehending and Responding to Domestic Terrorism

Why Study the Violent Far Right?

In the morning hours of August 5, 2012, the Sikh temple in Oak Creek, Wisconsin, was crowded, filled mostly with children and young mothers engaged in preparations for the Langar, a traditional Sikh communal meal that was to be held later that day. Paramjit Kaur was one of them. While her kids were already grown (her youngest was eighteen years old), she did not want to miss the opportunity to join her community and help in the preparations. Around 10 a.m., while Paramjit was praying with her sister inside the temple, they both suddenly heard gunshots. Paramjit and her sister stood, hoping to find a safe place to hide, and a bullet hit Paramjit in the back, inflicting fatal injuries.[1]

The shooter was Wade Michael Page, a forty-year-old man from the nearby town of Cudahy, Wisconsin, who, upon his arrival at the temple, started firing at its inhabitants using his Springfield XD(M) 9-millimeter automatic pistol, which he had purchased several days earlier. During his shooting spree, he killed Paramjit and five male worshipers. When, around 10:25 a.m., the first police officers arrived and engaged with Wade, he was able to return fire and injure one of them before being shot in the stomach. He then aimed his pistol at his head and committed suicide.[2]

The subsequent investigation by law enforcement linked Page to various far-right associations, mainly from the skinhead subculture and the white power music scene.[3] His first significant exposure to the white supremacy movement occurred in 1995 at Fort Bragg, the home of the 82nd Airborne Division and the U.S. Army's Special Forces command. In the mid-1990s, it was also a hub for neo-Nazis who were engaged in recruitment efforts for the National Alliance, the most prominent American neo-Nazi organization of the 1980s and 1990s. When three paratroopers from Fort Bragg killed a black couple in Fayetteville in 1995, the army initiated an investigation of far-right associations at the military base, and Page was one of nineteen paratroopers discharged for participating in hate activities. Since the end of his military career, Page increased his involvement in hate activities, primarily as part of various skinhead associations, where he was able to combine his love of music with the promotion of white supremacy.[4] Page's life story reflects that he was not a conventional lone wolf but a representative of a broad and influential subculture that spans various facets of American society.

Just a few weeks after the attack in Oak Creek, in an unrelated incident, law enforcement discovered that several soldiers from Fort Stewart, a military base in Georgia, were part of a militia that had been involved in the killing of at least two people and was actively stockpiling weapons and explosives "to give the government back to the people."[5] It was later determined that the militia also comprised nonmilitary members who, among other things, were plotting to assassinate President Barack Obama.[6]

During the final days of summer 2012, I was closely following these events. Beyond my long-term professional interest in political violence, I was in the final stages of a two-year study that sought to decipher the current landscape of far-right violence in the United States. Whereas most of the information on these events was made public at an infuriatingly slow pace, as is usually the case when law enforcement agencies are reluctant to release information before the completion of a criminal investigation, media outlets and policy makers wasted no time in warning us about another wave of far-right violence, expressing various opinions and ideas regarding the root causes and nature of this phenomenon. Many such discussions also reflected and promulgated common misconceptions and fallacies that dominate the popular discourse about the American violent far right, such as an inability to distinguish among its various components, a lack of understanding of its ideological tenets, and the tendency to ignore that the violent far right had always been present in American society. If anything, the level of far-right violence had been rising steadily for the last two decades.

I never stopped studying the American far right, and it was clear to me that the dynamics visible during and after the 2016 elections necessitated a new effort in order to understand the dramatic rise in far-right violence, as well as its new characteristics: the rise of what I term "spontaneous violence," the further decentralization of far-right groups, and the growing tendency to focus on attacks against religious targets. Moreover, more terrorist attacks—such as the attack on the worshipers at Pittsburgh's Tree of Life synagogue on October 27, 2018, in which eleven people were killed and another six injured, and the attack on an El Paso Walmart on August 3, 2019, which led to the death of twenty-two shoppers—were perpetrated by individuals who were radicalized and exposed to white supremacy narratives online. Events such as these emphasize the growing importance of studying far-right online communities and the specific mechanisms by which they inspire militant activism. Finally, the surprising tendency of some militant far-right associations (such as some skinhead groups) to denounce the use of violence points to the fact that we need an in-depth exploration of how the penetration of far-right concepts and practices into formal, mainstream political processes affects the nature and causes of contemporary far-right violence.

This book aims to illustrate, analyze, and explain the recent developments in American far-right violence while also providing a broad historical and geographical context. Several major insights drive this approach. To begin with, like many other social and political movements, the American far right is influenced by and cooperates with foreign actors. Close relationships have evolved between American neo-Nazi and skinhead groups and similar groups in European and other Anglo-Saxon countries (such as Australia and Canada), and some U.S. white supremacy groups also provide active support to foreign nationalist militias (for example, far-right activists from U.S. organizations such as the Atomwaffen Division and Rise Above Movement joined ultranationalist militias operating in eastern Ukraine).[7] Moreover, some components of the American far right originated in other countries. The Christian Identity movement, one of the popular streams within the American far right, is a descendant of an ideological movement that emerged in nineteenth-century Britain. Similarly, the American skinhead subculture was initially "imported" from Europe and in turn was "exported" to other Anglo-Saxon countries. Thus, the examination of historical and geographical vectors is necessary in order to decipher the various dynamics that affect the nature of the American far right. Second, even when focusing on the United States, it is clear that different elements of the American far right prospered in specific regions and communities in different historical periods, which further emphasizes the importance of geographical and historical context in the exploration of the American far right.

This book also aims to bridge some specific gaps in our understanding of contemporary far-right violence. An overview of the existing literature on the American far right shows a relatively high number of historical studies on specific groups, movements, and events.[8] Less common are comprehensive and comparative studies that use the tools of the quickly expanding literature on political violence and extremism. Moreover, the relatively small number of texts that have tried to provide a panoramic analysis of the American far right are becoming dated or lack empirical data about the magnitude of the phenomenon and trends within it.[9] I strive to fill this gap by using high-resolution data to produce a comprehensive ideological, operational, and organizational analysis of the various streams of the violent American far right and by developing a multifaceted explanatory framework based on elements from social movements, far-right politics, and political violence literature.

Finally, whereas the existing literature tends to focus on the actors, whether organizations or individuals, and traditionally puts less emphasis on analyzing trends in the characteristics of the violence, this book devotes significant efforts to identifying relations between the operational universe and the ideological and organizational ones. In other words, how is violence shaped by the changing environment and characteristics of the various far-right groups?

Far-Right Violence: A Threat to the American Ethos?

On June 4, 2019, the FBI's assistant director provided a statement to the House of Representatives subcommittee on Civil Rights and Civil Liberties (part of the Oversight and Reform Committee) regarding the need to confront white supremacy. In that statement, he emphasized the rise in hate crimes and related acts of violence, as well as the impact of such incidents on communities.[10] Six weeks later, Christopher Wray, the FBI's director, stated, "I will say that a majority of the domestic terrorism cases that we've investigated are motivated by some version of what you might call white supremacist violence, but it does include other things as well." These statements are an indication that American law enforcement acknowledges the need to address the rise in the level of violence from the far right of the political spectrum. Nonetheless, in other parts of those statements, it was made clear that the FBI does not necessarily see this threat as any different from other types of terrorism. The director of the FBI stressed that "we the FBI don't investigate the ideology, no matter how repugnant. We investigate violence. And any extremist ideology, when it turns to violence, we're all over it."[11]

The question of whether the response of the criminal justice system to domestic terrorism needs to be different from its response to foreign terrorism is not the focus of this book, but it is important nonetheless to understand the unique challenges that domestic acts of terrorism represent to the social and political fabric of the American republic. Most foreign terrorism seeks to shape American policy abroad, but domestic far-right terrorism is aiming to change American political constructs and societal norms and practices fundamentally. Thus, domestic far-right terrorism does not just represent a more close and immediate physical threat for most Americans but also affects their immediate social and political environment and behavior. More important, the majority of foreign terrorism is perpetrated by non-Americans and in most cases takes place outside the continental United States; it is perceived as part of a global ideological struggle rather than something necessarily a product of American politics or society. Far-right terrorism, as will be established in chapter 3, was always part of the American political landscape, and, thus, its intensity was always an indicator of the country's stability and health of its democratic and liberal practices. Therefore, understanding the factors that lead to a rise in support for far-right ideology and violence is crucial for ensuring that American society maintains its liberal, democratic, and inclusive ethos and can address groups that aim to undermine those virtues.

Far-right terrorism also represents a substantial threat in terms of its ability to shape political discourse and related civilian norms. The effectiveness of terrorism is not determined only by its direct impact (casualties and damage to property) but also by how effective the violence is in instilling doubts in the minds of people regarding the legitimacy or utility of existing political values, norms, and practices. And while it seems reasonable to assume that foreign terrorism's ideological frameworks will have limited appeal to most Americans, domestic terrorism, which focuses on domestic policies and value-based issues at the center of the political debate in the United States, represents a more substantial threat in terms of its ability to mobilize popular support for militant practices. In this context, it is important to emphasize the relatively positive connotation that violent civilian resistance has in the American popular (historical) mindset, as such groups were crucial in the struggle for American independence, as well as in some of the subsequent conflicts in which the United States was involved. Thus, violently confronting and challenging a central rule is not automatically perceived as illegitimate, as it is in many other democracies.

The threat from domestic terrorism is also more acute as a result of the increasing political polarization within American society since the late 1990s. As the book will depict in chapters 4, 5, and 6, this polarization intensifies some core factors that are responsible for the rise in far-right violence. The growing popularity of the view that competition in the American political system is a zero-sum game, with limited space for political compromise, leads to extreme interpretations of the political reality, which in turn can inspire violent political activism. Moreover, since this polarization emphasizes the need to maximize any political victory or to avoid by all means political defeat, extremists will be inclined to use violence to further push their preferred policies or to take advantage of what they perceive as a tolerant political environment (in the case of a victory for their political camp).

The overlap between political and ethnic divisions in the United States further facilitates a rise in domestic political violence. The accumulating evidence that minorities and immigrants are more inclined to support left-wing policies intensifies interethnic and interracial tensions that lend themselves to the popularization of extreme far-right views, which are more permissive toward violence against minorities. As the analysis in chapter 5 confirms, there is a direct correlation between the increase in the population's diversity and the rise in far-right violence. And since most demographic predictions forecast an even more diverse U.S. population, identifying mechanisms that can counter such tendencies is a crucial step if Americans want to curb the rise in far-right violence.

Finally, as political polarization intensifies, political leaders naturally tend to move to the extreme of the ideological spectrum (where they believe most voters are located) and in the process absorb and disseminate provocative and more extreme ideological narratives that will help them solidify their new ideological image. Indeed, chapter 7, which explores the new discourse of the American far right, illustrates the growing overlap between far-right ideological narratives and those of what is considered the mainstream right. Tropes of conspiracy theories that in the past were the sole domain of the far right appear today in expressions of many mainstream right-wing ideological platforms and leaders, and at the same time far-right groups, seeking to appeal to larger audiences, are not hesitant to promote policies that are the bread and butter of the American right (such as positions on gun legislation and environmental policies).

Organization of the Book

The dynamic nature of the far right in the United States and its multitude of ideological and operational facets can be perplexing to many students of this ideological sphere. Hence, the first part of the book will strive to provide some clarity about the historical origins of the different streams of the violent American far-right, as well as their unique ideological and operational characteristics. Specifically, chapter 2 will introduce readers to the main concepts and theories used to describe and explain far-right politics and violence and how they can be beneficial for studying the American case. Additionally, I discuss the main ideological pillars of the American far right and their intellectual origins. Chapter 3 discusses the history of the various ideological streams of the American far right and how their organizational and operational facets evolved over time.

The second section of the book focuses on an empirical examination of contemporary violent manifestations of the American far right and attempts to illuminate the social, economic, and political facilitators of far-right violence and how, in turn, these also influence American political and social dynamics. Chapter 4 presents the comprehensive dataset of far-right violence constructed for this book and discusses the various tactics and forms of violence that are utilized by far-right groups, how they have changed over time, and how tactical choices of the groups are in many cases reflections of their ideological inclinations. Chapter 5 uses the dataset and other sources to test various theories for explaining trends in the level of far-right violence in the United States. Additionally, it discusses the main facilitators of the recent rise in far-right violence while also exploring how the characteristics of various geographical areas and demographic changes play a role in this process. Chapter 6 tries to identify the potential demographic and psychological profile of the perpetrators of far-right violence and examines the fundamental difference between "spontaneous" and "calculated" perpetrators.

The last section of the book provides a window to the contemporary dynamics and rhetoric of the American far right. Chapter 7 uses a broad range of primary sources to examine the goals, rhetoric, propaganda, ideological discourse, and future plans of American far-right groups and explain how these may shape the future evolution of this ideological sphere. Chapter 8 summarizes the main findings of the book and provides a broader overview of their implications both in terms of the challenges the United States is facing in ensuring the stability and competency of its political system and the security of its citizens; it also offers a theoretical and analytical perspective, to provide some insights about the path forward for those interested in further studying the American violent far right.

2

An Ideological Typology of
the Violent Far Right

The Jewish Community Center of Greater Kansas City is located in Overland Park, an upscale and mostly peaceful suburb of Kansas City, Missouri. On most days, the center's facilities holds various activities and celebrations of the local Jewish community; the center also hosts an array of nondenominational cultural events. In the early afternoon hours of April 13, 2014, the center was crowded with teenagers who had arrived to audition for KC Superstar, a singing competition, and by actors and crew members of a local theater group, who were preparing for a 2 p.m. performance of *To Kill a Mockingbird*. Around 1 p.m., sounds of gunfire reverberated in the center's parking lot. A gunman tried to shoot at two bystanders, who luckily were able to escape before getting injured, one by foot and the other in his car. Subsequently, the shooter shifted his attention to a car parking nearby, driven by Dr. William Corporon, who was bringing his fourteen-year-old grandson, Reat Griffin Underwood, to audition for the KC Superstar competition. Dr. Corporon was shot in the head and died shortly afterward. His grandson was also wounded and was rushed to a local hospital, where he died a few hours later.[1]

After shooting several rounds at the center's building and the horrified crowd, the gunman returned to his car and drove to the parking lot of the Jewish retirement community of Village Shalom, located less than a mile from the Jewish community center. He resumed his attack by shooting at several people who were in the parking lot, killing Terri LaManno, an occupational therapist who had just arrived for her weekly visit with her mother.

The massive manhunt by local police relied on a description of the gun-man's car, which had been provided by witnesses. By 3 p.m. that day, two police officers identified the shooter's car near a local elementary school and were able to detain the gunman without him causing additional harm.

The name of the gunman was Frazier Glenn Miller Jr., a seventy-four-year-old resident of Aurora, Missouri, and a figure familiar to law enforce-ment, given the various leadership roles that he had assumed within the white supremacy movement in North Carolina and Missouri for more than thirty years. The recent history of the violent American far right is exemplified by Miller's life story, which illustrates some of its dominant characteristics: its organizational heterogeneity and its tendency for opera-tional and ideological fragmentation.

Miller joined the military in the late 1950s and retired in 1979 as a mas-ter sergeant. During those years, the U.S. military struggled tremendously to control the presence and proliferation of white supremacist views and activities within its ranks. Thus it is not surprising that Miller was forced to retire after it was exposed that he was distributing racist texts and publica-tions. Upon retirement, he joined a neo-Nazi group, the National Socialist Party of America, which was mainly known for its involvement in the 1979 Greensboro Massacre, where marchers from the Communist Workers Party were attacked and killed by neo-Nazi activists in Greensboro, North Carolina.[2]

While there are no indications that Miller was involved directly in the execution or planning of the Greensboro Massacre, he did receive death threats in the following months from some left-wing activists. This clearly didn't deter him from deepening his involvement in the white supremacy movement. In the late 1980s, he established the Carolina Knights of the Ku Klux Klan.[3] Even though the name of the group associated it with the traditional KKK, Miller preferred to adopt practices that characterized two other segments of the American far right. First, he promoted the group's embrace of military practices and activities, styling them on the American Nazi Party's parades and ceremonies. Moreover, in a fashion that usually characterizes American neo-Nazi groups, he preferred that his followers wear uniforms, rather than the KKK's traditional white robes. Second, as with many of the militia groups of that time, he aspired to engage in military training so the organization could eventually establish a "free territory." Specifically, he aspired to establish a "Carolina Free State" in areas of North and South Carolina.[4] In these ways, his organization reflected the growing ideological and operational overlap between the traditional KKK, neo-Nazi groups, and militia movement.

By the mid-1980s Miller had changed the name of his organization to the White Patriot Party, emulating similar initiatives by other leaders of the far right such as Thomas Metzger and David Duke, who were trying to shape a "cleaner" and more sophisticated image for the white supremacy movement by adopting a civil rights rhetoric focused on what they perceived as a violation of the rights of white people. Miller followed suit and declared that his party would aim to achieve the "unification of white people" and would act peacefully unless the federal government infringed on the rights of white people.[5] But Miller didn't wait, and between 1986 and 1987 he faced a series of investigations related to his militant activities, which included the stockpiling of military weapons and technology (such as hand grenades, C-4 explosives, and automatic guns), organizing military training drills for his supporters, and promoting actual attacks. For example, in a letter to his supporters that was tracked by the FBI in 1987, Miller ordered his followers to kill "our enemies" and introduced a point system for different targets. African Americans counted for 1 point, "White race traitors" and Jews counted for 10 points, judges for 50 points, and Morris Seligman Dees (a known civil rights activist and one of the founders of the Southern Poverty Law Center) for 888 points. In 1987, Miller pleaded guilty to illegal use of weapons and mailing of a threat and received a five-year prison sentence; he was released after three years.[6]

After his release from prison, Miller shifted his focus, again like many of his generation's leaders, to online propaganda. And while he was never as well known as Thomas Metzger, the founder of Stormfront, the most popular far-right website, he was still able to draw traffic to his website and his commentaries. Eventually, in 2014, Miller returned to his violent practices. When he was caught after his shooting spree, he left no doubt about his motives, shouting "Heil Hitler" and asking the arresting officers, "How many fucking Jews did I kill?"[7] The answer is zero—none of Miller's victims on April 13 was Jewish. Even in his last act, Miller illustrated one of the more common features of far-right violence in the United States: its amateurish, unplanned, and sloppy nature, especially in comparison to similar manifestations of political violence in other parts of the world.

Miller's life story reflects several important features of the American far right. First, it is inspired by multiple distinct ideological traditions. Even though the KKK, neo-Nazis, skinheads, and Christian Identity groups all tend to promote ideas of white supremacy, it is still possible to identify some differences in their logic and ideological reasoning. For example, the neo-Nazis base their support for racial segregation on pseudoscientific ideas and believe in social engineering, while Christian Identity's followers rationalize such views via their interpretations of religious texts. Miller, like other far-right leaders, was perpetually attempting to identify which of these movements' rationalizations resonated best with potential followers. Second, the American far right is extremely fragmented: numerous organizational splits and merges have characterized the far-right landscape over the past few decades. Many existing groups experienced multiple internal divisions or merged into new or other veteran groups. In many cases, groups that completely changed their characteristics and ideological tendencies maintain their original names. These dynamics present significant challenges for those interested in mapping the various organizational platforms comprising the American far right. Finally, the different types of American far-right groups tend to be operationally distinct. This is reflected in their target selection, tactics, and framing of their political rivals. For example, skinheads almost never attack law enforcement. Similarly, while leaders of militia groups never attempt to engage in formal politics, as a result of their fundamental delegitimization of the federal government, Miller's stint in formal politics, as a candidate for Congress in Missouri's seventh district in the mid-1980s, is a reflection of a wider trend among leaders of the KKK to compete for political offices.[8]

Miller's complex backstory illustrates that, before engaging with a review of the American far right, some introductory discussion is necessary. This chapter will present the main concepts and theories that dominate the current academic discourse about far-right politics and violence and unpack the major categories into which violent far-right actors in the United States typically fall.

Challenges in Studying Far-Right Politics and Activism

The study of far-right politics and activism presents a number of challenges. Some are an extension of the traditional challenges of studying

social or political phenomena; others stem more from the specific characteristics of far-right politics. To begin with, as with many other political
phenomena (for example, terrorism, political participation, radicalization),
the discourse on the far right seems to suffer from inconsistent and fluid
terminology. A quick overview of the literature shows that different terms
have been employed to describe political associations on the far right of the
political spectrum, such as "far right," "extreme right," "right-wing populism," and "radical right."[9] This trend reflects the inclination of different
scholars to emphasize distinct elements of this political realm. In this book,
I will use the terms "far right" and "right wing." The first term designates
groups and individuals whose ideology is located at the extremities of the
ideological spectrum and who seek substantial changes in the sociopolitical order, while right-wing groups are parties and movements placed to the
right of the center of the ideological spectrum but not necessary at its edge.
It should be noted that both categories can manifest violence, as will be
further illustrated.

A related controversy is associated with the similarities and gaps
between far-right ideology and fascism. While some argue for the need for
conceptual distinction, others are more disposed to see a significant overlap, considering fascism to be a specific form of government based on far-
right principles.[10] The dispute reflects both the tremendous influence that
the rise of fascism in the early twentieth century and its consequences still
exerts on the study of extreme political ideologies and a larger debate
about what the core components of far-right ideology and practices are.

The particularities of different political and cultural settings also present a challenge for those aspiring to promote a universal conceptualization of far-right politics. For example, in the Israeli political system, the
"far right" designation is almost exclusively used to describe a political
ideology that aims to preserve Israel's control over the West Bank and the
promotion of exclusionary policies that emphasize the Jewishness of the
state.[11] Moreover, while in both Israel and the United States numerous far-
right groups employ distinctive interpretations of holy texts for their ideological justification, in Europe and Latin America the role of religion is
more marginal within the far-right scene.[12] In some places (for example,
most European countries), far-right parties take an active part in the formal political system and political institutions, while in other countries such
cases are rare (the United States). This has ideological and operational

ramifications and further illustrates how the specifics of political settings can impede attempts to provide a universally accurate conceptualization of far-right politics and ideology.

Finally, the study of the far right presents moral and ethical challenges. Traditionally, the study of extreme political groups was associated with scholars' desire to understand the risks that such groups present to the stability and durability of liberal democracies and the necessity to counter their proliferation. Consequently, many of the frameworks that were developed to understand the ideological constructs of far-right groups and the factors that help them mobilize support were embedded in a paradigm that inherently posits them in a direct contradiction to liberal democratic principles and practices. While acknowledging the challenges that the far right presents to the sustainability of liberal democracy, I will also try to identify cases in which the far right presents an *extension* of some inherent features of democratic structures and show how contemporary far-right groups adapt to exploit democratic practices and modern liberal discourse.

Conceptualizing Far-Right Ideology

Two conceptual approaches can explain what distinguishes far-right ideology from other doctrines. The first, what I call a minimalist approach, looks for the maximum number of elements that have characterized all manifestations of far-right's political activism. The other, which I term the inclusive approach, uses the "most similar system design," seeking the greatest number of possible similarities among at least some far-right associations.[13]

When adopting the first approach, we can identify at least two major elements that appear in all cases of far-right activism and ideology: extreme versions of nationalism and nativist sentiments. And while these concepts may seem to be closely related, they actually refer to a distinct set of political views and behaviors. Nationalism is usually understood as the association between ethnic, cultural, and/or linguistic identity and political expression, that is, the desire for promoting or preserving a convergence of a cultural framework with a political entity.[14] In the ideological streams that are part of the far right, nationalism takes an extreme form of full convergence between a single polity or territory and a single ethnic, religious, or cultural group.[15] To reach this full convergence, far-right ideologists will usually advocate for maximizing internal homogenization of society (the aspiration that all residents of the polity will share the same national origin and ethnic characteristics) and external exclusiveness, which reflects the aspiration that all individuals belonging to a specific national or ethnic group will reside in the "homeland."[16]

Nativism represents a wider implementation of internal homogenization by not just rejecting the incorporation into the nation of those embodying different ethnic and national backgrounds but also opposing various types of foreign influence. Nativist arguments assert that the integration of foreign customs, norms, practices, and cultural expressions threaten the identity and cohesiveness of the nation and thus its resiliency and durability.[17] The concept of nativism explains why in many cases the activities of far-right groups oppose not only foreigners but also those citizens who promote what are perceived as non-native norms, practices, or values. Therefore, by expanding the concept of internal homogenization as it is manifested in the concept of nativism, promoters of far-right ideology establish comfortable ground—and moral justification—for actions against the "nation's enemies from within."[18]

The maximalist approach for drawing the boundaries of the far right seems to be partly a result of an effort to reduce the extent of gray areas between the mainstream right and the far right. Hence, it integrates additional ideological elements that, while present in the platform and discourse of many far-right groups or parties, are not consistent across the far-right landscape, and the emphasis they receive tends to fluctuate. These ideological elements are both related to attempts to enhance the separation and qualitative differences between in-groups and out-groups, as well as to attitudes toward the state and society.

Xenophobia, racism, and exclusionism are the most prominent practices that fall under this category. Xenophobia involves behaviors and sentiments derived from fear, hate, and hostility toward groups perceived as alien or distinct, including people with alternative sexual preferences, styles of living, and behavior.[19] Racism, which in popular discourse became a catchall term for any discrimination based on collective attributes, refers to similar sentiments as xenophobia but on racial grounds, such as the belief in the national and moral significance of natural and hereditary differences across races and the conviction that certain races are superior to others.[20] Finally, exclusionism is the practical manifestation of these sentiments in various spheres of public life. For example, outsiders are prohibited from accessing specific domains of the social, economic, and political arena, such as the labor market, educational system, and residential areas.[21]

The far right also engages with ideas that at their core strive to shape the political and social climate and, more broadly, the relationships between the state and its citizens. A common perception is that liberal/left-wing and conservative worldviews are different in their time orientation. While liberal worldviews are progressively oriented and see political and cultural changes as a positive opportunity for societal development that can benefit both the individual and his community, conservative perspectives see important qualities in preserving the status quo and ensuring the sustainability of social and normative principles that are (perceived as) part of the collective's identity. Thus, conservatives are usually more inclined to cooperate with and support social institutions that have a vested interest in preserving social and normative practices (for example, religious organizations and pro-life movements).[22] The far right usually manifests more radical versions of such tendencies. Many far-right groups justify their political vision through the aspiration to restore or preserve values and practices that are part of the idealized historical heritage of the nation or ethnic community.[23] In many cases, these past-oriented perspectives help formulate a nostalgic and romantic ideological aura, and this makes these groups attractive to many who wish to restore the halcyon days of a clear hierarchy of values and norms.[24] While this strong commitment to traditional values is an important distinction between the far right and other political streams, it should be noted that the new waves of far-right groups, especially those emerging since the 1980s, do not always adhere to traditional values or tend to emphasize them.

An additional trend among many far-right groups is the rejection of core aspects of liberal democracy and related concepts of freedom. There are both intellectual and practical reasons for this tendency. In terms of realpolitik, the liberal-democratic legalistic framework's emphasis on civil and human rights, protection of minorities, and the overall promotion of universal practices presents inherent difficulties for the advancement of policies compatible with far-right ideology.[25] From a strictly intellectual perspective, the fundamental contradictions between core nationalist ideas such as internal homogenization and nativism and the liberal-democratic school of thought and value system compel far-right groups to adopt an "antisystem" stance and revisionist views of the democratic system.

There are numerous definitions and conceptual frameworks for understanding the ideological paradigm of far-right groups. As indicated by the political scientist Cas Mudde, by the mid-1990s no fewer than twenty-eight different definitions were introduced, which included close to sixty different components. This terminological fluidity continues to characterize the field.[26] For example, it is not difficult to identify the recent growing prominence of concepts such as "populism" and "alt-right" both in the academic and nonacademic analysis of the far-right scene. However, in many cases, these new terms present more a reflection of generational changes within the community that study the far-right rather than in the features of the phenomena. In other words, while some of the ideological elements are sometimes termed differently or being constructed via a different methodological or theoretical construction, they still represent in the majority of cases the core ideological foundations of far-right politics. Therefore, they will be used in this study to sketch the boundaries of the American far right. At the same time, attention will also be given to more recent and specialized characteristics (such as antifederalism) or features that are referring to practices of mobilization (for example, populism), internal structure, and organizational culture (for example, authoritarianism).

A Typology of the American Far Right

The American far right was associated for many years with the militant activism of the Ku Klux Klan. While the KKK in its modern form is still active, since the mid-1960s other varieties of ideological groups have begun to populate the American far-right universe. Among these are militias, Christian Identity groups, skinheads, and neo-Nazis. From an analytical perspective, this evolution has had two major consequences. First, the American far right has become more vibrant and more ideologically and structurally diverse than ever before. Second, the boundaries of the American far right have grown less distinct, with many of the new groups occasionally taking inspiration from ideas and practices originating from outside conventional far-right discourse. Both these outcomes reflect the need to develop an effective typology in order to portray a more accurate and nuanced picture of the American far right and to understand its ideological development.

A useful analytical instrument for the construction of such a typology is the classification proposed originally by John McCarty and Mayer Zald to differentiate between a social movement, a social movement organization, and a social movement industry.[27] A *social movement* is defined as a set of opinions and beliefs of a segment of the population and represents preferences for changing some aspects of social or political constructions or policies; a *social movement organization* is the formal organizational manifestation of the social movement. The *social movement industry* is a collection of social movement organizations that have as their goal the fulfillment of the broadest preferences of the social movements. To illustrate, the skinhead subculture in the United States can be seen as a social movement because it includes a collective of individuals who share a set of social norms and behavioral practices while trying to promote compatible political policies via multiple organizations, such as the Hammerskin Nations and Keystone United. The collection of skinhead organizations can be described as a social movement industry.

An examination of the movements and organizations that are located at the right side of the American political spectrum identifies four major social movement industries that seem to meet the maximalist definition of far right and also manifest violent tendencies. These are the white supremacy, antigovernment, fundamentalist, and pro-life social movement industries. These all include organizations that utilize violent practices to promote or force nativist and extreme nationalist ideas. Naturally, many of them also include organizations that embrace various xenophobic, segregationist, racist, and antidemocratic inclinations.

White Supremacy

The groups that are part of the white supremacy social movement industry are interested in preserving or restoring what they perceive as the natural racial or ethnic hierarchy by enforcing social and political superiority over minority groups such as African Americans, Jews, and members of various immigrant communities. They aim to promote policies, norms, and social practices that sustain or elevate the privileges enjoyed by whites. Ideas of nativism, internal homogeneity, racism, exclusionism, and xenophobia are highly visible in the ideological discourse of these groups.[28] While other popular elements of far-right ideology, such as traditional values and anti-democratic dispositions, are also occasionally exhibited by some white supremacy associations, they are clearly secondary to their core ideological pillars of nativism and racism. The declared goal of the first KKK convention, which was held in 1867 in Nashville, Tennessee, reflects clearly the focus on racial superiority: "To maintain the supremacy of the White Race in the Republic."[29] Indeed, since the mid-nineteenth century, the KKK used its political influence and violent tactics to obstruct policies that would increase integration between white and nonwhite communities, provide nonwhite ethnic/racial groups more access to material and political capital, and promote greater cultural and demographic diversity.[30]

Since the mid-twentieth century, many white supremacy groups that were influenced by the emergence of Nazism and similar fascist movements in Europe have adopted Nazi symbols, rhetoric, and practices to promote anti-Semitic and nativist ideas and exclusionism.[31] Therefore, conforming to the conventions of National Socialism, it was not uncommon to see the leaders of neo-Nazi groups presenting programs for the promotion of enforced segregation (in the case of African Americans), the elimination of inferior races (for example, Jews), or for dividing the United States' territory into racially homogeneous areas.[32] All these proposals were and remain in the spirit of preserving the purity and supreme status of the white race, which was considered paramount for the ongoing survival and flourishing of the Aryan people.

The rise of younger and more educated leadership within the white supremacy movement in the 1970s and the 1980s led to some adaptation of the movement's rhetoric. David Duke, at that time one of the emerging leaders of the KKK, described this transition as a move from the "cow pastures" to the "hotel meeting rooms."[33] This phrase described the transition from a language focusing on degrading other ethnic or religious groups to a protectionist language focusing on the need to protect the civil rights and heritage of the white people while also asserting that segregation and exclusionist policies will benefit nonwhite groups as well. An excerpt from a 1983 article authored by Duke further conveys the spirit of the new rhetorical paradigm:

> Immigration along with non-white birthrates will make white people a minority totally vulnerable to the political, social, and economic will of blacks, Mexicans, Puerto Ricans, and Orientals. A social upheaval is now beginning to occur that will be the funeral dirge of the America we love. I shudder to contemplate the future under nonwhite occupation; rapes, murders, robberies multiplied a hundred fold, illiteracy such as in Haiti, medicine such as in Mexico, and tyranny such as in Togoland.[34]

In the early 1980s, the skinheads started to populate the white supremacy arena as well, infusing new cultural and social practices. The skinhead subculture, which originated in the United Kingdom and "immigrated" to the United States in the mid-1980s, absorbed traditional neo-Nazi elements and merged them with practices that emphasized antisocial and taboo-breaking behaviors inspired by a strong sense of economic and cultural marginalization.[35] Via a strong focus on the development of white power music, intensive use of National Socialist sentiments, and violent attitudes toward ethnic and religious minorities and people with alternative lifestyles and political ideas (including communists and libertarians), the American manifestations of the skinheads aspired to represent the interests of the youth of the Aryan American working class.[36]

To conclude, the traditional and more recent manifestations of the American white supremacy movement adopted rhetorical and ideological notions of nativism, support for ethnic/religious internal homogeneity, and racist and exclusionary tendencies. It also should be noted that in recent years white supremacy groups have intensified their attempts to link these sentiments to contemporary political discourse; thus they tend to be vocal in their opposition to multiculturalism, illegal immigration, interracial marriage, black-on-white crime, Jewish (and other ethnic) influences in society, and affirmative action. Their attempt to maintain their relevancy and to exploit divisive issues at the center of contemporary political discourse is illustrated effectively by the following statement from the Brotherhood of the Klan website from the mid-2000s: "Are you prepared to FIGHT AGAINST ILLEGAL IMMIGRATION? The time for ACTION is NOW! Our Government won't stop them so we will. It's time to declare war on these illegal Mexicans. The racial war is among us. Our blissful ignorance is over. It is time to fight."[37]

Antigovernment

Antigovernment sentiments have been present in American society since the establishment of the Republic, and they involve diverse movements and ideological associations promoting antitaxation, gun rights, survivalist practices, and libertarian ideas.[38] Yet most scholars agree that the modern antigovernment movement, usually designated as the militia or patriot movement, emerged in the early 1990s as a result of a combination of economic conditions (primarily the "farms crisis" of the 1980s) and a response to cultural changes in American society such as the growing political influence of minority groups and attempts to implement gun control and environmental legislation.[39]

Scholars also tend to point out two waves of militia activity, the first from 1993 until the early 2000s and the second from 2006 onward. However, from an ideological perspective, both waves promote similar ideas, which originate from the conviction that it is crucial to counter the increasing powers of the federal government and its tendency to expand into various spheres of the civilian arena.[40] More specifically, militia groups are concerned with three major issues: constitutional rights, the growing influence of foreigners in U.S. policy, and maintaining the tradition of civic activism.

Militia organizations usually justify their focus on the protection of constitutional rights by pointing out what they perceive as the ongoing intentional attempts of the federal government to erode these rights. Their concern is with policies and legislation that they feel (1) limit civil liberties, especially in the context of individuals who are detained or under investigation, concerns that intensified following the legislation of the PATRIOT Act and similar antiterrorism bills; (2) empower federal law enforcement in their ability to monitor and conduct searches in people's possession and property; (3) attempt to limit or increase the monitoring of gun ownership; (4) promoting restrictive policies related to land ownership; and (5) enhance environmental regulation.[41] The Militia of Montana's manual exemplifies these sentiments: "False is the idea of utility . . . that would take fire from men because it burns and water because one may drown in it; that has no remedy for evils except destruction (of liberty). The laws that forbid the carrying of arms are laws of such nature. They disarm only those who are neither inclined nor determined to commit crimes." Another quote, from a Missouri Militia member, reflects the fear of government tyranny: "One of the things that people really fear from the government is the idea that the government can ruin your life; totally destroy your life . . . split your family up, do the whole thing and walk off like you're a discarded banana peel, and with a ho-hum attitude."[42]

Many militia groups also adhere to the idea that the U.S. government, including its fundamental institutions, were already or were in the process of being hijacked by foreign powers looking to promote a "New World Order." According to popular narratives among militia members, the transition to the New World Order has already begun, as in recent years there has been a transfer of powers from local to federal institutions (in many cases undermining local law enforcement). The weakening of local law enforcement, combined with the merger of American federal forces with some kind of a multi-/international peacekeeping force, will lead eventually to the loss of American sovereignty and independence (the New World Order).[43] More specifically, the deployment of foreign forces on U.S. soil will be rationalized by pointing out the moral collapse of American society and the growing incompetence of the American political system and law enforcement. The last stage will include the complete merging of the United States into a transnational entity (a world government).[44] Most militia groups believe that the only way to thwart these upcoming developments is by armed resistance, which explains their engagement in military training. The militia members' concerns about the possible realization of the New World Order also explain their opposition to what they see as the increasing oppression of local institutions and to the growing influence of international NGOs on American politics and policies (such as the United Nations or the International Monetary Fund).[45] This hostility in some cases also serves as a breeding ground for nativist sentiments and practices and occasionally also facilitates cooperation between militias and racist/ white supremacy elements.

Finally, the militias' rhetoric exploits traditional American sentiments, which tend to treasure the role of militias and paramilitarism in American history. Thus, militia members in many cases will legitimize their military training and opposition to the government by drawing similarities to the struggle of similar groups during the American Revolution and Civil War.[46] A more extreme manifestation of this line of thinking seems to facilitate the emergence of the latest ideological extension of the antigovernment social movement industry, the Sovereign Citizens.

While the origins of the Sovereign Citizens are not completely clear, they can be traced to the late 1970s and early 1980s, which were characterized by the emergence of several militant antitaxation groups. At some point, various figures within the antitaxation movement, which were also inspired by the emergence of New World Order conspiracy theories, Y2K theories, and general animosity toward the government, started to develop a more comprehensive ideological platform that rejected the very concept of a "citizen of the United States."

Sovereign Citizens reject the legitimacy of the federal government and, in some cases, also state authorities to regulate any aspect of civilian life. This view stems from their conviction that the Founding Fathers never intended that there would be a legitimate notion of a "citizen of the United States." Hence, while all people who live in the Union should be considered a "citizen of a state in the Union," any later attempts to construct a new concept of citizenship (such as the Fourteenth Amendment) are in contrast with the true intentions of the Founding Fathers and their vision regarding the relationships between Americans and the political authorities.[47] These sentiments explain why some Sovereign Citizens believe that local authorities have the right to reject any act of Congress and to oppose federal regulations, including, if necessary, by the use of force.

The Sovereign Citizens' intense animosity toward the federal government was also facilitated by the adoption of additional narratives that further emphasized the instrumental nature of the relationships between the federal government and the American people. For example, many Sovereign Citizens assert that at some point the original legal system that was constructed by the Founding Fathers ("common law") was secretly substituted by "Admiralty Law" or "Commercial Laws."[48] This new set of laws is supposedly more restrictive and intrusive and managed by powerful forces within the government interested in exploiting the American people via various governmental mechanisms, including the transformation of the U.S. government to a commercial corporation.

Eventually, the popular belief among Sovereign Citizens about the transformation of the U.S. government into some kind of for-profit corporation also led to the popularization of the concepts of "straw man" and "redemption." Many members of the Sovereign Citizens believe that subversive actors within the government were behind the decision to abandon the gold standard in 1933. Since this decision led the United States to bankruptcy, the solution, so this argument goes, was the construction of a complex system in which American foreign debt is paid for using American citizens as collateral.[49] Thus, Americans' birth certificates and driving licenses are tools for creating a corporate shell (the "straw man") in which American money is being invested. Many sovereign citizens have tried over the years via the extensive filing of financial and legal paperwork ("redemption") to manipulate and expose this system and to gain access to this supposed sum of money, which is being invested into their identical (by name) corporate shell.[50]

Fundamentalist White Supremacy

The academic literature on fundamentalism usually refers to ideological doctrines that promote practices based on literal interpretations of religious texts. Thus, in most cases, the concept has been used to describe militant religious groups that exercise coercive means in order to promote their interpretations of their sacred texts and related norms and way of life.[51] While some groups within the white supremacy social movement industry associate nativist and xenophobic sentiments with religious narratives, their religious dimensions are secondary or just one element of a wider ideological discourse. In contrast, the Christian Identity movement, which is an extension of the British Israelite religious movement that emerged in the United Kingdom in the nineteenth century, uses exclusively distinctive interpretations of religious texts to advocate ideas of nativism, exclusionism, and Aryan superiority.[52] The various groups that make up the movement use spurious religious heritage, symbols, rituals, and norms to popularize their beliefs and ideology. They also use such mechanisms to formulate a moral justification for activism against groups, communities, and individuals perceived as a threat.[53]

Most Christian Identity groups share several prominent ideas, although in some cases they take different forms. The first is a unique interpretation of the holy texts, especially the Old Testament, which argues that in contrast to the accepted convention, Aryans are the true chosen people, descendants of the Hebrew (or Israelite) people, and not those who identify as Jews. Thus Aryans enjoy superior qualities and attributes and should lead the nations of man.[54] Relatedly, identity narratives also assert that a racial war between the white Anglo-Saxon nations and various non-Anglo-Saxon ethnic groups such as the "Children of Satan" (Jews) and "mud-people" (nonwhites) is imminent and that this conflict reflects the ongoing struggle between the forces of light and forces of evil as described in various religious texts.[55] The war will end with the restoration of the dominance of the Aryan people. To support such narratives, many identity leaders tend to associate current events with the intensification of this "war." In the past, for example, Identity leaders referred to the Cold War and the Israeli-Palestinian conflict as indicators or signs of the upcoming collapse of the existing international order and the approach of a full-scale apocalyptic war.[56]

Finally, from its earliest stages the identity movement manifested extreme anti-Semitism. Several factors may explain this tendency. First, in the Identity school of thought, adherents perceive Jews as the descendants of Eve and the Serpent, while Aryans are the descendants of Adam and Eve. Other races are usually designated as pre-Adamic (thus existing before God created Adam, the first white man, and Eve). Relying on this interpretation, identity thinkers oppose race mixing, since in their view the sexual relationship between Eve and the serpent was the original sin that led to the expulsion of the white man from the Garden of Eden.[57] The narrative identifies Cain, the first murderer, as the son of Satan and the first Jew. Second, in the eyes of many Identity leaders, the Jews represent a threat because they compete for the title of the chosen people. Most identity narratives solve this dispute by indicating that while the Aryans are descendents of the ten tribes of the Kingdom of Israel, the Jews are the descendants of Judea, which according to Identity thinking was the least advanced of the Hebrew tribes.[58] Finally, the Identity movement perceives Jews as the promoters of social deficiencies such as socialism and abortion.

Thus, these groups consider Jews as an imminent threat to the morality of white people, as illustrated, for example, in the following argument of an Identity thinker:

> The wicked of the earth, the enemies of Christ, have grown strong and arrogant in our land. They have infiltrated our schools, news media, churches and government in their attempts to keep you in ignorance of your identity as Israelites. They are attempting to steal your heritage. The heritage their father Esau despised and sold; that they might conquer America and take rule over the whole earth, and destroy, if they can, the very name of Christ, Christians and Christianity. But God Almighty has decreed the destruction of those who hate Jesus Christ and His True Israel People [Obadiah 18].[59]

Antiabortion Violence

One of the ideological pillars of the far right is the yearning to restore or preserve values and practices that are part of the idealized historical heritage of the nation.[60] Some far-right groups are even willing to use violent tactics to express their desire to preserve specific cultural and normative practices. A case in point is groups and individuals who engage in violence to undermine what they consider the "abortion industry." Since pro-life violence is an extension of a broader spectrum of far-right violence, it is not surprising that there is evidence of overlap in membership between white supremacy groups and pro-life organizations.[61] Moreover, occasionally operational cooperation between pro-life organizations and neo-Nazi groups will occur, as the latter see abortions as an attack against the growth of the white race.[62]

Since the late 1970s, Americans have witnessed an increase in the number of violent attacks against abortion clinics and their personnel. Most of these violent acts were motivated by religious and fundamentalist sentiments. This is not a surprising trend when considering that the pro-life movement has been dominated by religious leaders and associations and that religious sentiments have been a significant, even dominant, part of its ideological construction. For example, the United States Catholic

Conference invested significant efforts in thwarting the growing impact of the *Roe v. Wade* Supreme Court decision and in 1974 sent four cardinals to Washington, D.C., to convince Congress to legislate a national prohibition on abortion.[63] At the same time, other associations with orthodox orientations, such as the Life Amendment Political Action Committee, the Committee for the Survival of a Free Congress, and the Committee for Pro-Life Affairs, promoted a pro-life agenda via engagement in electoral processes, usually by focusing on thwarting the election to public office of pro-choice candidates.[64]

Toward the late 1970s, some pro-life leaders began to justify the pro-life agenda by utilizing concepts drawn from Manichean dualism, which were familiar from the ideological rhetoric of the Identity movement. Simply put, they portrayed the pro-life struggle in apocalyptic and absolutistic terms.[65] During 1979, for example, two well-known speakers of the evangelical movement at that time, Dr. C. Everett Koop and Francis Schaeffer, consistently claimed during a speaking tour that *Roe v. Wade* "symbolize[d] the triumph of evil over good."[66] The operational implications of such rhetoric were not late to come. On February 15, 1979, twenty-one-year-old Peter Burkin ignited a gasoline can in a nonprofit abortion clinic in Hempstead, New York. In the following years, similar attacks were perpetrated, mostly by individuals affiliated with the Army of God (AOG), the organization that would become the public face of the violent campaign against abortion clinics and their staff during the 1980s and 1990s.

The Army of God's organizational manual, which was uncovered in 1993 in the backyard of one of its activists, Shelley Shannon, provides a glimpse into the ideological principles of pro-life violence. It includes the portrayal of the supporters of the right to choose as representatives of the devil and evil and argues that the pro-life struggle is part of an ongoing war between Satan and God's children. To justify such views, and to eliminate any nuance, the manual describes the abortion "industry" as a mechanism for the methodical killing of innocent and pure human beings, which practically causes a "new Holocaust." Moreover, since every human being is created in the image of God, it is by definition a sin to end any human being's life before it is able to "enjoy love and life of this planet."[67]

The manual also discusses the individuals who participate in the pro-life struggle and identifies them as members of a clandestine avant-garde, regarded as a remnant, a small minority among the communities of believers. The reason for this minority status is that the fragmentation of the Christian religious establishment prevents any likelihood of unity behind the cause of preventing abortion. Finally, the manual also provides specific rationalizations for the use of violence: the need to demolish the murder weapons, that is, destroying the structures within which abortions are being committed; disarming the individuals who are participating in the crime of abortion by inflicting severe physical harm on them; to deter those who continue to engage in and be part of the abortion industry by advocating the view that "the only rational way to respond to the knowledge of an imminent and brutal murder is direct action," thus defining the violence as an act of rescue or defensive action, not a murder; and to ignite the public discourse regarding the immorality of abortion. As explained in the Army of God manual: "It is easy at this time for the media as a whole to hold the position that they do: they can comfortably be for death. Not so when the honorable citizens of any given community begin to rise up in righteous indignation and destroy these miniature Dachaus. All of a sudden, apathy is gone. The average reporter says to himself, 'Wow! Maybe there are a few people that really believe all this jargon about abortion being murder.'"[68]

To conclude, pro-life violence is driven by several ideological building blocks that are enhanced by religiously based convictions, that is, that fetuses are human beings created in God's image, as such they should be accorded the rights of humans from the moment of conception, and thus any violent acts to end their lives are immoral and should be prevented. Prevention includes damaging the physical tools of the crime as well as shaping a moral and political environment that will convince people of the immorality of the abortion industry and deter people from becoming part of it.

Implications of Ideological Diversification

Recognizing the ideological nuances within the American far right is not just important from a conceptual and theoretical perspective (since ideological distinction may allude to the possibility that different theoretical constructs may be applicable for explaining the behavior of the different groups) but also from a practical policy perspective. Ideological differences were translated in many cases to distinct organizational structures and modi operandi. Thus, countering the violence of the far right cannot be successful without understanding how ideological tendencies are associated with operational features such as recruitment methods, propaganda, organizational structure, and target selection.

While there is much similarity in the policies promoted by the different far-right groups, they originated from distinct ideological traditions and rationales. Moreover, while some of the far-right groups are merely extensions of ideological movements that emerged initially in other Western countries (for example, neo-Nazism, skinheads, Christian Identity) and at some point in time were imported to the United States, some of the groups are a product of the specific political and social dynamics of the American polity (for example, KKK, "patriot" militias). Both types of groups cannot be understood without diving into the details of the evolution of American society and the political system and historical developments that facilitate the emergence or import of far-right ideologies. The next chapter will delve into the multiple histories of the American far right.

3

Historical Pillars of
the Violent American Far Right

The Permanent Presence of the Far Right
in American History

Rutledge M. Dennis, one of the most important sociologists to study race relations in America, stated that "in order to understand the dynamics and the impact of racism, we must view it as a faith—and, for the American society, a permanent belief system rather than a transient apparition. Its longevity has been tried and tested. It now occupies a place in the American value pantheon alongside such concepts as democracy and liberty."[1] This is a controversial assertion, even offensive for some Americans, since it argues that sentiments of hatred toward out-groups—and the need to exercise these sentiments in the public sphere—are a fundamental aspect of American political culture.

While this book does not engage directly with Dennis's contention, the historical evolution of the American far right, starting with the quick emergence of the Know-Nothing Party in the middle of the nineteenth century, reflects that nativism, exclusionism, and bias toward "others" were part of the American political landscape from early on. This chapter will discuss how we arrived at the current diverse and fragmented landscape of the American far right and how various historical, political, and societal events shaped the far right's ideology and activities. Such an overview will allow us also to gain a better comprehension of the current challenges that the far right presents and to contextualize more effectively many of its current trends.

The First Seeds of American Nativism: The Know-Nothing Party

In the mid-1850s, the American political system was becoming increasingly polarized with regard to several issues that had a direct effect on the lives of most Americans at that time. Long-standing divisions regarding the extent of the states' powers and rights vis-à-vis the federal government were exacerbated further by growing tensions about the question of the expansion of slavery to new territories and future states.[2] Additionally, ethnic and religious divisions became increasingly contentious and eventually spilled over into the political arena. For example, controversies arose in many northeastern metropolitans with regard to the growing number of new Catholic schools, which advocated for public funding and adopted their own version of Bible studies. Similar controversies also emerged when in some northeastern states political leaders were willing to pursue the growing Catholic vote by nominating Catholics to various public and political positions.[3] These dynamics led to the emergence of strong sentiments of anti-Catholicism and to protests of the Protestant majority in places such as New York, Philadelphia, and Baltimore. Many Americans were sincerely fearful of what they perceived to be the growing influence of Catholics in various areas of public life.[4]

Many who were concerned about the erosion of Protestant dominance in America pointed a finger at the massive wave of immigrants, many from Catholic countries such as Italy and Ireland, which the country absorbed in the late 1840s and early 1950s. Between 1845 and 1854, nearly 3 million immigrants settled in the United States, more than one-eighth of the country's population at that time.[5] The difficulties of assimilating this high number of newcomers in such a short time amplified concerns among many Americans about the country's ability to maintain the "American way of life," with its unique cultural, political, and economic characteristics.

Economic concerns also played a role in the growing hostility toward immigrants and minorities. Between 1850 and 1855, the American economy fluctuated between depression and rapid growth; the rapid rise in inflation in 1855, which coincided with the highest number of immigrants that the United States absorbed in one year (more than four hundred thousand), generated stiff competition over jobs between immigrants and "veteran" Americans.[6]

The Know-Nothing Party was just one of many nativist groups that emerged in the northern United States in the 1850s aiming to counter the perceived threat from immigrants and Catholics. The party originated in New York in 1949 as a secret brotherhood but quickly spread all over the Northeast in the following years via the formation of secret societies and local councils, designated by terms such as "wigwams" and "lodges." While initially aiming to support and promote politicians with anti-immigration and anti-Catholic tendencies, the party's growing resentment toward and distrust of the two established parties—the Democratic Party and the Whig Party—as well as its unprecedented success in expanding its ranks (between the years 1850 and 1855, it was the fastest-growing political party/organization) led it eventually to enter the political arena in the 1854 elections, under the label of the American Party.[7]

The Know-Nothing Party's success in the 1854 elections was mainly manifested at the state and local levels. It enjoyed a landslide victory in the Massachusetts legislature and swept local councils in the prominent cities of the state, including Boston and Salem. In addition, the party gained significant electoral achievements in Maine, Indiana, and Pennsylvania and won nine gubernatorial competitions.[8] Nonetheless, these achievements were not a sign of things to come. Less than a year after it was formally established, the party suffered from internal divisions (mainly on the issue of slavery) as well as from growing backlash from prominent political leaders and public intellectuals who detested its militant and toxic rhetoric against immigrants and other groups. The inability of the party's elected officials to curb immigration and the growing dominance of the slavery issue within American politics seem also eventually to have pushed most Know-Nothing Party voters to shift their support either to the Republican or Democratic parties.[9] In the 1856 elections, the party lost thirty-eight of its fifty-two seats in the House of Representatives; it lost all of them by 1860.

The rhetoric employed by the Know-Nothing Party resembles many rhetorical strategies used by contemporary far-right and populist parties. These include the construction of a dichotomist and populist framing of society, ideological cooptation of historical and national symbols, and placement of the needs and well-being of the "Nation" at the center of the political discourse. More specifically, party leaders constructed a vision that sharply differentiated between in-group and hostile out-groups. They consistently portrayed immigrants and Catholics as foreign agents conspiring to transform the American culture and way of life and therefore needing to be confronted by Protestant Americans committed to the preservation of the true nature of America. In many cases, the delegitimization of Catholics and immigrants included toxic descriptions. Posters circulated in the Boston area circa 1854 described Catholics as "vile imposters, liars, villains, and cowardly cutthroats."[10]

The cooptation of American historical and symbolic narratives was promoted by associating the party with the historical ethos of the American collective and thus, by interpretation, with idealized and admired past and political principles. This process helped the party enhance its political legitimacy and mobilize support by exploiting the emotional and cognitive attachment of Americans to their nation's history and ethos. Leaders of the Know-Nothing Party used the Founding Fathers' rhetoric of republicanism to justify their political agenda and to bridge the moral gap between their views and American principles of freedom, democracy, and human dignity. They particularly preferred to present their struggle as a continuation of the Revolutionary War, as illustrated in the following sentences from an 1855 advertisement of the party in the *New York Mirror*:

> America for Americans. We say. And why not, Didn't they plant it, and battle for it through bloody revolution . . . Why shouldn't they shape and rule the destinies of their own land? . . . Why not rule their own particularly when the alien betrays the trust that should never have given him, and the liberties the land are thereby imperilled?[11]

Finally, the Know-Nothing Party was successful in constructing a tangible and organic sense of the "Nation." As with many of the fascist movements that emerged in the first half of the twentieth century, it adopted an ideological approach that identified the American nation as an independent organ, unique and ideal, which needs to be protected. The spirit, norms, and practices of the original Americans were the foundations of the American nation's success, grandeur, and uniqueness. They created "A Nation of the Century, and yet mightier than the oldest empire on earth."[12] Consequently, leaders of the Know-Nothing Party concluded that the infusion of what they perceived as "foreigners" represented a direct threat to the American spirit and thus to the Republic.

Beyond these contextual and rhetorical factors, an important organizational characteristic also seemed to help the Know-Nothing Party mobilize significant support. The secret nature of the party, at least in its initial stages, helped its leaders foster an aura of heroism around the party's activities and leaders, an element that attracted many supporters. The secret nature of the party also allowed many Americans to distinguish themselves from the "crowd" and to gain a sense of empowerment, which was further enforced by party leaders who presented the secrecy of the organization as a manifestation of their constitutional freedom and of the rejection of established politics.[13] Thus the secrecy was both a source of personal empowerment and a demonstration of support for the right to free political expression. Consider the following excerpt from a Know-Nothing communiqué:

> Who will say that the people—the sole depositories of political power— discontented with existing parties, may not, even in this mysterious manner, make new combinations for the transaction of their own affairs, and erect new standards of policy for themselves? Is it not their right? Who says no! . . . Is it secrecy that makes them wrong? Sir, secrecy is their right. It belongs to them. No man and no power can justly take it from them.[14]

The Know-Nothing Party can be seen as a prototype. Many of its features eventually appeared in the populist far-right movements and parties that followed it in the twentieth century and beyond. However, a combination of political and social dynamics prevented the movement from developing long-term relevancy or establishing a loyal base of support. This was, however, not the case with most of the American far-right ideological streams that succeeded it.

The Last Breath of Southern Resistance:
The First Incarnation of the KKK

The resolution of the U.S. Civil War did not end the deep cultural, economic, and normative divisions between the South and the North. Moreover, it can be argued that the abolition of slavery triggered among many southerners' further devotion to preserve and cherish other aspects of the Southern socioeconomic order. Such feelings were a dominant force behind the first incarnation of the Ku Klux Klan during the second half of the 1860s and early 1870s.

After its formal establishment by six former Confederate officers in Pulaski, Tennessee, between December 1865 and April 1867, the KKK spread across the South, growing quickly, with chapters established in Alabama, Mississippi, Kentucky, Virginia, West Virginia, South Carolina, and Georgia. The new movement maintained limited coordination between its chapters, which operated independently.[15] In April 1867, during the first convention of the KKK in Nashville, Tennessee, there was an attempt to institutionalize the movement with the appointment of Ret. General Nathan Bedford Forrest as the KKK's national leader (the "grand wizard"). Under his leadership, what was referred to as the "Invisible Empire" was divided into realms (under the leadership of "grand dragons"), dominions (under the leadership of "grand titans"), provinces (under the leadership of "grand giants"), and dens (under the leadership of "grand cyclops"). It also was decided that the imperial headquarters would be based in Memphis.[16]

Despite the efforts to centralize the KKK's operations and to establish some formal chain of command, established hierarchy was never consolidated. Regional branches continued to shape their violent campaigns independently and to determine the types of activities and targets they preferred to undertake. The failure to solidify movement-wide formal practices seems to have been a result of the limited logistical capacity of the leadership to monitor the operations of the different regional branches and Bedford's tendency to empower local leaders of the KKK; the local sentiments of the activists, who usually believed they knew best how to enforce their values in their town, county, or state, also didn't help facilitate coordination between the different KKK factions.[17]

Most of the KKK's violence during its early days was aimed at African Americans, representatives of organizations based in the North, and local individuals involved in interracial social activities. While some of the Klan chapters claimed to focus on regulation rather than punishment, brutal violence was a recurring component in most regional Klan activities.[18] In Tennessee alone, in the early fall and summer of 1867 regional Klan associations were involved in 140 violent incidents; twenty-five of them ended with fatalities, and thirty-five included extreme assaults, which involved branding of their victims, mutilation with acid, flogging, or physical beatings.[19] While these kinds of activities encouraged the perception in the North that the KKK was a violent and subversive group, in the South many still viewed these activities as patriotic retribution. This was also reflected in the growing popularity of the movement in that region. While there is no clear evidence regarding the size of the overall movement at that time, Forrest claimed in an 1868 interview that the Tennessee Klan had more than forty thousand members and that the overall number of KKK members in the South was over half a million.[20] It is unclear how reliable these numbers are, but there is broad consensus that at that time much of the white population in the South was sympathetic toward the KKK.[21]

While the decentralized structure of the KKK helped overcome ideological and operational disagreements between different regional chapters, it also crippled the leadership's ability to enforce movement-wide practices and policies when necessary. Hence, despite that in late 1869 and early 1870 the federal authorities intensified their pressure against KKK violence, small cells of the movement all over the South continued to engage in brutal attacks against African Americans and white supporters of African American rights. This in turn further legitimized federal scrutiny and actions against the Klan. Eventually, after acknowledging the limited authorization and control he had over the different chapters of the KKK—and facing federal charges—Forrest announced the disbandment of the KKK in January 1869.[22] The violence continued until the end of 1871, when a combination of military, administrative, and legal measures led to the gradual decomposition of most regional Klans.[23]

The Rise and Collapse of the Pre-World War II KKK

Several factors led a group of Atlanta-based entrepreneurs, headed by Colonel William Simons, to reestablish the KKK in 1915. Anti-immigrant sentiments were proliferating within American urban centers, as a result of waves of new immigrants arriving in the United States in the hopes of escaping the horrors of World War I. These new immigrants were perceived as another strain on a struggling labor market,[24] sentiments that were further intensified when the American masses were exposed to one of the most successful and influential films of the twentieth century. The movie, *The Birth of a Nation*, depicted an alternative historical narrative, one in which the KKK fulfilled a heroic role during Reconstruction by protecting white people from African American violence.[25] Simons and his associates used two major mechanisms in order to exploit this renewal of nostalgia for the old South and the growing hostility toward immigrants to mobilize support and expand the reach of the reestablished organization. The first was the use of the growing popularity of the printed media for the publication and distribution of propaganda. The public relations firm Southern Publicity Association (SPA) was the main driver behind the KKK's use of a variety of media platforms to promulgate its message.[26] The second mechanism that proved effective in expanding the ranks of the KKK was a pyramid recruiting system, in which recruiters benefited directly from enlisting new members, who in turn were incorporated into the pyramid structure.[27] After a modest start, which included several hundred members in 1915, the KKK grew to several million in the mid-1920s (most estimates range from 1.1 million to close to 5 million members).[28]

The KKK also was able to enhance its presence in areas where it had had limited influence in the past, including the Northeast and Midwest. The dissatisfaction expressed by returning African American soldiers' at the continuation of their marginalization in American society, as well as massive migration of African Americans from the South to the North, served as the breeding ground to growing racial tensions in many northern urban centers.[29] Increasing discontent caused by postwar immigration and its effect on the labor market and other structural economic changes also facilitated KKK efforts to develop grassroots support in northern states.[30] Finally, the relatively mild image of the KKK, which was perceived by many at that time as an "American Movement" focused

on national issues, also convinced many northerners that the organiza
tion was legitimate.[31]

By the mid-1920s, as the new KKK transformed into a mass movement,
Simmons adopted a hybrid structure that included rigid formal hierarchy
but also gave significant autonomy to the regional Klans. The imperial
wizard was assisted by fifteen imperial officers ("Kloncilium") and a legislative body ("Klonvokation") consisting of the imperial officers, specially
elected delegates, and grand dragons. The latter were appointed to lead
particular "realms" (states); the realms, in turn, were divided into provinces where several regional Klans could potentially operate, each in its
own "Klanton." A pyramid-style financial model helped sustain and
expand the new KKK. Recruiters (mainly "Kleagles" and Protestant ministers) were paid a fixed percentage of the initiation fee (ten dollars) for each
new Klansman they recruited.[32] The new Klansman was able in turn to
earn money by introducing individuals from his own social network to his
original recruiters. An additional source of income was the large quantity
of KKK clothing and accessories that were sold to members and nonmem-
bers, including flags, knives, swords, and even "Klan waters."[33]

The growing profitability of the KKK allowed its leaders gradually to
adopt a luxurious lifestyle, which was exemplified more than anything else
probably by the purchase for $200,000 of what was referred to as an "Impe-
rial Mansion" for Simmons.[34] As expected, Simmons and his closest companions eventually met with popular disdain over the corrupt and exploit-
ative nature of their lifestyle. These public perceptions, combined with
criticism toward Klan relations with fascist groups and the outbreak of the
Great Depression—which made the business model of the movement
untenable—culminated in a mass departure from the movement, especially of its middle-class members.[35]

Even a leadership transition and the appointment of Hiram Evans as
Simmons's successor in 1922 could not reverse the trend, and by the early
1930s the KKK was left with only core supporters from relatively poor
southern agricultural areas. As a result, the KKK was forced to liquidate
assets, including its Imperial Mansion property. When in spring 1944 the
IRS presented a bill of more than half a million dollars to the KKK, which
was on the verge of bankruptcy and claiming fewer than ten thousand paying members, the imperial wizard at that time, James Colescott,
announced his decision to disband the organization.[36]

Despite its relatively moderate image and its ability to gain mass popularity, it would be a mistake to assume that the second incarnation of the KKK was not engaged in violent practices. Different estimations and anecdotal evidence enable a reliable approximation that between 1915 and World War II the organization was responsible for at least several hundred attacks.[37] The violence was aimed at enhancing whites' social control over minority communities by a process of violent retribution and intimidation. This social control was manifested by the enforcement of all-white elections, in which African Americans were prevented from participating, as well as forcing segregation by attacking individuals, government institutions, and commercial bodies that did not ban African Americans from the public sphere.[38] Hence, it is not surprising that in 1947 the U.S. Attorney General's Office included the KKK on its list of subversive, totalitarian, fascist, and communist organizations.[39]

During the late 1940s, there were attempts to rebuild the national framework of the KKK under the charismatic leadership of Samuel Green, Georgia's grand dragon.[40] However, this ceased with his sudden death in 1949, and in the first years of the 1950s, the movement continued its gradual decline into irrelevancy. Except for a few active chapters, the KKK was dormant until the mid-1950s, when the delicate status quo in the South was challenged by the U.S. Supreme Court rulings in 1954 (against "separate but equal" policies in education) and in 1955 (the requirement of racial integration of schools at the district level).

The Rise of American Nazism

While National Socialist groups have been part of the American political and social spheres since the early 1930s, unlike the KKK, they were never able to transform into a mass movement or gain access to the formal political system. Moreover, the fact that most Americans associated National Socialism with the German Nazi regime further prevented American Nazi groups from establishing significant grassroots support. It is not a coincidence that in 2017 the largest contemporary neo-Nazi organization in the United States, the National Socialist Movement, decided to cease using the swastika in its formal publications and as one of its symbols.[41]

The first American organization to support Nazi ideology was the Chicago-based Friends of the New Germany (FotNG), which was formed in 1930 to bring together German Americans who identified with the new rising German National Socialist Party.[42] As the latter gained political prominence in Germany, FotNG's popularity surged, and in the mid-1930s it included between ten thousand and twenty thousand members, mostly first- or second-generation German immigrants from Chicago or New York City.[43] In 1936, FotNG transformed officially into the German-American Bund, and under the leadership of Fritz Kuhn (a World War I German Army veteran and member of the Nazi Party) it aspired to serve as the American branch of the Nazi Party. It focused mainly on spreading anti-Semitic, anticommunist, and antiliberal propaganda at rallies, demonstrations, and in its recreational/indoctrination camps in New York and New Jersey.[44] The Bund also created its own version of the Hitler Youth, aimed at preserving and enhancing the familiarity of future generations of German Americans with German heritage and culture.[45]

The Bund never gained the same level of traction as the KKK or some of the far-right movements that succeeded it. This seems to be a combination of internal and external factors. The Bund failed to convince the Third Reich's leadership to support it financially or ideologically. Moreover, the Nazi regime, recognizing that the Bund's actions intensified anti-German sentiment in the United States, consistently refused to allow German citizens to join the Bund and condemned the use of Nazi emblems and symbols by its members. The German ambassador to the United States described Bund activities as "stupid and noisy activities."[46] Internal issues also undermined mobilization efforts by the Bund. Kuhn's poor English and limited understanding of American culture was rarely relatable to German Americans and was a liability for an organization looking to gain sympathy within the American German public. Finally, as the United States became more involved in the Second World War, there was a growing perception in the law enforcement community that the Bund harbored subversive potential. A series of federal and local investigations against the organization led to its dissolution in December 1941.[47]

Despite the Allies' defeat of Nazi Germany, Nazi ideology never entirely disappeared from the political realms in the West. Europe saw the formation of far-right fascist parties shortly after the end of the war, and in the United States, several highly centralized neo-Nazi groups emerged in the 1950s and 1960s. The first among these was the National Renaissance Party (NRP), which was established in 1949 by James Madole. This cult-like organization, which ceased to exist after the death of Madole in 1978, focused primarily on conducting public rallies and demonstrations and producing National Socialist propaganda via the "National Renaissance Bulletin."[48] Although the NRP formed its own elite guard, which was mostly used for protecting Madole from angry protesters during NRP rallies, there are no indications that party members were involved in violent activities or that it was able to garner support beyond its core of several dozen supporters in upstate New York.[49]

In contrast to the limited influence of the NRP, the American Nazi Party, which was established in 1959, became not just the face of American neo-Nazism in the 1960s but also served as the incubator that produced some of the most prominent leaders of American neo-Nazism in the following decades. Thus it is difficult to understand current trends within the American neo-Nazi movement without an examination of the American Nazi Party and its glory days.

The American Nazi Party (ANP) was founded by George Lincoln Rockwell, a Navy veteran and a charismatic and skilled speaker who understood the power of the mass media in drawing attention to his ideas and ANP activities.[50] He invested much of his effort into organizing ANP rallies, demonstrations, and public speaking events in "controversial" locations, where he was confident that he could exploit a potential backlash from locals in order to publicize the ANP and draw attention to its activities.[51] In addition, he advanced his ideas and his image as an "American Nazi hero" via two ANP bulletins, the *Stormtrooper* and the *Rockwell Report*. Both aimed to promote conspiracy theories with regard to alleged cooperation between American Jewry and communists, as well as to advance ideas of racial segregation.[52]

As is the case with most Nazi organizations worldwide, and in the spirit of the traditional structure of the German Nazi Party, the ANP adopted a paramilitary hierarchical structure in which "Commander" Rockwell was the only meaningful authority. Accordingly, the ANP headquarters in Arlington, Virginia—the base of the "Stormtrooper" rank-and-file members, also known as "Hatemonger Hill"—was managed as a military base under the leadership of Rockwell.[53] The members were assigned ranks, wore uniforms, and subjected to strict discipline. New members participated

in three days of ideological training, which concluded with a commence-
ment ceremony.[54]

Despite Rockwell's charisma and comprehension of the machinery of
modern media, he was less effective in constructing a stable constituency
and financial base for the ANP. The organization was able to establish
several branches outside Virginia (Fighting American Nationalists groups
were formed in Chicago, New York City, Pennsylvania, Ohio, Maryland,
California, Dallas, and Illinois, and some branches of the ANP youth
movement, White Youth Corps, were established in California, Chicago,
Washington, and New York City); however, most indications are that the
party was never able to grow its constituency beyond a few hundred members. It is not surprising, then, that Rockwell's campaign for the governor-
ship of Virginia during 1965 garnered less than 1 percent of the vote. The
campaign nonetheless reflected Rockwell and his followers' conviction
that the party's road to power would go through nonviolent political
means, a principle also articulated in the ANP's political program.[55]

Facing recruitment and funding challenges, Rockwell concluded that
the association with Nazi Germany was the main obstacle preventing the
ANP from gaining the support of the masses. Therefore, in January 1967
Rockwell changed the party name to the National Socialist White People's
Party (NSWPP) and changed its slogan from "Sieg Heil" to "White Power."
He issued also the party's ten-point program, which emphasized the need
to fight for an all-white America and to eradicate the control of American
Jewry over American culture, finance, and politics.[56] These steps, however,
did little to halt the decline of the organization. Upon the assassination of
Rockwell in August 1967 by John Palter, a former ANP member who had
been expelled from the party by Rockwell several months earlier, some
prominent members decided to depart to form their own organizations.[57]

The ANP, suffering from the exodus of prominent members and without its charismatic leader, became a dying organization. Branches in many
major cities were shut down, such as in Los Angeles and Chicago; the bar-
racks were abandoned; and the headquarters was eventually relocated to
Milwaukee.[58] In 1984, Matt Koehl, Rockwell's successor, decided to
restructure the party's ideology by adding religious and Christian Identity
components and adopting structures and norms similar to those of a
cult. He claimed that Hitler had been the gift of an inscrutable divine
providence sent to rescue the white race from decadence and extinction.

In this context, he announced that the party would be renamed New Order. These changes had limited effect, however, and the party found it difficult to expand beyond its several dozen members and close to a hundred supporters. Today, the name "American Nazi Party" has been adopted by a group run by Rocky J. Suhayda, a former member of Rockwell's original ANP. Based in Westland, Michigan, Suhayda's ANP website sells nostalgic reprints of Rockwell's 1960s-era magazine *Stormtrooper* and holds semiprivate annual meetings in Laurens, South Carolina.[59]

The inability of the ANP to mobilize significant support stemmed from several factors, including its reliance for many years on foreign National Socialist heritage and jargon; a rigid ideological framework that made the party less competitive in the far-right universe; the military culture of the party, which intimidated many potential supporters; the avoidance of violent/action-oriented initiatives, which alienated those seeking a militant framework; and the limited funds available to sustain party operations.

The vacuum left by the decline of the ANP was filled by organizations led by Rockwell's former followers, such as the National Socialist Movement, National Socialist Vanguard, Nationalist Socialist White American Party, National Socialist League, and Euro-American Alliance.[60] Thus the decline of the American Nazi Party facilitated the breakdown of American National Socialism from a relatively cohesive framework in the late 1950s and early 1960s into an accumulation of smaller fragments, many of them consisting of only a handful of members with no operational or political capabilities. As a consequence, these small groups focused mainly on the distribution of neo-Nazi literature.[61] The limited capabilities of the groups were also a result of their reluctance to engage cooperatively with one another. Considering the limited cadre each group possessed, the leaders of the different groups were careful when engaging in joint operations, fearing that these would promote defections.[62]

The Third Rise of the KKK and the Transformation to the "Klean Klan"

The growth of the civil rights movement and the Supreme Court rulings in 1954 (against "separate but equal" policies in education) and 1955 (the requirement of racial integration at the district level of schools) facilitated sentiments of frustration and social anxiety among white Americans in many southern states in the second half of the 1950s and 1960s. Many of them manifested their desire to maintain the status quo in the South by joining the KKK, which provided a platform for a militant and violent struggle against integration. Thus, by the end of the 1950s, KKK membership climbed to around one hundred thousand members.[63]

Consequently, new KKK organizations were established that aspired to provide a coordinating framework for the growing movement, such as the Americans for the Preservation of the White Race and United Klan of America (UKA), which became increasingly influential in the mid-1960s and eventually took on a Klanlike hierarchical structure, with branches in different states.[64] In most southern states there was a statewide organizational framework divided into "Klaverns," which included between ten and forty members.[65] Transferring between Klaverns was only permitted with permission from both Klaverns, and attending other Klavern meetings was not allowed without special authorization. Rules and protocols existed for most aspects of a Klavern's activities, including clothing stipulations, admission requirements, Klan ceremonial rituals, and in-group hierarchy; most Klans continued to use the same terminology for designated ranks, for example, imperial wizard, dragon, etc.[66]

The KKK chapters at that time served as an organizational facilitator of innumerable acts of violence against African Americans, Jews, and civil rights activists. Beyond hundreds of incidents of lynching and arson per year, KKK members also engaged in several dozens of more sophisticated attacks every year, such as bombings of religious facilities and coordinated shooting attacks. The violence increased in particular between 1956 and 1958 and again between 1963 and 1966.[67] One of the explanations for the high levels of "productivity" of the KKK chapters is that in many localities they were able to forge close "relationships" with local law enforcement personnel, who were willing to turn a blind eye and in some cases even to take an active role in Klan activities.[68]

Considering the limited effectiveness of local law enforcement, the Federal Bureau of Investigation became the main actor in countering KKK violence. FBI efforts were aided by several processes, the combination of which led eventually to a decline in KKK membership. These were the growing exposure and criticism of the brutal violence of many

Klansmen in the burgeoning new media of television, contrasted against the growing popularity of the civil rights agenda. In addition, the American military involvement in Vietnam shifted the American public's mindset from local issues to external threats. Hence, most estimates indicate that by the early 1970s the KKK consisted of no more than a few thousand members.

Facing declining membership and losing political relevance, several new and young leaders tried to revive the KKK by introducing some reforms both in terms of its operations and its rhetoric.[69] These new leaders, such as David Duke and Thomas Metzger, who emerged in the 1970s and early 1980s, were not just charismatic and communications-savvy but also interested in mainstreaming the KKK into a legitimate political force. The "Klean Klan" attempted to attract educated, urban-based activists from mid- and high-level sociodemographic echelons by engaging in publicly visible events, not just operate in secrecy. At the same time, the new leaders adopted pseudoliberal rhetoric that focused on the need to protect the rights of white people rather than on the exertion of social control over other ethnic and religious groups.[70]

Many of these emerging leaders, such as David Duke, Louis Beam, Thomas Metzger, Donald Black, and Bill Wilkinson, were able not just to expand their Klan significantly but also become familiar figures nationwide. Some also exploited their substantial popularity and publicity to establish their own independent white supremacy groups, free from the shadows and constraints of the KKK's traditions and problematic and violent image. Tom Metzger established the White Aryan Resistance and David Duke the National Association for the Advancement of White People.[71] These new organizations were also a symptom of the growing fragmentation of the movement and of the attempt to break its boundaries to increase mobilization and cooperation with other far-right groups outside the realm of the KKK. In the mid-to-late 1980s, for example, neo-Nazi skinhead groups in California cooperated with and were guided by Metzger's California Knights and later WAR.[72] During this period, KKK leaders also forged close ties with Christian Identity groups such as the Criminal Extremist Coalition (CEC) and the Aryan Nations. These changes indicate that the KKK was not only experiencing an ideological facelift but had also adopted cooperative practices that helped it gain access to ideologically related movements.

The leaders of the Klean Klan held different perspectives regarding the importance and effectiveness of violence for enhancing the popularity and influence of the KKK. Whereas David Duke usually rejected the use of violence, others, such as Thomas Metzger, Bill Wilkinson, and Louis Beam, continued to support and to emphasize the importance of militant activism. Metzger established the Border Watch, a militia group that patrolled the Mexican border with California and other southwestern states, and Wilkinson and Beam founded military camps in their Klan territories.[73] Beam was also one of the first to introduce the concept of "leaderless resistance," based on the idea of abandoning the attempts to create a nationwide hierarchical KKK organization and instead forming a leaderless organization consisting of small cells of six to eight individuals who could operate independently and thus maintain relative immunity from external infiltration and legislative and administrative counterterrorism measures. It is clear that Beam, the Texas Klan leader, believed that this was the most efficient structure in response to the strategies employed by the FBI against American far-right groups.[74] Other leaders joined him in advocating leaderless resistance, especially following successful operations against their own organizations. For example, after the White Aryan Resistance collapsed in the early 1990s, Thomas Metzger rejected attempts to establish a new group and supported decentralized resistance.[75]

These different approaches to violent activities reflect a tension between two mobilization tactics. Duke believed that the future survival of the movement depended on its ability to mobilize support from the more mainstream conservative audience, emphasizing the clean and new intellectual nature of the Klan. Other leaders, such as Beam and Wilkinson, believed that the mobilization potential of the movement existed among those who were looking for channels to actively manifest their frustration and resentment toward minorities and the government: their investment in the creation of paramilitary recruiting and training camps served exactly that goal.

By the 1990s, it was clear that the efforts to revive the KKK had only enjoyed limited success. Moreover, the political and social climate became more challenging for the movement. The blossoming of the mainstream conservative right under the Reagan administration and its transformation into a powerful political force provided more legitimate alternatives and platforms for those conservative Americans who felt disenfranchised and were interested in engaging in political activism. Additionally, the use of civilian lawsuits by civil rights organizations such as the Anti-Defamation League (ADL) and the Southern Poverty Law Center (SPLC) proved to be a highly effective tactic in shuttering far-right groups. Wilkinson's Louisiana Knights, for example, eventually collapsed after they were unable to deal with the growing torrent of civil lawsuits; the same process led to the disbandment of Robert Shelton's United Klans of America.[76] And while the 1995 Oklahoma City bombing directed most of the attention of law enforcement authorities to the militia movement, the KKK also suffered from increased scrutiny and public backlash. Indeed, in the mid-1990s most assessments indicated that the KKK's nationwide membership was under ten thousand. There are no indications that, since then, the KKK has been able to return to its former peak membership numbers, and it remains overshadowed by its competition, mainly new neo-Nazi groups and the skinheads.

The Ascent of the Skinheads

The collapse of the American Nazi Party led to the fragmentation of the American Nazi movement. That also meant that the new groups were no longer restricted by Rockwell's legacy of nonviolent practices. The 1979 Greensboro Massacre, in which National Socialist Party of America activists were involved in a shooting attack against marchers from the Communist Workers Party, in Greensboro, North Carolina, was probably the most known manifestation of this new trend but definitely not the only one.[77] In a similar incident a year later, National Socialist Liberation Front members were involved in a shooting of African Americans at Metairie, Louisiana, and SS Action Group (SSAG) members were frequently involved in violent confrontations with members of different liberal and left-wing organizations.[78]

It is possible that the increasing violence from American Nazis was also a reflection of their growing willingness to cooperate with other far-right groups, including adopting their violent practices. Indeed, in the post-Rockwell era, many neo-Nazi groups assumed a more pluralistic nature, avoiding restriction of their ideology to National Socialism and willingly merging it with neighboring ideological creeds. For example, both the Social Nationalist Aryan Peoples' Party and the National Socialist Liberation Front were highly populated by, and cooperated with, local KKK members and associations. Matt Koehl, Rockwell's successor, explained this development in an issue of the NS *Bulletin*: "In the past, the New Order/NSWPP has been very hesitant to hold joint activities with other racialist organizations. But, as part of our new outreach, we felt that this occasion would be the perfect one in which not merely to give lip-service to White Unity, but rather to give a practical demonstration of it."[79]

It should be noted that this was not a one-directional process: some white supremacy and Christian Identity groups started to adopt National Socialist concepts. Perhaps the most glaring example is the Aryan Nations, which, although initially formed as a Christian Identity organization, increasingly absorbed National Socialist elements to the point that some experts argue that it has become a version of neo-Nazism and is no longer an Identity group.[80] The two trends of an increasing propensity toward violence and toward cooperation with other far-right organizations have further intensified in the past two decades. As recently as 2017, for example, the National Socialist Movement "signed" a cooperation treaty with some regional KKK groups.

In the early 1980s, a younger and more class-oriented version of National Socialism emerged in the United States. While the skinheads shared several similarities with the more veteran American neo-Nazi groups—they embraced Nazi symbols, regalia, and terminology, and like the neo-Nazi groups, they were also an American extension of a sociopolitical phenomenon that emerged initially in Europe (in this case, the United Kingdom)— they developed a distinct and unique counterculture. The first appearance of skinheads in the streets of urban America occurred in the early 1980s, in the Midwest and Texas.[81] Those skinhead associations were small and relatively unorganized groups of youths who embraced European skinhead subculture and punk music while espousing only limited support for white supremacy ideology. It is therefore not surprising that some of the early American skinhead groups included African American and Hispanic members.[82]

In the mid-1980s, some skinhead groups began to absorb white supremacy sentiments and engaged in violent racist activities. Some of them also benefited from forging relations with other far-right organizations. In late

1984 in the Chicago area, for example, influenced by Hitler's *Mein Kampf* and exposed to British white power punk music, Clark Reid Martell and twelve of his close friends established a group they initially named Romantic Violence and later CASH: Chicago Area Skinheads. In the following months, Romantic Violence became involved in a series of violent incidents perpetrated against Hispanic and Jewish victims, and they collaborated with the local American Nazi Party's branch in spreading racist propaganda and white power music. Very similar dynamics led to the formation of the American Front in 1985 in the San Francisco area, by Robert Heick, who, with several companions, distributed white power punk music and propaganda and engaged in severe attacks against interracial couples, Jews, and other minorities.[83]

In early 1986, Thomas Metzger, the longtime KKK leader, started to realize that the skinheads could provide a significant boost to the declining American far right. He used the new organization that he had formed upon his departure from the KKK, White Aryan Resistance (WAR), to produce outreach propaganda operations and mobilize hundreds of skinheads to adopt white supremacy ideology. The outreach operations included forging connections with dominant figures from the European skinheads and white power music scene and introducing them via WAR to American skinhead groups;[84] the production and distribution of a youth magazine, the WAR *Zine*, which combined National Socialist and white supremacy messages with reports and news from the white power music scene;[85] the broadcasting and distribution of "Race and Reason" white supremacy propaganda videotapes, which featured speeches by Metzger and other prominent members of WAR;[86] frequent appearances on nationally syndicated television shows presenting the fundamentals of the skinhead subculture; and the creation and management of an electronic bulletin board known as the WAR board and hotline services with information about White Aryan Resistance and skinhead activities.[87] Finally, Metzger intensified WAR's presence on college campuses via collaboration with the Aryan Youth Movement (AYM), which had roots in a number of academic institutions, and through nationwide tours, which also helped establish ties with local skinheads in different parts of the country.[88]

It is not a coincidence that the first skinhead event on a national level that White Aryan Resistance organized was a white power music festival.[89] The original skinhead scene emerged from ska, reggae, and punk music clubs. The racist skinheads eventually separated from the mainstream by following a specific branch of punk music dedicated to white supremacy and neo-Nazi messages. The first and most prominent of the bands performing this style of punk rock was Skrewdriver. Led by one of the most prominent figures of the European skinhead movement, Ian Stuart Donaldson, it inspired the formation of similar bands and became in many ways the ideological beacon of the movement.[90]

With the growth of the skinhead subculture, white power music filled three key social roles. The first was its function as a tool of mobilization. For many would-be skinheads, white power music was their first encounter with the ideological and cultural foundations of the skinhead way of life. Thus the music served as a catalyst for their further familiarization with the subculture.[91] White power music also became the main instrument for the consolidation of white supremacy ideology as an inherent part of the neo-Nazi skinhead subculture. In a subculture that for many years was composed of isolated, informal, and unstable cells, white power music was the unifying medium that enabled the formation of a cohesive ideological framework, including consolidation of the movement's fundamental values, norms, practices, and main adversaries. In this context, the music also facilitated the emergence of what can be described as the skinhead "language," which includes shared concepts, terms, and framing of political and social reality. Moreover, in many cases, the music provided operational blueprints for skinhead activity, especially in terms of legitimizing violent tendencies.[92] Finally, the music was also an instrument used by the movement's elites—and by far-right organizations interested in linking themselves with the skinheads—to enhance their influence and control within the skinhead scene and to shape its ideological development. Hence, it is no coincidence that White Aryan Resistance and similar associations were engaged in organizing hate rock festivals and concerts and in the establishment of white power record labels.

The consequences of the American skinheads' ideological embrace of white supremacy sentiments were quickly visible. During the late 1980s, skinheads were involved in several hundreds of acts of vandalism against Jewish stores and synagogues, as well as violent attacks against LGBT and ethnic minorities. Paradoxically, even though the skinhead ideology focused on the need to defeat what they believed to be Jewish-controlled government institutions, attacks were usually aimed at different representations of out-groups, such as minorities and people with alternative lifestyles and rarely if ever directed against government targets.[93] Moreover, while many of the skinhead groups' social activities enjoyed a high level of coordination and planning, their violent attacks were typically opportunistic. Skinheads would typically refer to their assaults as fights, implying spontaneous incidents, and framed them in the context of self-defense. In his study of the skinhead subculture of the 1980s and early 1990s, the criminologist Mark Hamm was unable to identify even one skinhead interviewee who admitted that he was involved in a premeditated violent incident.[94] The rapid growth in skinhead violence led the U.S. attorney general in 1989 to emphasize the government's commitment to spare no effort to counter the "shocking reemergence of hate group violence."[95] Indeed, in the late 1980s and early 1990s federal law enforcement agencies and political actors enhanced their efforts to counter the skinheads' subculture, including implementation of the Hate Crime Statistics Act, which requires the attorney general to collect data on criminal incidents committed because of the victim's race, religion, disability, sexual orientation, or ethnicity.[96]

While most skinhead groups lacked any clear hierarchy, several of the WAR-associated skinhead groups (WAR Skin) did assume a paramilitary structure. These groups employed military ranks and held roster sheets and a report/activities card on each of their members. Apparently, these were used for assessing suitability for promotion. Some of the groups possessed tangible assets such as headquarters and living quarters for their members.[97] It is also important to note that despite WAR propaganda efforts, recruitment remained mainly based on secondary social ties and differential association, that is, social interactions were the primary mechanism used for learning and internalization of values, attitudes, and motives.[98] WAR attempts to create a nationwide organization of neo-Nazi skinheads stumbled, mainly as a result of the collapse of WAR in the late 1980s. However, into the vacuum left by White Aryan Resistance stepped a Texas-based skinhead organization that eventually would unify the entire American skinhead movement.

The Hammerskin Nation (also known as the Hammerskins, or HSN) arose from the Confederate Hammerskins (CHS), which had begun to consolidate in Dallas between 1985 and 1987.[99] This group was not merely one of the more violent skinhead groups at that time but was also highly efficient at publicizing its activities, engaging in successful recruitment from among the developed nonracist skinhead scene in the Dallas area and in developing sources of revenue.[100] The quick expansion of the Confederate Hammerskins was both a result of planning but also coincidence and luck. The latter was reflected mainly by the decline of other major actors in the skinhead subculture, primarily White Aryan Resistance, as well as the growing economic struggles of the American middle class in the Midwest and the South. In this environment, Confederate Hammerskins leaders were able effectively to pursue cooperation with other groups. They attended events of similar groups all over the country and promoted cooperation; indeed, many of these groups would eventually become Hammerskin Nation's branches during 1988 and 1989, especially in Oklahoma, Tennessee, and in several cities in Texas. Confederate Hammerskins leaders also exploited large-scale regional events organized by far-right associations to attract new groups to join under their organizational umbrella. In 1988, following SKINFEST in Milwaukee, several major skinhead groups from Wisconsin joined the emerging Hammerskin Nation. Similarly, the Aryan Fest in Oklahoma the same year provided significant momentum for the recruitment of groups based in the South, and the Aryan Woodstock in California planted the seeds for the emergence of Hammerskin Nation chapters in southern California.[101] Finally, interpersonal relations and the migration of Confederate Hammerskins members to other parts of the country also assisted in forging ties with new groups and persuading them to join the Hammerskin Nation. Cases in point are groups in Maine, northern California, and Chicago, which joined the Hammerskin Nation during 1989.[102]

HSN continued to grow at a fast pace in the early 1990s. After the formal establishment in 1988 of the Northern chapter of the Hammerskin Nation (NHS), similar regional branches formed in the following years in other areas, and by the mid-1990s the Hammerskin Nation included more than thirty branches throughout the United States, which were grouped into several regional organizations, including the Western Hammerskin (WSN), Rocky Mountain Hammerskin (RHS), and Eastern Hammerskin (EHS).[103] In 1994, the organization also looked outside the United States, forming relations with European skinheads, initially with groups in Switzerland and Northern Ireland but later with groups from other European countries, mostly in Western Europe, including Germany, Spain, and Italy.

In the late 1990s, while further Hammerskin Nation international branches formed in Canada, Australia, and New Zealand, the organization started to experience some internal strains. Two major developments facilitated the growing tensions within the organization. The first was the changing balance of power between the local branches and the national leadership. The latter introduced in 1994 a strict recruitment procedure for those interested in joining the organization, as well as codes of conduct, including restrictions on violent behavior. This represented an attempt by the Hammerskin Nation leadership to transform the skinheads into the elite force of the American white supremacy movement. The counter-response to these attempts to "mainstream" the movement was the defections of several regional branches, mainly in Indiana and Ohio, such as the Outlaw Hammerskin and Hoosier State Skinheads. The new skinhead groups were usually more violent, less reluctant to engage in criminal activities, and tended to absorb elements of African American street gang subculture (in many skinhead circles, they were designated simply as Outlaw Hammerskin). In an attempt to prevent further defections, the Hammerskin Nation leadership in 1999 and 2000 decided to provide more freedom and flexibility to the local chapters and reshaped the borders between the different regional organizations, which included the creation of a new branch, the Midlands Hammerskin (MHS). The effectiveness of these steps was limited. The skinhead scene continued its fragmentation, and more groups distanced themselves from the Hammerskin Nation in the following years.[104]

The New Patriots

The American collective mindset traditionally associated the "militia" concept with the important role played by civilian paramilitary groups during the violent American struggle for independence and later in providing security during times of territorial expansion. However, whereas Americans continue to remember and admire the role militias played in the Revolutionary War, for example, the Minutemen in the battles of Lexington and Concord, growing numbers of scholars, policy makers, and practitioners express concern at the modern manifestations of American militias and the threat they represent.

While attempts by the far right to promote paramilitary subcultures could already be witnessed in the 1960s,[105] several catalysts transformed these attempts into a mass movement in the early 1990s. In the second half of the 1980s, the sharp decline in crop and agricultural land value led to a quick growth in American farm debt and overall to what was designated as the "1980s farm financial crisis."[106] Many Americans, especially in the rural Midwest, felt betrayed and abandoned by the federal government, which only provided limited support during the crisis. These sentiments of marginalization were further intensified as the coastal areas experienced a high-tech-driven economic boost, which contributed to the growing cultural and normative schism between rural and urban America.[107] The Ruby Ridge and Waco[108] incidents, both of which the federal government mishandled, leading to the deaths of American civilians, were not just responsible for an escalation in the hostile perceptions toward the federal government among people from rural and mid-America but also engraved in the minds of the future militia members the understanding that self-defense of their way of life and values inevitably meant acting against, or vigilantly protecting themselves from, the federal authorities.[109]

The immediate impact of the Ruby Ridge incident was reflected in a movement-wide conference—which became a mythical event among far-right activists[110]—held at Estes Park, Colorado, between October 23 and 25, 1992. Around 160 members and leaders of various American far-right groups convened in order to discuss the appropriate response to, and the implications of, what they perceived to be an increasing tendency of the American government to invade segments of the civilian sphere that are supposed to be constitutionally protected.[111] Some accounts maintain that at this meeting a consensus was reached that public concern regarding the threat to constitutional rights should be exploited to help mobilize far-right organizations and enhance their recruitment efforts.[112] Another consensus consolidated around the need to encourage the formation of a loose network of mostly independent militias, in accordance with Louis Beam's doctrine of leaderless resistance. Beam had participated in the event and that year published his famous manifesto regarding the need of the American far right to shift to an organizational structure and strategy of leaderless resistance/phantom cell.[113] Also attending the meeting was Larry Pratt, the head of Gun Owners of America (GOA). Pratt recommended the creation of units of freedom fighter militias that would fight against "communist death squads."[114] Both decisions reflected the understanding of many within the American far right that the Ruby Ridge incident was not an isolated occurrence but a reflection of a growing tension between some parts of the American society and their government and that the anti-institutional tendencies of most of the potential recruits lent themselves to the creation of a new antifederal movement.

Following the Estes Park meeting, United Citizens for Justice (UCJ) was formed, in order to "return . . . to a position of service to the people, and the defender of individual rights as our forefathers had intended."[115] Although most of its leaders were members of organizations such as the KKK and the Aryan Nations, the organization avoided sliding into the usual racist and nativist agenda and focused mainly on antifederal rhetoric. And although UCJ was in decline by 1994, its ideas had taken hold, and three of its members founded what is now considered the first modern American militia.

The Montana Militia (MOM) was established by members of the Trochmann family—the brothers John and David and David's son, Randy—in early 1994. In contrast to many of the militias that followed, it was engaged mainly in propaganda and public relations initiatives and much less, if at all, in violent or paramilitary activities.[116] The effective manner in which the Montana Militia's leadership was able to attract media attention and publicize and disseminate its ideological vision made it a beacon for people with similar views throughout the country. The Montana Militia's "productions" included the journal *Taking Aim* and other highly popular publications, such as the *Blue Book*, a binder with media excerpts supposedly confirming New World Order conspiracy theories; special guides for military activities and newsletters; militia accessories and videotapes; and endless public appearances at gun shows, in gun clubs, and at survivalist workshops and expos. Some within the militia movement criticized the Trochmanns' avoidance of militant activism. However, they were able to provide a voice and, more importantly, an inspiration to the many Americans sharing the same frustrations regarding what they perceived as the changing nature of America and especially the expanding influence of federal authorities.[117]

New militias continued to form during 1994 and 1995. Most of the groups emerged as local initiatives in rural areas, characterized by small and isolated communities and based on dense and relatively small extended families and social networks of white men from the lower and middle classes.[118] As in many cases of social networks based on close and long-term social ties and operating on the fringes of the legal sphere, recruitment was invariably based on previous acquaintanceship rather than on any institutionalized recruitment process involving stages of identifying potential recruits, indoctrination, and operational training.[119] This facilitated trust between the militia members, promoted ideological cohesion, and made the group harder for authorities to infiltrate. When attempts were made to expand the militia beyond its core network of founders, a variety of mechanisms were used to garner recruits, including the introduction of NWO theories and the exploitation of recruits' sentiments concerning specific political issues such as the expansion of gun control, environmental legislation, government promotion of liberal social policies (for example, Clinton's health reform initiative), and the changing demography of American society.[120] The prevailing view is that in late 1995 the movement was composed of militias in at least thirty states and included tens of thousands of supporters and active members.[121]

While many of the new militias, such as the Montana Militia and Linda Thompson's Unorganized Militia of the United States, were careful to stay within legal boundaries and focused mainly on ideological propaganda, other militias took a different path. The most well-known of these groups was the Michigan Militia. Established by the firearm-store owner Norm Olson a few months after the formation of the Montana Militia, it assumed a paramilitary organizational structure. Four divisions were created, and these, in turn, were divided into brigades that conducted military-style training and stockpiled military equipment; raids on militia compounds in the mid-1990s frequently uncovered dozens if not hundreds of firearms and thousands of rounds of ammunition.[122]

The Michigan Militia and Montana Militia represented the two faces of the militia movement as it developed during the 1990s. On the one hand, defensive and nonviolent militias leveraged legitimate means in order to protect their members' civil liberties and generally did not directly challenge the sovereignty of the federal government. On the other hand, offensive, violent, and underground militias encouraged their members to engage in direct actions against the federal government, including illegal initiatives and retaliatory attacks. The latter, naturally, were those that attracted most of the attention of local and national law enforcement, who exposed most of the violent militias' plots before they materialized. For example, the Arizona-based Viper Militia plot to bomb the IRS, ATF, police, and National Guard facilities in Phoenix was exposed before its members were able to execute any of the attacks. Similarly, the members of the Oklahoma Constitutional Militia were arrested while preparing explosive devices intended to destroy the Southern Poverty Law Center (SPLC) offices and abortion clinics.[123] Successful plots were relatively rare; nonetheless, the few successful ones had a direct negative impact on the movement.

The public, media, and law enforcement associated the bombing of the Alfred B. Murrah Federal Building in Oklahoma City on April 22, 1995—which led to the death of 168 people, including nineteen children—to the militia movement almost immediately, since the main perpetrator, Timothy McVeigh, was linked to the Michigan Militia and similar groups in Arizona and expressed the views advocated in their propaganda. This association had a multilayer impact on the militia movement. The movement leaders were placed on the defensive; many of them were quick to claim that the attack was a government-sponsored ploy perpetrated in order to justify increasing scrutiny of the movement by authorities.[124] Others were critical of the media and government use of the event in order to delegitimize the movement and to color it as racist, anti-Semitic, and inherently violent.[125] On the other hand, the event greatly magnified the movement's public exposure, facilitating recruitment and expansion. Reports by the SPLC and the ADL concluded that in late 1995 and early 1996 the movement consisted of more than two hundred militias in more than thirty-five states. Nonetheless, and despite the short-term boost to its numbers, the overall trajectory of the movement was downward during the second half of the 1990s. The attack in Oklahoma led law enforcement organizations to increase their efforts to infiltrate and thwart militia group operations. Hundreds of militia members were arrested; many of them were prosecuted for the illegal manufacture and distribution of firearms, explosives, and ammunition. Dozens of violent plots were uncovered, and, in general, the authorities grew much less tolerant of paramilitary activities conducted by civilian associations. A growing number of states in the

1990s also enacted anti–paramilitary training statutes, which restricted unauthorized military-style training.[126]

Several other developments intensified the decline of the militia movement in the second half of the 1990s. Millenarian conspiracy theories swamped the movement in the late 1990s. Most of these theories included a variation of the following narrative: the collapse of the country's infrastructure during the first weeks of the year 2000, as a result of the Y2K software bug, will lead to social and economic havoc, which will be exploited by the government to declare martial law and perpetrate mass violations of constitutional rights, ultimately resulting in the restoration of law and order with the assistance of international forces and their connivance in creating the New World Order.[127] Many also argued that collaborators supported this scheme from among the major parties and from within the U.S. Armed Forces.

However, the fact that the year 2000 passed without any catastrophe and even included some positive developments (from a conservative perspective), such as the election of a Republican president, led to a dramatic decrease in the credibility of the movement and its leaders. The militia members, who expected a watershed event that would substantiate their ideological foundations, instead witnessed a rise in the standard of living and the election of a president identifying with small government and strong and independent local authorities. For many militia members, America was on the right track; thus, the incentive to prepare for war against the New World Order's forces evaporated. Reversed dynamics, which culminated in 2008—the election of a Democratic president with a liberal background, the economic recession, and the introduction of policies and reforms threatening the independence of local political authorities—led to the revival of the militia movement, and new groups, such as the III Percenters and the Oath Keepers, started to gain momentum.

The III Percenters was established by Michael Vanderboegh in 2008, focusing on the protection of the Second Amendment and named after the 3 percent of American colonists who took up arms against the British to fight for political independence. The rapid growth of the group since 2010 should be attributed to Vanderboegh's ability to connect with an issue predominant in the public discourse and that enjoys significant legitimacy among large parts of the American public and definitely within the Patriot movement, as well as his ability to effectively make use of new media platforms.[128] The influence of Vanderboegh on the Patriot movement is also reflected in his ability to inspire illegal and sometimes violent activism. His call for throwing bricks at Democratic Party offices in 2010 led to attacks all over the country. A year later, it was exposed that a plot by four members of the Georgia Militia to poison government officials with ricin was associated with some of Vanderboegh's writings.[129] Following the Newtown school attack[130] in 2012, the III Percenters sent threatening emails to law enforcement in Connecticut,[131] and in 2014 Vanderboegh and members of the III Percenters actively participated in a armed stand-off in Bunkerville, Nevada, between a local cattle rancher, Cliven Bundy, and his supporters and federal agents from the Bureau of Land Management, who were looking to prevent Bundy from using federal land to feed his cattle because of his refusal to pay grazing fees.[132]

The Oath Keepers was also formed in 2008. Its founder, Stewart Rhodes, focused on the recruitment of military personnel, which upon their joining took an oath that they will not assist or accept actions of the federal government that may undermine the Second and/or Fourth Amendments, facilitate the use of foreign forces on U.S. soil, or expand the powers of the government to regulate various elements of the civilian sphere.[133] The rapid growth of the Oath Keepers also elevated the willingness of Rhodes to actively use the "troops" of the organization in various events. Oath Keepers showed up in Ferguson, Missouri, to "support" the city during the unrest of summer 2014,[134] as well as in Medford, Oregon, in April 2015 to support gold miners who were in dispute with the federal authorities.[135] Oath Keepers also arrived to support Cliven Bundy during his standoff with agents of the Bureau of Land Management in Clark County. The growing popularity of the organization among a population with significant military and security experience, as well as the willingness of its members and Rhodes to actively oppose federal authorities, illustrated the potential threat of the group and made it in the eyes of many a symbol of the revival of the militia movement in the twenty-first century.

American Fundamentalism

For many years, the Christian Identity movement did not produce violent groups but rather functioned as a source of intellectual inspiration and moral justification for the violent activities and operations of ideologically related groups. Hence, it is not surprising that many of the prominent leaders of the racist and antifederal movements intensively cooperated with— and at times saw themselves as part of—the Identity movement. This dynamic allowed the penetration of non-Identity ideas into the ideological framework of the Identity movement and vice versa, thereby overall narrowing the ideological gap between Identity groups and other streams of the American far right.

The Christian Identity movement was never able to develop an effective nationwide organizational framework. This could be attributed to the inherent reluctance of highly charismatic and authoritarian pastors to share power with others and to the tendency of each pastor to engage in the development of his creed, a process that worked against the formation of a consensual ideological paradigm. This corresponds with theoretical frameworks that emphasize the process whereby isolated constituencies, as is typical of the various Christian Identity churches, which have limited face-to-face interactions with other constituencies, facilitate fragmented social movements.[136]

By the mid-nineteenth century, the British Israelite ideology had already crossed the Atlantic, and the writings of its prominent thinkers, such as John Wilson and Edward Hine, had attracted the attention of a small but devoted group of adherents. Nonetheless, most of them—such as Pastor Joseph Wild from Brooklyn or the Kansas-based novelist M. M. Eshelman—were local figures who lacked the resources or the aspirations to create a nationwide theological movement.[137] This dynamic began to change in late 1884, with the arrival of Hine to the Northeast and the Great Lakes areas on a five-year lecture tour he conducted among his American followers. The tour, from which Hine produced published materials aimed specifically at his American audience, was a stimulus for the emerging movement and spurred the further expansion of British Israelite ideas in the United States.[138] Thus, in the late 1890s, British Israelite congregations could be found in most of the major cities of the Northeast, as well as in the Midwest, where the ideology attracted a significant number of evangelical Protestants. When Protestants moved in great numbers to the Far West in the late nineteenth and early twentieth centuries, California also became an important stronghold of the movement.

While lacking a centralized organizational framework, several popular publications advanced the crystallization of the movement's principles, which in later years would become the ideological building blocks of the Identity movement. These publications, such as C. A. L. Totten's *Our Race* and A. A. Beauchamp's *Watchman of Israel*,[139] were also effective tools in the early 1920s for the expansion of the movement and provided a platform for the rise of national leaders such as Reuben H. Sawyer, who eventually became one of the founders of the British Israelite World Federation, which was established in London in 1920.[140] In the late 1920s, Sawyer was joined by Howard Rand, a prolific writer and publisher not only devoted to spreading British Israelite ideas but also convinced of the need to coordinate the activities of the movement's different branches and to link its ideological principles to modern-day political agendas.[141]

Rand's efforts bore fruit in 1930, when the first convention of the Anglo-Saxon Federation of America was held in Detroit, and in following years branches of the federation were established in California, Illinois, Florida, Oregon, Washington, Idaho, Nevada, Utah, Michigan, and most northeastern states. The rapid expansion was aided by the production of an immense amount of published material: close to fifty thousand pieces of relevant literature were produced in the early 1930s alone. The use of print media and radio, during this period of extreme hopelessness and at the height of the Great Depression, increased the mobilization potential of millenarian and religious movements. The rise of William J. Cameron to the presidency of the movement in the mid-1930s, with his excellent organizational and public relations skills and political and financial connections to Henry Ford and the Detroit business community, also provided the movement with significant momentum.[142]

Along with Rand, Cameron was responsible for the growing anti-Semitic tendencies of the movement and its increasing cooperation with the American right. He was highly active in producing anti-Semitic publications reliant on British Israelite ideas and formed a mechanism for the distribution of the federation's material to prominent political operatives on the American political right.[143] There are various views and contradicting evidence regarding how other members of the movement felt about these ideological and political shifts; it seems, however, that the growing dissatisfaction by some ultimately led to the replacement of Cameron in 1937 and the decision to relocate the federation's headquarters from Detroit—Cameron's power base—to Haverhill, Massachusetts. In any case, the federation as an effective organization deteriorated during World

War II and the following decade. The departure of Cameron, the aging of its leadership, and the dramatic improvement of the economy in the 1950s made it difficult for the federation to recruit a new generation of follow-ers.[144] Nonetheless, in terms of the massive amount of published material, organizational structure, and conceptual articulation between far-right and religious notions, the ideological and organizational foundations were secured for the emergence of Christian Identity.

The first Christian Identity groups emerged on the West Coast in the late 1940s. Their origins can be traced to a series of conventions organized between 1937 and 1947 in the northern Pacific by a British Israelite associa-tion from Vancouver. These conferences led to the formation of a network of groups on the Pacific coast that was relatively isolated from the British Israelite World Federation as well as its American branch. The isolation was not only a reflection of the geographical distance between the Pacific groups and the center of the federation in the east but also of an ongoing political struggle and hostility between the Pacific branches of the move-ment and some of the East Coast associations, especially between the Vancouver and Toronto branches.[145] In any case, this isolation allowed the Pacific groups to depart from the traditional British Israelite ideological tradition and develop unique ideological notions focusing on extreme anti-Semitism, racial conspiracy theories, and apocalyptic visions.

This new coalition of groups moved further from the British Israelite ideological tradition with the rise of Gerald K. Smith to a leadership position within the movement. Smith was a Southern political operative who had been Louisiana senator Huey P. Long's main aide during the Great Depression.[146] He moved to Los Angeles in the early 1950s and quickly became the major organizational force behind the emerging Iden-tity movement via its own organization, the Christian Nationalist Cru-sade. Smith magnified the importance of anti-Semitic ideas in the move-ment's ideology and worked intensively to tighten its ties with the American political far right by recruiting Identity activists for campaigns against the civil rights movement and the perceived communist threat. He was also able to mentor and nurture a new cadre of leaders, including Conrad Gaard, Jonathan Perkins, Bertrand Comparet, and, most importantly, Wesley Swift.[147]

Swift became the most influential ideologue of the Identity movement in its early days. He founded his church around 1948 under the name

Anglo-Saxon Christian Congregation—which was quickly replaced by the name The Church of Jesus Christ Christian—in Lancaster, California. It soon became clear that he was one of the more charismatic and talented speakers of the Identity movement as well as a highly capable organizer able to form ties with other Identity associations.[148] These relationships enabled him to engage in frequent lecture tours all over the West Coast and the Midwest as well as to develop a popular weekly radio show. In his lectures, he did not just use biblical texts to justify the racial superiority of the Aryan people but also to raise the anti-Semitic rhetoric of the movement to new heights, as typified by a statement he made in the early 1950s in one of his lectures: "All Jews must be destroyed. I prophesy that before November 1953 there will not be a Jew in the United States, and by that I mean a Jew that will be able to walk or talk."[149]

Swift's blunt anti-Semitism also made him a popular figure among members of the KKK and other white supremacy groups, many of whom had found their way into the different organizations Swift helped establish or sponsor in the 1950s and 1960s. These organizations incorporated Identity ideology with violent activism. The Christian Defense League (CDL), for example, was involved in paramilitary activities, and its members were accused of being involved in violent attacks against minorities and of planning to assassinate Rev. Martin Luther King Jr.[150] While the Christian Defense League declined in the late 1960s, two of its main leaders, Colonel William Porter Gale and Richard Butler, would become the face of the movement from the late 1960s to the late 1980s via their respective organizations: Gale's Posse Comitatus and its militant offshoots and Butler's Church of Jesus Christ Christian and its political wing, the Aryan Nations.

From an ideological and operational perspective, Posse Comitatus shared some similarities with the 1990s militias and set the stage for the more contemporary Sovereign Citizens movement. Its origins could be traced to Colonel William Porter Gale's Ministry of Christ Church and its journal *Identity*.[151] During 1967, Gale used the journal's pages to endorse an emerging tax-rebellion movement and its leader, a Kansas-based building constructor by the name of Arthur Julius Porth.[152] After Porth was arrested in 1970, Gale organized rallies, seminars, and a public campaign for his release. This campaign gained momentum in terms of public support, which, along with the vacuum created by the death of Swift and the arrest of the Minutemen's leader Robert Depugh that year,[153] seems to have driven Gale to establish a new organization that could continue the struggle against what he saw as the attempt by governmental authorities to impose inappropriate practices, values, and norms on the American people, or, in his own words—"to (prevent the Congress from) subverting the Constitution of the United States and violating the Laws of its Christian Constitutional Republic."[154]

What emerged was a network of Posse associations that combined racist and anti-Semitic Identity ideas and practices with active hostility and militancy toward the federal authorities, especially the Internal Revenue Service. Between the years 1972 and 1974, Posse chapters were formed in the states of Oregon, Idaho, Michigan, Alaska, Washington, Virginia, and Arkansas. Many of them, however, were relatively small and founded by individuals who believed this would help them fight their own personal struggle with the IRS.[155] While some members in these chapters did not just engage in publicizing their beliefs and ideas but were also willing to practice them and "protect" their rights, a fact that triggered several violent clashes with federal authorities, overall it is difficult to claim that Posse activities escalated into an organized violent campaign. While the organization gained considerable attention from the authorities and the media until its decline in the late 1970s and early 1980s, it was never more than a loose network of frustrated entrepreneurs and farmers who found a common "enemy" and usually engaged in active protest. The picture was fundamentally different, however, in the case of the Aryan Nations and its offshoots.

When Swift died in 1970, Richard Butler established his own Church of Jesus Christ Christian in a deserted compound near Hayden Lake, Idaho, after his attempt to be recognized as Swift's successor was rejected. His goal was to "expand the Kingdom Identity program and form the foundation for a call to the nation or Aryan Nations."[156] Shortly after the move to Idaho, Butler and his close associate Robert Miles, who headed the Mountain Church of Jesus, agreed to form an organization that would promote the idea of transforming the "white bastion"—comprising most of the territory of the states of Washington, Oregon, Montana, and Wyoming—into the base of a future Aryan nation. This organization became known as the Aryan Nations Church of Jesus Christ Christian, or simply Aryan Nations.[157]

Under Butler's charismatic leadership in the 1970s and early 1980s, the Aryan Nations quickly expanded by establishing chapters in other states and promoting various recruitment initiatives. Maybe the best known of these efforts was the annual World Congress of Aryan Nations, which attracted several hundred members and was basically a summer festival focusing on white supremacy and paramilitary and weapons training.[158] The annual youth conventions were another initiative that was eventually followed by the formation of the Aryan Nations Academy, which included several dozen full-time students, ranging from preschool to eighth grade. Finally, relying on the growing number of Aryan Nations members serving long prison sentences, the organization also became active during the 1980s in recruiting support from the inmate populations in correctional facilities.[159]

While all of these strategies expedited the spread of Identity ideas and raised public awareness of the organization, the most important element that transformed the Aryan Nations and its Idaho compound into the organizational, ideological, and operational center of the Identity and the broader American far right—or, as Butler termed it, "the International Headquarters of the White Race"—was the fact that the Idaho compound became a safe haven for many of the leaders of the various far-right associations in the country.[160] It was a place isolated and distant enough to discourage the intrusion of law enforcement, the media, and the general public, and it also offered the freedom and intellectual stimulation of a wilderness environment. Thus, major thinkers of the American far right, figures such as the KKK's Louis Beam, WAR's Tom Metzger, and even the founder of the Montana Militia, Jon Trochmann, felt free to develop their ideological visions, to improve coordination and cooperation, and to mobilize new recruits while spending significant time at the Aryan Nations compound in Idaho.[161]

Ideologically, the Aryan Nations promoted what could be termed radical localism. In many ways similar to the visions promoted by the militias in the 1990s, these ideas centered around the desire to create a network of Aryan farm communities that would be run according to "Biblical/Aryan" laws, independent of federal authorities. However, unlike the case of the militias, the idea behind this vision was driven less by hostility toward the authorities and more by the desire to promote racial segregation. Aryan Nations promoted a militant and activist version of Identity's traditional anti-Semitic and racial principles, which, while still based on a revisionist interpretation of biblical texts, was also facilitated by the incorporation of National Socialist elements and symbols.[162] This statement by Pastor August Kreis, the leader of Aryan Nations until 2012, reflects this amalgam of ideas: "We, as your elect, will carry out your wrath against your enemies on this, the great battlefield, called earth. . . . We look forward to the destruction of your enemies on this earth and to the establishment of your kingdom." In another statement, he was more explicit: "We firmly believe that until every last Jew Yehudi-Shataan is dead, there will be no peace in earth. There is no room for negotiation; we want no peace with them; there is no living with them. We will accept nothing less for Edo/Esau Jewry than explained in Matthew 13."[163]

Some Aryan Nations members who were exposed to these statements and texts engaged in violent and illegal activities. Some acted alone and without organizational assistance, such as Buford Furrow. A former Aryan Nations security guard, Furrow fired more than seventy rounds from a submachine gun at children and teenagers at the North Valley Jewish Community Center in Los Angeles, California, on August 10, 1998; he injured three boys and a teenage girl.[164] Others exercised violence by creating offshoot organizations. The Order is probably the most well-known example of such Aryan Nation offshoots.

The Order was founded in 1983 by Robert Mathews, an Identity activist from Idaho. He planned to form a small cell in Arizona that would first acquire financial resources and then engage in guerrilla warfare against the federal government. Specifically, it would target what Identity followers term "ZOG"—the Zionist Occupation Government—which in turn would ignite a mass uprising. After recruiting several dozen members, mostly from the Aryan Nations but also from other far-right groups including the National Alliance and the KKK, the Order initiated a campaign of counterfeiting, armed robberies, and violent attacks between 1983 and 1986.[165] The most successful robbery was of a Brinks armored vehicle near Ukiah, California, which netted $3.8 million. Other violent attacks conducted by the Order were the assassination of Alan Berg, a Jewish liberal radio host at KOA radio, as a response to Berg's tendency to ridicule the far right; the bombing of a pornographic theater in Seattle, Washington, and of a synagogue in Boise, Idaho, in April 1984; and the bombing of the house of a Catholic priest in August 1986 in Coeur d'Alene, Idaho. The

FBI succeeded in penetrating the group and detaining most of its members in less than a year after it was formed. Mathews was located in December 1984 on Whidbey Island in Washington State and killed during a shootout with FBI agents. No fewer than seventy-five people, including forty-eight who were active members of the group, were convicted on numerous charges related to the Order activities.[166]

Another well-known and violent group that arose from the Identity movement at that time was the Covenant, the Sword, and the Arm of the Lord (CSA). In the early 1980s, members of the group were mainly involved in a series of insurance fraud, arson attacks, and robberies in order to garner resources for what they saw as the inevitable "Armageddon." In late 1983, the group escalated its attacks with a series of bombings of civilian infrastructure, including water supplies and electric facilities. In mid-1985, the FBI and other agencies took control of the group's compound, located close to Bull Shoal Lake in Arkansas. Following the trials of the group's members, it was revealed that they were planning a mass-scale poisoning operation of the United States' main water supplies.[167]

Since the early 1990s, the Aryan Nations' prominent position within the Identity movement has eroded. While Butler's age and declining health played a role in this, its eclipse was also a result of Butler's success in nurturing a skilled cadre of potential future leaders and operatives. Many of them preferred to leave the Aryan Nations to establish their own churches and organizations. For instance, Butler's chief of staff, Carl Franklin, and the Aryan Nations' security chief, Wayne Jones, established the Church of Jesus Christ Christian of Montana, and Charles and Betty Tate, the chiefs of Aryan Nations' printing operations, left to promote a new group in North Carolina. Furthermore, several successful civilian lawsuits against Aryan Nations members in the late 1990s and early 2000s—including a verdict that forced the organization to pay a sum of $6.3 million to Victoria and Jason Keenan, a mother and son who were attacked by Aryan Nations members—crippled the organization financially.[168]

The emergence of competing organizations was another factor that facilitated the declining status of Aryan Nations and Butler (Butler died in 2004, leaving the organization under the leadership of August Kries III, with smaller factions still operating in Texas and New York). The most prominent of these competing organizations was established by Pastor Pete Peters, who, via his Colorado-based La Porta Church of Christ and its outreach arm Scriptures for America, became one of the most notable speakers and leaders of the Identity movement until his death in 2011. Although La Porta Church of Christ had been founded in 1977, only in the late 1980s and early 1990s did Peters begin to expand his influence within the Identity movement. He became highly effective in promoting the Identity arsenal of extreme anti-Semitism, apocalyptic conceptions, and white supremacy ideology via the mass media, including the *Scriptures for America* shortwave radio program and website.[169] Moreover, by hosting Scriptures for America Bible retreats, family Bible camp conferences, seminars, and other activities, Peters, like Butler before him, was able to transform his Colorado compound into an organizational and ideological hub for the movement, attracting prominent Identity and other far-right figures. The contemporary Identity movement continues today to maintain its relatively fragmented nature, with more than sixty ministries and around fifty thousand supporters nationwide.

General Historical Trends Within the American Far Right

An initial analysis of more than 150 years of political activism reveals several cyclical trends within the American far right. In terms of their popularity, American far-right groups enjoyed several peaks in their lifespan, which were usually followed by relatively quick and dramatic declines. Thus, mobilization and growth were seldom a continuous long-term gradual process but rather a response to specific historical processes or events and sociopolitical conditions that were exploited by capable political entrepreneurs. However, these entrepreneurs rarely were able to maintain the attractiveness or influence of their organization and ideology in the face of changing political conditions. So, for example, while the KKK was able to take advantage of economic and social conditions several times in order to enhance its relevance, it was almost never able to adapt when the environment became less favorable.

Trends in popularity have also been reflected in the level of violence produced by the different groups, as a rise in the numbers of members has consistently been reflected by a rise in the level of violence, even in cases when the leadership objected to violent practices. This increase in violence despite leadership's reluctance confirms the inherently violent and militant nature of the far right and implies an incapacity in maintaining operational discipline during times of organizational growth. Furthermore, it affirms the validity of theoretical frameworks linking growth in the level of social interactions within groups with an escalation in the militancy of organizational practices. Finally, it appears that in many of the groups, repeated attempts by the organizational leadership to enforce a rigid hierarchical structure have been relatively unsuccessful and have eventually led to the opposite result, that is, increased fragmentation of the group or movement.

These insights correspond with existing organizational and political violence literature, which tends to associate a group's adaptability and its durability and associate its level of violence and its organizational cohesiveness. Yet identifying the specific factors that prevented American far-right groups from developing effective mechanisms of adaptation and the environmental factors responsible for fluctuations in the level of violence demands a more rigorous empirical exploration of the operational and rhetorical dimensions of the American far right. The following chapters will use comprehensive databases to facilitate such an exploration.

4

Tactics of the American Far Right

In the morning hours of April 19, 1995, an old yellow Mercury Marquis with no license plates caught the attention of Oklahoma state trooper Charles J. Hanger, who was patrolling highway I-35. After signaling the driver to park the car on the shoulder, Hanger approached the car and noticed that the driver was behaving unusually. Instead of waiting within the car, as most people would do, he stepped out and admitted that he had neither insurance nor license plates. The driver also admitted that he had a knife and a loaded handgun in his possession, the latter unlicensed. In the state of Oklahoma, these infractions result in immediate detention. To complete the unusual picture, the driver was wearing a shirt printed with intriguing phrases. The front of the shirt quoted the words shouted by John Wilkes Booth after shooting Abraham Lincoln, "Thus, always, to tyrants." On the back was Thomas Jefferson's "The tree of liberty must be refreshed from time to time with the blood of patriots and tyrants."[1] The driver, Timothy James McVeigh, was arrested and taken to the Perry District Detention Center to await trial for illegal possession of a firearm. However, three days later, the FBI concluded that this was the least of his crimes. McVeigh was responsible for what was then the most calamitous terrorist attack on U.S. soil.

Little more than an hour before he had been arrested, McVeigh had driven a Ryder truck loaded with over 6,500 pounds of explosives and parked it near the Alfred P. Murrah Federal Building in Oklahoma City.

The subsequent explosion, two minutes after 9 a.m., had almost completely destroyed the northeast side of the building, although it failed to obliterate the entire building, as McVeigh had hoped. One hundred and sixty-eight people, including nineteen children, were killed. Hundreds were injured. The city of Oklahoma and large parts of the country were in a state of shock and disbelief.[2] The FBI investigation revealed that the attack was not the act of a single fanatic but an operation planned by a small network consisting of four people,[3] all with ties to the militia movement. Motivated by their rage, bitterness, and animosity toward the federal government, they decided to take matters into their own hands. For them, the only way to raise the awareness of the American public to what they perceived as the growing corruption of the federal government and its increasing tendency to violate constitutional rights was by conducting a dramatic mass-casualty attack against the government's workers and facility.[4]

The case of McVeigh's network seems to be exceptional in terms of its planning, execution, and impact. No American far-right group had ever been or was subsequently able to produce an attack comparable to the one perpetrated in Oklahoma City. For years, far-right groups had been known for their fairly unsophisticated acts of violence, which usually failed to produce a high number of casualties. But was this really the case? And if so, can we identify the reasons for such a trend of incompetence? Moreover, considering the fragmented and diverse nature of the American far right, it is important to examine if different ideological streams are inclined to engage in specific types of violent tactics. Finally, it seems valuable also to track changes over time in the operational characteristics of far-right violence in the United States. Gaining a better comprehension of the tactics of American far-right groups will enable us not just to better understand their capabilities and identify specific concerning trends but also to develop more nuanced insights about the appropriate response to the threat they represent.

To decipher the current landscape of the violent American far right, my team and I constructed a dataset that documents all violent attacks between 1990 and 2017 by groups or individuals affiliated with far-right associations or were intended to promote ideas compatible with far-right ideology. The methodological appendix provides further details on the compilation process of the dataset and offers related methodological considerations.

Targets of Violence

Students of political violence usually employ several popular parameters for assessing the effectiveness and impact of violent campaigns. These parameters aim not just to assess the direct physical damage the attack produced but also its potential symbolic and psychological impact.[5] For example, while arson attacks against religious facilities such as synagogues and mosques end in many cases without casualties, the psychological effect on the community can be substantial given the symbolic importance of the site and its communal function as a place of gathering and worship. Therefore, it is important to examine not just casualty numbers but also other operational parameters so as to determine both the symbolic and direct impact of the attack.

Probably one of the more important operational elements that can teach us about both the specific political goals and the capabilities and levels of ideological commitment of the perpetrating organizations is the nature of the target being attacked. Theories of terrorists' target selection usually identify an association between the ideological goals of the perpetrators and the type of targets they prefer to focus on.[6] Thus, for example, it was common among European far-left groups during the 1960s and 1970s to engage in attacks against symbols of capitalism such as businessmen and financial institutions.[7] Similarly, we should expect some variation in target selection among the various ideological streams of the American far right.

As can be observed in figure 4.1, more than half of the attacks are conducted against individuals or groups of minorities (usually one of the significant minority groups in the United States, such as African Americans, Jews, Mormons, Muslims, etc.) or those who are members of the LGBTQ community. Religious sites, antiabortion-related targets, and immigrants also are among the more popular targets.

These findings confirm that there is a clear association between the dominant themes in the ideology of the American far right and the targets of its violence. The core components of the far-right ideology—internal homogeneity and nativism—and other commonly shared ideological components—xenophobia, racism, and exclusionism—refer to practices that aim to shape and more precisely define the boundary between ostracized out-groups (minorities, immigrants, and LGBTQ) and the "true"

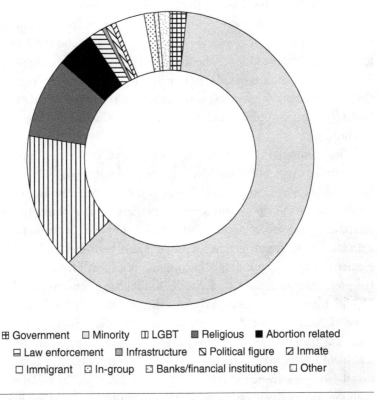

Figure 4.1. Targets of far-right violence in the United States, 1990–2017

members of the nation (white Protestants). Therefore, it is not surprising that "outsiders" are the main targets of far-right groups and individuals.

Moreover, attacking outsiders also serves as a signal. The literature regards terrorist attacks as symbolic violence used to communicate a political message aiming at challenging the hegemonic construction of political reality.[8] A symbol is "an object or a phenomenon used to provide a meaning not inherent in the object itself."[9] In the case of terrorism, we are dealing with a violent act whose various components—targets selected, tactics used, and timing—are used to convey a message to different audiences in order to affect the perception of reality and one's place in it. In the case of the American far right, violence is practiced in order to prevent the continued blurring of the boundaries between "Americans" and "non-Americans" by communicating a clear message of who constitutes legitimate members of the collective and the nation and who do not. This rationale also helps explain the positive correlation between the size and relative proportion of minority populations in a specific state and the level of violence in that state (which will be discussed in the following chapter), since it is precisely in these types of states—with a high proportion of minorities—that we find both higher levels of ambiguity regarding the definition of "outsiders" and "insiders" and a broader pool of available targets (that is, minorities).

From a more rational-operational perspective, immigrant and minority communities typically constitute a more vulnerable part of society: they have limited access to political power and economic resources and, as a result, are unable to secure severe sanctions against those threatening them; they are easy to identify and are likely to have contentious relations with law enforcement agencies. Thus, it is easy to understand why far-right elements might assume that attacking minorities will have limited potential costs in comparison to the costs of attacking other types of targets. Despite the extreme negative rhetoric directed against the government by some elements of the American far right (militias, Sovereign Citizens), attacks against proxies of the government are fairly rare and only constitute 2 percent of the overall number of attacks. Naturally, this doesn't mean that these attacks were not influential or significant (as the Oklahoma City bombing exemplifies) but that the great majority of attacks are not aimed against representatives of the federal government. This may be explained by the costs associated with attacking such targets, as they are usually better protected. Also, the profile of these targets can lead to harsher sanctions against the perpetrators.

Another interesting observation is the relatively substantial number of attacks against members of the LGBTQ community (more than 15 percent). This is somewhat surprising considering that other segments of the population usually receive more attention in the ideological discourse of the far right; there also tends to be a relatively limited number of LGBTQ-associated targets "available" to potential perpetrators (in comparison to the number of available targets associated with ethnic and religious groups).

Religious sites are the third most popular target, which seems reasonable considering both the far right's strong animosity toward specific religious traditions and the fact that religious facilities are usually highly visible targets, and thus striking them can help enhance the symbolic impact of the attack. But no less of an interesting question is why religious sites became more popular targets just in the last few years. As figure 4.2 illustrates, while until the beginning of the current decade individuals/groups affiliated with a minority group were by far the most popular targets, since the beginning of the current decade religious sites have become equally popular and in some years even more popular.[10]

Moreover, while we see in the last few years a decline in the number of attacks against other targets (in comparison to the last few years of the previous decade), the number of attacks against religious sites broke a new

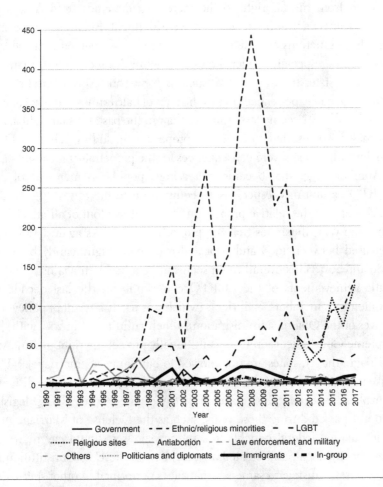

Figure 4.2. Main targets of far-right violence by year, 1990–2017

record in 2017. Several factors can potentially explain such a trend. First, the September 11 attacks, as well as the rapidly expanding perception that Islamic terrorism is becoming one of the most significant security threats to the United States, facilitated among many Americans sentiments of Islamophobia and fear of anything associated with Islam.[11] Thus, it is not surprising that mosques became a popular target for many far-right groups. Indeed, the first spike in attacks against religious sites occurred in the early 2000s. But the more significant spike has occurred since 2012. Thus, additional factors may be the growing influence of religious rhetoric in the American political arena, as well as within the far right, and the related backlash from the far right to the increasing demands from American Islamic leaders not to be treated as a security threat. Finally, as more and more legal sanctions on hate crimes have been implemented over the last two decades, especially under the Obama administration and in many of the "blue" states (many of them, such as New York, Massachusetts, and California, had experienced rises in the rates of hate crimes), attacks against people probably became less attractive than in the past; thus far-right activists may have resorted to attacking properties, including religious sites, which result in less severe consequences for the perpetrators if caught.

Another target that became increasingly popular is members of the LGBTQ community, especially in comparison to the 1990s. Figure 4.3, which portrays the relative proportion of each target (out of all attacks) in a specific year, illustrates that the proportion of attacks against LGBTQ increased between 1998 and 2001 and even more significantly between 2009 and 2013. This overall trend seems to be a backlash against the dramatic achievements of the LGBTQ community in the last decade in advancing its members' civil rights (which was partly a result of policy initiatives of the Obama administration), which culminated in 2015 with the Supreme Court's decision to constitutionally protect the right to same-sex marriage (that is, states are not allowed to ban same-sex marriage).[12] The spike in attacks against LGBTQ during the late 1990s seems more difficult to explain, especially since some of the more direct anti-LGBTQ legislation was passed during these years, such as the Defense of Marriage Act, which denied federal benefits to same-sex spouses should gay marriage ever become legal, and created an exception to the U.S. Constitution to allow states to disregard same-sex marriages performed in other states. On the other hand, in 1996's *Romer v. Evans* ruling, the Supreme Court struck

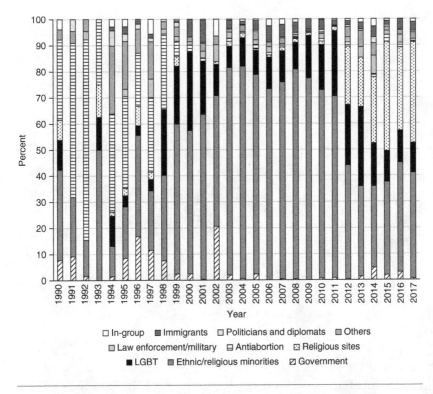

Figure 4.3. Portion of far-right attacks against specific targets by year

down Colorado's Amendment 2, which denied gays and lesbians protections against discrimination, calling them "special rights." It is clear that more research needs to be conducted to understand further the trends in attacks against LGBTQ individuals.

Targets and Ideology

To examine how the specific ideological tendencies of American far-right groups are shaping their target selection, it is beneficial to look into the specific targets chosen by each type of far-right group. As can be seen in figure 4.4, there is indeed a strong correlation between the ideological

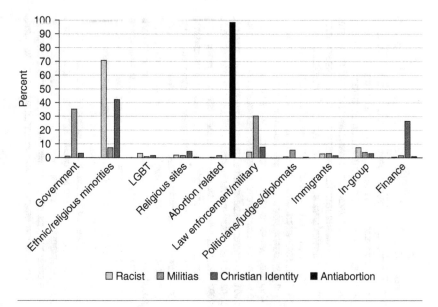

Figure 4.4. Targets of far-right violence by type of group

agenda of the groups and the targets against which they are operating. Groups focusing on racist ideology, such as the KKK, neo-Nazi groups, and skinheads, are perpetrating more than 80 percent of their attacks against minorities, immigrants, and LGBTQ individuals or their related institutions. Similarly, militias and other groups whose ideology is hostile to the federal government (such as the Sovereign Citizens) are perpetrating two-thirds of their attacks against government institutions, law enforcement, or military targets. If we also add their direct attacks against politicians and infrastructure, which in many cases also represent, at least symbolically, the government, then more than 80 percent of their attacks are aimed directly at the government and its various proxies.

Unsurprisingly, the most significant reflection of the target-ideology association can be found among antiabortionists, in which close to 100 percent of their attacks are against what they occasionally designate as the "abortion industry" (physicians, nurses, abortion facilities). In contrast, target selection by Christian Identity followers is somewhat puzzling. As we would expect, a significant portion of their attacks are perpetrated against minorities (more than 40 percent); however, their second most popular target, by a large margin, is financial institutions. This may be a reflection of several factors. The first is the limited violent or operational infrastructure that exists within many Christian Identity communities. While the KKK and many neo-Nazi groups had a tradition of operating underground and maintaining related supporting infrastructure, Christian Identity groups, lacking such resources, directed their attention first to the acquisition of financial resources. For example, the Order, the violent group that emerged from the Aryan Nations (see chapter 3), initially focused on attacks against banks and the theft of a Brinks truck.[13] Another possible explanation is related to the uniquely strong presence of narratives in the Christian Identity discourse that link world and American Jewry with the control of financial markets and institutions (see chapter 7). Thus, in the eyes of members of Christian Identity groups, operating against financial institutions reflects an additional way to manifest their anti-Semitic sentiments.

But can we identify even more specific tendencies of far-right groups, beyond these general ideological trajectories? The answer is mostly positive. Moreover, many of these trends can reveal important dynamics within these groups. To begin with, skinheads seem to have a higher tendency (almost 10 percent of their attacks) to engage in internal violent disputes. This seems to be attributed to their young demographic and the spontaneous nature of many of their violent incidents. It is also a consequence of the outbreak of internal competition between different skinhead groups following the disintegration of the Hammerskin Nation in the early 2000s. Other groups that are highly engaged in in-group violent incidents are prison gangs (almost 25 percent of their attacks)—hardly a surprise, considering the high level of interactions between the group's members as a result of their isolated environment, the related stress factors of that environment, and the high volume of individuals with violent and aggressive tendencies in correctional facilities.

Considering the increase in attacks against LGBTQ over the last few years, it is interesting to see that most attacks against this segment of the population are perpetrated by individuals who are not members of a formal group. This seems to suggest that these attacks are more triggered by individual factors and tend to be more spontaneous in nature (a concept further discussed in chapter 6). Another interesting related finding is that the neo-Nazis and skinheads are the main groups that target LGBTQ, while the more traditional white supremacy groups, such as the KKK, are much less involved in such attacks. This may be a result of the fact that the former groups are more concentrated in areas with a higher availability of LGBTQ targets, such as the Pacific Coast and the Northeast, while the latter is still mostly concentrated in the traditional South. It may be also a reflection of the ideological discourse of the different groups (a domain that will be explored in chapter 7): KKK groups' rhetoric tends less to focus on LGBTQ in comparison to the discourse of the skinheads and neo-Nazis.

To conclude the discussion about target selection, it is interesting to note that attacks against perceived enemies from within—that is, political competitors such as left-wing or liberal political elements—a trend visible in far-right violence in other countries, is not discernible in the American case. One reason for that is the relative ideological volatility within American political parties. Until the mid-1960s, the Democratic Party aligned itself with discriminatory policies and hence was highly popular in Southern states that implemented racial segregation and discrimination, but since the late 1970s it has become increasingly more identified with liberal and progressive policies, while the Republican Party became the preferred party for most far-right activists. One of the results of such ideological shifts is that the two main parties are fairly ideologically diverse; thus moderate Democratic candidates can become popular in fairly conservative states and vice versa. The bottom line is that political identification does not completely overlap with a specific ideological domain. In contrast, in other parts of the globe, especially in Europe, such shifts in party ideology is virtually nonexistent, and so political parties have more effectively become symbolic targets for militant political rivals.

Another reason for the relative absence of attacks against political rivals seems to be related to the constraints of terrorism and its role as a tool of psychological warfare. The costs of acquiring the comprehension regarding the nature of a specific political/social organization, and in the process of framing it as a viable target, are higher than those related to attacks against "natural" enemies of the far right such as minorities or the LGBTQ community. Simply put, a far-right organization that wants to attack a political party and ensure that this attack will have the same level of symbolic/psychological impact as an attack against obvious "enemies" of the far right needs to invest significant additional resources in framing the new type of target as a legitimate enemy. Thus, from a resource-calculation perspective, it is more beneficial to continue to focus on operations against "traditional" enemies.

Lethality, Sophistication, and the Iceberg Theory

An overview of the inner workings of the violence produced by the American far right can help in evaluating its productivity, effectiveness, organizational patterns, and overall capabilities. After all, the capacity to influence social and political processes fundamentally depends on the effective use of violent tactics. As mentioned earlier, one of the more popular measurements that academics and practitioners employ to assess the effectiveness of terrorist campaigns and the capabilities of terrorist actors is the number of casualties that result from their attacks.[14] The ability to generate a high number of victims can increase the psychological and symbolic impact of a terrorist attack by reflecting the incompetence of the authorities and heightening the perception of the threat in the eyes of policy makers and the public.

Figure 4.5 provides data about the number of injured and fatalities as a result of far-right violence between 1990 and 2017. With the exception of the casualties of the 1995 Oklahoma City attack, it is possible to identify several distinct phases. The first, between 1990 and 1998, is characterized by a relatively low number of fatalities and injured. Between 1999 and 2002 we can see a significant rise in the number of casualties attributed to far-right violence: the number of injured spiked to over 100, and except for 2002, over 150 per year. The number of fatalities was usually a few dozen. Between 2003 and 2006 there is a decline in casualties: in those years the number of victims drops below 100 injured and 20 fatalities. Between 2007 and 2011, there is again a rise in the number of victims, to the highest levels documented so far. This is followed by another decline until 2017, where there is again a rise in the number of casualties.

To get a better sense of the lethality of the attacks, it is not enough to observe the overall numbers; the average number of victims per attack must also be calculated (see figure 4.6). Interestingly, the picture now is a bit more complicated. Far-right attacks were more prone to generate

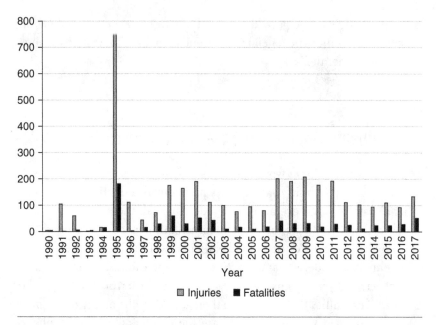

Figure 4.5. Number of injured and fatalities from far-right violence per year

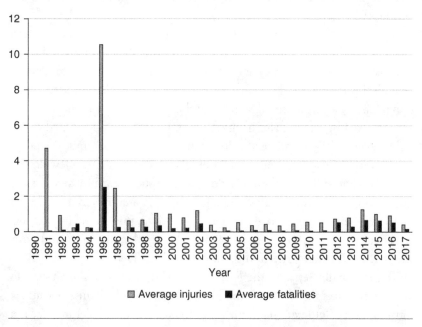

Figure 4.6. Yearly average number of injured and fatalities per attack

victims between 1999 and 2002 and since 2012 (with some decline in 2017 and, again, with the exception of the Oklahoma City bombing). Several conclusions can be drawn based on these findings. The years 1999 through 2002 reflect not just a rise in the number of casualties but also in the lethality of far-right violence. In contrast, the rise in the number of casualties starting in 2008 is more reflective of the rise in the number of attacks than in the sophistication or lethality of far-right violence. Finally, while the overall number of casualties declined in the last five years in comparison to the 2008–2011 timeframe, the lethality and sophistication increased. The latter trend is a source of concern, since it indicates that far-right groups overall are currently more inclined to engage in lethal tactics than in previous periods.

Nonetheless, it is important to note that, overall, far-right attacks generate a low number of casualties, especially in comparison to other types of terrorism. Even in the years in which far-right attacks were especially lethal, the average number of injured per attack didn't rise much above 1, and the average number of fatalities was around 0.5. Examination of the tactics employed by the perpetrators of far-right violence further clarifies the reasons for the relatively low number of victims. More than 44 percent of the attacks were acts of vandalism, and close to 10 percent were acts of intimidation (such as cross burning). Moreover, less than 2 percent of the attacks were intended to generate or resulted in mass casualties. Hence, it is evident that, for the most part, the American far right resorted to limited violence by using tactics rarely intended to generate mass casualties. Yet when looking at the distribution of tactics by year (see figure 4.7), we can see further support for the conclusion that in the last decade the American far right has become more inclined to engage in lethal tactics that could substantially increase the number of victims. For example, since 2008, the number of attacks against human targets is at higher levels than in previous years (except for a spike in 1999–2002).

How can we explain the tendency of perpetrators of far-right violence to resort to nonlethal tactics or operations that generate a limited number of casualties? One possible explanation is that since most far-right activists see themselves as part of the American collective, they are reluctant to engage in operations that can delegitimize them in the eyes of most Americans. Thus, they understand that operations that lead to the mass killing of innocent Americans can undermine rather than help their attempts to mobilize support.

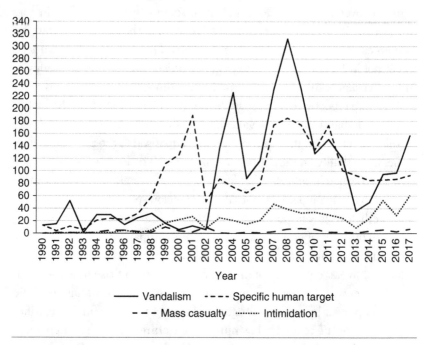

Figure 4.7. Tactics of far-right violence by year

However, a more empirically based approach, which is also based on the fact that there is a correlation between the different types of tactics (in other words, an increase in nonlethal tactics is accompanied usually by an increase in other tactics, the one exception being during the years 1999–2002), suggests that the operational-social framework of the violent American far right could be better understood—with some modifications—via the framework of the iceberg theory, which was originally developed by Ehud Sprinzak more than forty years ago.[15] In the context of the American far right, it seems that we have a large base of supporters—the base of the iceberg—who are usually engaged in low-level violence, such as minor incidents of vandalism or low-sophistication attacks against individuals. The tip of the iceberg includes a relatively small number of individuals or groups who are responsible for producing lethal and mass-casualty attacks. Further developing the analogy, we can say that most of the low-level attacks have received relatively little attention from the media, political authorities, and law enforcement: this is the submerged, unseen part of the iceberg. The few mass-casualty attacks, represented by the visible tip of the iceberg, attract most of the attention. Nevertheless, the common wisdom is that the most damaging and dangerous mass of the iceberg is the proportionally larger submerged segment. Thus the high volume of violence reflected in acts such as vandalism should be worrisome, considering that such attacks are likely to lead eventually to more sophisticated attacks.

Ideology and Tactics

By looking at the types of tactics being used by different types of groups (see figure 4.8), we can learn about their operational inclination and about the level of threat posed by each of the far-right groups. Several important insights can be gleaned from the data. While some attacks against physicians gained significant publicity, the great majority of antiabortion violence is against property (abortion clinics and similar facilities). Furthermore, among racist groups, a significant portion of the attacks (close to a third of all attacks) are acts of vandalism. In contrast, members of Christian Identity and militia groups seem to focus more on attacks against human targets; they also are significantly more inclined to engage in mass-casualty attacks. The latter seems to be a reflection of their tendency to attack law enforcement and government facilities, hardened targets that can, in high probability, lead to casualties.

That militias emphasize attacks against physical targets associated with the government may provide another explanation for the growing concern regarding their activity, and especially of the Sovereign Citizens, despite their relatively limited number of attacks. Inflicting damage on symbolic targets enhances the sense of vulnerability of the existing political order, but, more importantly, it is perceived by policy makers as a threat to their ability to maintain a political and social discourse that supports democratic practices and the principle of the government's monopoly on the use of force.

Attacks against symbolic targets have the potential to increase hostility toward the perpetrating groups and to expand the social and emotional distance between terrorists and the collective. This can have the result of legitimizing or encouraging a harsher government response. However, militia groups do not seem to suffer from a decline in their ability to mobilize support (for example, the expansion in recent years of groups such as

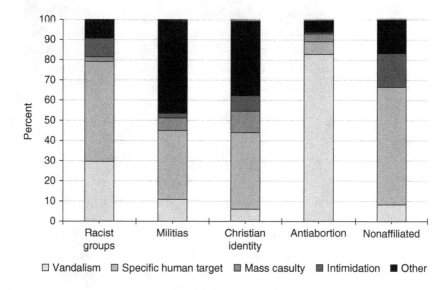

Figure 4.8. Tactics of different far-right groups

Note: The category of "Nonaffiliated" refers to attacks by individuals in which
their organizational affiliation is not clear or where they operated independently.

the Oath Keepers and III Percenters). The main reason for that is the
unique demographic composition of the new militia groups, which rely on
former law enforcement and veterans to fill their ranks. Thus the background of their members and its symbolic meaning help these groups
maintain public legitimacy despite their involvement in violent incidents.
This also reflects another concern: the notable presence of active-duty
military and veterans allow militia groups to use more sophisticated weapons and employ more sophisticated tactics, which may also generate high
levels of casualties.

Indeed, as figure 4.9 illustrates, attacks by antigovernment groups are
by far more lethal and harmful than attacks by any other type of group.
Christian Identity groups are also fairly effective in generating casualties
in their attacks, but all other far-right groups represent a significantly lesser
threat in terms of lethality. It is important to note that even when we omit
the Oklahoma City attack, militia groups are still the ones whose attacks
generate the highest number of fatalities, although the margin from other
types of groups is substantially smaller.

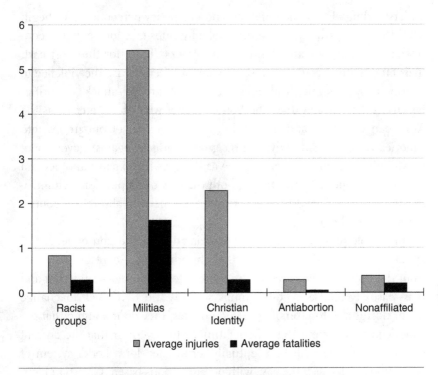

Figure 4.9. Average casualties from attacks of different far-right groups

The relatively high lethality of Christian Identity groups corresponds with a global trend in which religious groups tend to engage in more lethal, mass-casualty attacks on average, in comparison to secular groups.[16] Most scholars emphasize that the lack of a necessity to mobilize support from communities of nonbelievers, the extreme dehumanization of rival groups or religions, and the tendency to adhere to an absolutist ideology (leaving limited space for negotiation or modifications) facilitate the tendency of religious groups to be more prone to maximize the number of casualties in their attacks.[17]

Theoretical Insights

This chapter focused on the various operational features of far-right violence and provides important insights that can inform both our theoretical understanding of this phenomenon and our policy perceptions. To begin with, the data further confirm that violent groups take ideology into consideration when they are plotting their attacks. Thus, for the most part, their targets are selected because they enable them to use the violence to convey a specific political message. Racist groups attack minorities because it helps them draw the boundaries of what they perceive as the American collective and undermine the integration of out-groups into American society. Similarly, militia groups' attacks against government proxies aim to counter what they see as the growing expansion of federal powers and policies by illustrating both the lack of support for such intrusive policies and the cost the government will need to absorb if it continues to pursue them.

But ideology also seems to be associated with the consequences of attacks. More specifically, the further the ideological core of the group from the political mainstream, the more it tends to engage in lethal and mass-casualty attacks. While groups such as the KKK seek to change social norms and to promote specific policies, they do not argue that the American government lacks the legitimacy to govern or that the current sociopolitical order will be eventually terminated for a better system of government, such as is the case with other religious-based (Christian Identity) or secular (Sovereign Citizens) groups. Hence, the more the group delegitimizes the sociopolitical order, the less it is concerned with how engaging in mass-casualty attacks will affect its ability to mobilize support from the public. The primary reason for this dynamic is related to the groups' perceptions of the collective. Unbelievers (using a Christian Identity narrative) or foreign elements hijacking the government (using the militias' narrative) are not part of the planned "revolution"; thus those elements' perception of the violence is irrelevant in the eyes of those groups. Furthermore, since their success will be part of an apocalyptic process, those Americans who criticize their violence will be forced to join them eventually, regardless of their current views of these groups.

Finally, the findings seem to support an iceberg model of far-right violence, in which the largest portion of the violence is fairly limited and unsophisticated. The number of violent acts produced by unaffiliated individuals is extremely high; moreover, these attacks are usually unsophisticated—only 1 percent of the attacks included the use of firearms or explosives, well below what could be observed in any other group or movement (see chapter 6). Thus, in most cases, we are concerned with the spontaneous beatings of minorities or the vandalism of facilities. It is possible to assume that the perpetrators of these attacks represent the future recruitment potential of the more institutionalized and formal violent movements. In other words, after crossing the line and performing minor attacks on their own initiative, at some point such individuals may seek more organized, systematic mechanisms to express their convictions and thus join more formal associations of the American far right.

It also appears that the KKK, with its current informal and fragmented structure and low level of operational sophistication, is the formal movement that is closest to the base of the iceberg and may be the first station for those joining the institutional American far right. Abiding by the same logic, the higher we climb the iceberg, the more lethal the group's attacks and the smaller they are in numbers. Thus, while the militia and Christian Identity groups were involved in the fewest number of attacks, on average these have generated the highest number of victims. The skinheads are ranked fourth in terms of the number of attacks and in terms of the likelihood of causing mortal harm. Neo-Nazis are ranked third in terms of the number of attacks and casualties. While the unaffiliated have a slightly higher level of lethality in comparison to the KKK and antiabortionists, overall the iceberg model fits the findings, as there is a clear base, which is wider in terms of the number of attacks, while the narrower parts of the iceberg are indeed sharper (more lethal). In the next chapter, we will explore whether these insights can also provide more specific explanations for the changing trends in the volume of far-right violence.

5

The Rise and Decline of Far-Right Violence in the United States

For many Americans, the results of the 2016 elections and the ensuing policies of the Trump administration reflected a rise in the influence of far-right ideology within the American political system. Many also felt that the growing political prominence of the far right led to a more permissive and tolerant environment for far-right activities. Indeed, since 2016, the number of violent attacks by far-right activists has spiked. The Southern Poverty Law Center, a nonprofit that researches U.S. extremism, reported nine hundred bias-related incidents against minorities in the first ten days after Trump's election—compared to several dozen in a normal week—and found that many of the harassers invoked the president-elect's name.[1] Similarly, the Anti-Defamation League, a nonprofit that tracks anti-Semitism, recorded an 86 percent rise in anti-Semitic incidents in the first three months of 2017.[2]

The data collected for this book also reflect a rise in the volume of attacks by the American far right since the 2016 elections. While in 2015 and 2016 the number of attacks was 265 and 230 respectively, in 2017 there was more than a 30 percent increase, to 326 attacks. But is it a coincidence that the 2016 elections triggered a rise in the number of attacks? Or is it a common side effect of most electoral processes? And more generally, which factors facilitate a rise or decline in far-right violence in the United States? This chapter aims to provide some insights regarding these questions and to engage with the existing theories on the rise of far-right extremism.

Elections and Far-Right Violence

A close examination of the yearly distribution of far-right attacks in the United States (see figure 5.1) reflects that while there are variations over the years, the overall trend of an increase in far-right violence is clear. If in the 1990s the average number of attacks per year was 70.1, the average number of attacks per year in the first 17 years of the twenty-first century was 286.4, a rise of more than 400 percent.

Equally important, the data reflect that an increase of far-right violence usually characterizes presidential election years and the preceding primary years. For example, the years 1999 and 2000 saw an increase of almost 70 percent compared to the number of attacks recorded in 1998. The years 2003 and 2004 witnessed an increase of over 300 percent compared to the number of attacks in 2002. And the years 2007 and 2008 saw an increase of more than 100 percent compared to 2006. Regarding the 1992 elections, the increase occurred only in the election year. The trend appears to repeat itself in 2011, although in 2012 there was a decline. Finally, 2015 and 2016 recorded substantial increases in the number of attacks in comparison to 2013 and 2014.

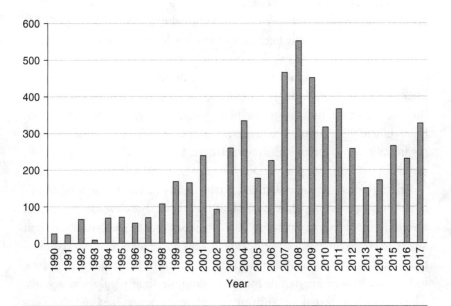

Figure 5.1. Number of far-right attacks per year

A decline in the number of attacks can usually be detected after elections. In 1993 there was more than a 70 percent decline from the 1992 figures; in 2005, a more than 80 percent decline from 2004, and in 2009 there was a decrease of almost 30 percent from the 2008 numbers. After the 2000 elections, the decline was visible only in 2002, but in 2013 there was a decline of close to 40 percent in comparison to 2012. The only outlier seems to be 2017, which may reflect the rise of an administration whose policies and rhetoric provided ideological legitimacy to the American far right.

These findings suggest that American far-right groups and individuals are more inclined to engage in violence in a contentious political climate. This helps explain the lack of an increase in the level of violence during 1996, one of the least competitive elections of the last several decades (in which Bill Clinton won 379 electoral votes in comparison to 151 by the Republican nominee Bob Dole).

What explains the rise of violence during election years? First, far-right groups may assume that during election years, the public is more receptive to political messages, including those conveyed via violent activism. This explanation, however, seems a bit problematic when considering that the competition over the public's attention during election years is more significant than in other years. Therefore, it may actually be more difficult to get the public's to attend to a specific political message. A more probable explanation is that exactly because of the crowded and competitive nature of the political arena during election years, political groups must engage in more extreme activities in order to get noticed and convey their political message. Consequently, they have an inherent incentive to escalate their activities, including the use of violence. Moreover, during elections there is usually a transfer of additional resources from formal partisan organizations to ideological street activists, thus providing the latter with more opportunities to plot various forms of political activism.[3]

An additional dynamic that can further lead to a rise in the level of violence during election years is the fact that as we get closer to the actual elections, many far-right activists have no choice but to recognize that their ability to shape the parties' political platforms and gain effective representation in the political system is marginal. The resultant frustration can drive individuals to seek alternative means to promote their ideological agenda. The relatively informal, opportunity-based, and unorganized nature of far-right violence over the last two decades seems in line with this explanation.

Further supporting this line of reasoning are the trends during and following the 2016 elections. Since for the first time after several decades, many far-right ideas found representation in the mainstream political discourse, especially during 2016, it seems that far-right activists were not as pressed to look for alternative means of activism. Therefore, it is not surprising that the level of violence actually declined slightly in 2016 (when Trump solidified his candidacy). Indeed, in contrast to the past two decades, for the first time, we did not see a rise in the levels of far-right violence during an election year.

But how can we explain the rise of violence in 2017? Two major schools of thought are gaining momentum with regard to explaining this development. The first is based on the assumption that policy makers and, by extension, government agencies are less inclined to apply severe sanctions to politically motivated crimes of groups that are ideologically close to them. Consequently, potential perpetrators of violence assume that the (new) ruling elites will be more tolerant to politically motivated (violent/illegal) acts originating from their own ideological camp. Indeed, we can find empirical support for such policy patterns. The Israeli right-leaning governments employed fairly moderate counterterrorism measures when they had to respond to the violence of groups that were close to them ideologically.[4] Likewise, studies focusing on the rise of left- and right-wing terrorism in Italy and white supremacy violence in the United States further established that political officials are more reluctant to operate against groups that are located on their side of the ideological spectrum. In Italy, during the 1970s and 1980s, right-wing governments adopted tolerant policies against nationalist and violent far-right organizations, while left-leaning politicians were fairly tolerant of the operations of the Red Brigades.[5] Moreover, in the early decades of the twentieth century, organizations such as the KKK were less worried about interference by law enforcement in states where public offices were held by sympathetic political elites (usually from the Democratic Party).

The second school of thought assumes that the increase in the political power of the conservative political camp provides a sense of empowerment, which leads individuals to engage in more daring forms of political participation. This perspective is in line with studies focusing on the concept of *political efficacy*, which describes the level to which a person believes in his/her ability to influence the political process.[6] When an individual feels that the surrounding environment responds to his/her political engagement, he/she will become even more convinced and empowered to believe he/she can further influence the political process. It is not surprising, then, that the literature usually associates high levels of political activism with increased individual political efficacy.[7]

The findings represent a contrasting perspective to prevalent perceptions regarding the association between political violence and democratic practices. Within the policy and academic domains, there is a tendency to assume that democratic processes are an effective mechanism to discourage groups from engaging in political violence, mainly since they provide nonviolent alternatives for advancing political agendas.[8] However, the case of the American far right indicates that under particular conditions the democratic process encourages violence; this is in line with other studies that also challenged this common perception.[9]

Theoretical Explanations for the Rise of Far-Right Politics and Violence

A theoretical framework that strives to explain fluctuations in the level of far-right violence must rely on two bodies of literature. The first is the academic discourse explaining the rise of far-right politics. Such studies usually tend to center on identifying the reasons behind the electoral success of far-right parties or the growing popular support for far-right ideologies. Some tend to discuss how the structure of the political system and changes in the political environment tend to facilitate the rise of far-right political actors; others focus more on how specific economic and demographic changes facilitate populist perceptions among some segments of the population.[10] The second is the academic literature that attempts to explore the root causes of political violence. This vast literature usually tends to emphasize political, social, and economic grievances as potential facilitators of conflict. Some studies use rational-choice frameworks to explain the cost-benefit analyses behind groups/communities' decision to adopt violent means;[11] others incorporate psychological and social concepts to explain how perceived grievances are translated into violent practices by individuals or groups.[12] At the same time, some studies focus on trying to identify how the political, ideological, and cultural characteristics of some collectives may facilitate the use of violence.[13] Finally, a growing stream of new studies is focusing on the dynamics of social networks and human interactions to decipher processes that lead to acts of political violence.[14]

Both corpora of literature are extensive and have experienced exponential growth over the last couple of decades. Testing each one of the theoretical approaches developed is beyond the scope of this book. However, some of the theories focusing on explaining far-right activism are closely related—or are more specific versions—of some theories of political violence. This is not a complete surprise, especially since violent practices have characterized far-right politics in many instances. Another similarity between the two bodies of literature is related to their evolution. In both cases, scholars initially focused on the personal/psychological traits that characterize those who join militant groups. For example, Theodor Adorno and his associates' study of the "authoritarian personality" is probably the most renowned in this context; it, like the many that followed it, argued that those who tend to support far-right ideologies have specific mental and personal traits that can be measured by using a set of criteria, also known as the "F Scale."[15] Similarly, since the 1970s, various scholars have tried to identify the "terrorist's profile," mostly with limited success.[16]

The mixed empirical support for Adorno's approach and the dramatic rise in the power of the European far right during the 1980s and 1990s, as well as the shockwaves of the 9/11 attacks, led to the emergence of alternative theories and explanations that departed from the individual psychological approach. Some of them, as mentioned earlier, share similar logic and are particularly beneficial for the study of far-right violence. These theories are presented in table 5.1.

Political Opportunities, Empowerment, and the Rise of Far-Right Violence

The data presented earlier, which indicate an association between the characteristics of the political environment and the level of far-right violence (times of increasing political competition, for example, election years, have on average higher levels of violence), reflect that a perceived

Table 5.1 Explanations for rising support in far-right ideology

THEORY	RATIONALE
Single-issue thesis	The narrow nature of the political message and its relevance explains success. The main examples that are usually mentioned are the success of far-right groups/parties that have focused on anti-immigration, law and order, and unemployment policies. Hence, far-right groups will be successful when one of these issues is at the center of public or political discourse. (Roger Eatwell, "Ten Theories of the Extreme Right," in *Right Wing Extremism in the Twenty First Century*, ed. Peter H. Merkl and Leonard Weinberg [London: Routledge, 2003], 47–73)
Protest thesis	The popularity of far-right groups is related to the level of societal discontent with the mainstream established political actors. Thus support is less ideological but more an expression of temporary frustration with established politics. (P. Knigge, "The Ecological Correlates of Right-Wing Extremism in Western Europe," *European Journal of Political Research* 34, no. 2 [1998]; Hans Georg Betz, "Conditions Favoring the Success [and Failure] of Radical Right-Wing Populist Parties in Contemporary Democracies," in *Democracies and the Populist Challenge,* ed. Yves Meny and Yves Surel [London: Palgrave Macmillan UK, 2002])
Social breakdown	Breakdown of the traditional social structure (class, religion) has weakened the sense of social integration, belonging, and solidarity; hence, people tend to be attracted to ethnic nationalism. This leads to an escalation of group relations and increases anomie, which leads to the loss of the foundations for standards of judgment and behavior. (William Kornhauser, *The Politics of Mass Society* [Glencoe, IL: Free Press, 1959]; S. Halebsky, *Mass Society and Political Conflict: Towards a Reconstruction of Theory* [Cambridge: Cambridge University Press, 1976]; Eatwell, "Ten Theories," 52–54)
Postmaterial thesis	Stresses the importance of traditional values over economic interests. Those who feel strongly attached to traditional values, when the latter are—according to their perceptions—in decline, are more inclined to join far-right groups. A counter-response to postmaterial politics, which focuses on issues such as the environment, gender relations, feminism, etc. (Paul Ignazi, "The Silent Counter-Revolution: Hypothesis on the Emergence of Extreme-Right Wing Parties in Europe," *European Journal of Political Research*, 26, no. 3 [1992]: 3–34)

Table 5.1 Explanations for rising support in
far-right ideology (continued)

THEORY	RATIONALE
Status theories and economic interests	Far-right groups emerge in order to maintain narrowing lines of power and privileges. Far-right activism intensifies when specific segments of the population feel that they are losing status and power as a result of economic/normative changes. Some theories directly link economic interests—or a sense of economic insecurity—with support for far-right ideology. (S. M. Lipset and E. Rabb, *The Politics of Unreason: Right-Wing Extremism in America, 1790–1970* [New York: Harper and Row, 1970]; Eatwell, "Ten Theories")
Political opportunity structure (POS)	Reflects the tendency to see political activism—particularly in the context of broad social movements—as a result of perceived changes in the political power structure. In the eyes of the movement's members, such activism presents an opportunity to promote significant political change. Combination of all or some of the following components (i.e., Perceived Opportunities) can facilitate the emergence and growth of far-right groups: weak political structure or turmoil in the political system, external pressure, existence of mobilization resources (when mainstream politics neglects central issues), and legitimization of far-right ideas by mainstream politics. (See H. Kitschelt, "Political Opportunity Structures and Political Protest: Anti-Nuclear Movements in Four Democracies," *British Journal of Political Science* 16 [1986]: 57–85; Joshua D. Freilich, *State Level Variations in Militia Activities* [El Paso, TX: LFB, 2003]; Kai Arzheimer and Elisabeth Carter, "Political Opportunity Structures and Right-Wing Extremist Party Success," *European Journal of Political Research* 45, no. 3 [2006]: 419–43)
National-tradition thesis	The success of far-right groups depends on their ability to portray themselves as part of the region/country's tradition and heritage. This way they can legitimize their discourse and penetrate the political and social spheres more easily. People are more reluctant to be excluded from political discourse groups that position themselves as part of the community's historical identity. (Roger Eatwell, "Ten Theories"; Arie Perliger, "How Democracies Respond to Terrorism: Regime Characteristics, Symbolic Power, and Counterterrorism," *Security Studies* 21, no. 3 [July 1, 2012]: 490–528)

political opportunity can trigger political violence from far-right activists. Further support for this conclusion is the strong correlation between partisan control of Congress and levels of far-right violence (see figure 5.2; to augment the analysis, I also included data before the 1990s, based on Christopher Hewitt's chronology of far-right attacks).

The data illustrate that there is a significant positive correlation between Republican control of Congress and the level of far-right violence. Both the number of Republican congressmen/-women and the number of Republican senators are positively correlated with the number of attacks. Not surprisingly, the numbers of Democratic senators and congressmen/-women are negatively correlated with the number of attacks per year (see statistical appendix).[17] The correlation between increased conservative political power and far-right violent activism need not imply causality. But it definitely supports the two possibilities mentioned earlier: that far-right groups may feel that conservative political authorities are more tolerant of their activities or that their actions have the potential to embolden their representatives to pursue a far-right agenda. More importantly, both these possibilities indicate that far-right activists see political dominance of the

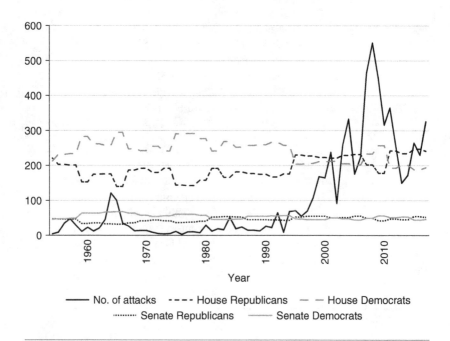

Figure 5.2. Number of far-right attacks and Partisan control of Congress

right as an opportunity that increases the potential benefits of violent activism while reducing potential costs.

The correlation between the level of far-right violence and the identity of the party controlling the executive branch is weaker than the linkage between far-right violence and the composition of the legislature (see statistical appendix). That said, the election of the first African American president had a significant effect on the level of far-right violence. Without taking Obama's years into account, the average number of attacks during the administrations of Republican presidents is around 25 percent higher than the number of attacks during Democratic presidents (87.3 attacks per year in comparison to 61.6 attacks per year, respectively). When including Obama's presidency, the balance is overturned. The average number of attacks during Democratic administrations is almost double (153.3) than the average number of attacks during Republican administrations (87.3).[18] Overall, the findings are in line with the conclusion that the level of violence is positively correlated with features of the political environment, and if we do not take into consideration the dramatic impact of Obama's election, they also correspond with the trend connecting Republican political dominance with higher levels of far-right violence.[19]

We can conclude by carefully arguing that these findings correspond with some aspects of theories grounded around the concepts of empowerment/political efficacy and Political Opportunity Structure (see table 5.1). The role of political efficacy and empowerment in facilitating activism was discussed earlier, but they also intrinsically link to Political Opportunity Structure. Having gained prominence in the study of social movements, Political Opportunity Structure reflects the tendency to see political activism—particularly in the context of broad social movements—as a result of perceived changes in the political power structure. In the eyes of the movement's members, such situations present an opportunity to promote significant political change, or, in the words of the sociologist Doug McAdam, "Any event or broad social process that serves to undermine the calculations on which the political establishment is structured occasions a shift in political opportunities."[20] Some students of this approach specifically emphasize the importance of the openness of political institutions to ideas of the movement as a factor that facilitates the rise of the movement. And while most scholars do not tend to see elections as a "classic" opportunity, it seems that this is the case in the eyes of far-right elements in the United States. The reason for this anomaly may be attributable to the idiosyncrasies of the American political system.

In most parliamentary systems, the results of elections are reflected in the restructuring of divisions of political power between existing sets of actors and their respective parties; thus, in many cases, the same actors may serve in various constellations of governmental coalitions. Therefore, the results of elections in many instances will lead to marginal changes in major policy issues, especially those related to society's core moral foundations. This is also a result of the fact that coalitions by definition demand compromises, which usually prevent dramatic changes in core policies after elections. There are significant caveats to these generalizations, and sometimes we do witness revolutionary electoral results. Nonetheless, general elections in most parliamentary systems can be described as more incremental in the way they affect public policies.

The United States, in this sense, is a different breed. Both the two-party system, which creates the political dynamic and perception of a zero-sum game, and the predominant nature of the executive branch, which channels the political game into one major electoral process—the presidential election—may shape a mindset that will perceive every presidential election as an opportunity to promote significant policy changes. Therefore, the positive correlation between a conservative political environment and high levels of far-right violence could indicate that in the eyes of far-right elements, periods of conservative political dominance are times of opportunity in which the political system is more accessible and open to pressure from groups on the right side of the political spectrum. Indeed, social movements' studies have emphasized the role of perceived success in increasing mobilization and activism.[21] Similarly, studies conducted in the European arena have identified correlations between an increase of support for the far right and legitimization of its ideas by mainstream political actors.[22]

The Effects of Policies on Far-Right Violence

Additional support for the explanations focusing on empowerment and Political Opportunity Structure can be drawn from an examination of the association between far-right violence and related decisions by the U.S. Supreme Court and executive branch. Table 5.2 includes a list of all relevant

Table 5.2 Far-right violence and civil rights policy initiatives and Supreme Court rulings

1954–1955	*Brown v. Board of Education*: Chief Justice Earl Warren, reading his first major opinion from the bench: "We conclude, unanimously, that in the field of public education the doctrine of 'separate but equal' has no place. Separate educational facilities are inherently unequal." *Brown v. Board II*: the Supreme Court holds that school systems must abolish their racially dual systems and should do so "with all deliberate speed."	Significant rise in far-right violence in the following years (1956–1957), when the decisions were formally implemented. The reemergence of the KKK.
1956	The Supreme Court, without comment, affirmed a lower court's ruling declaring segregation of the Montgomery bus system illegal, giving a major victory to Rosa Parks, Martin Luther King Jr., and the thousands of anonymous African Americans who had sustained the bus boycott in the face of violence and intimidation.	Significant rise in far-right violence in the following years (1956–1957). The reemergence of the KKK.
1963	Equal Pay Act: prohibits sex-based pay differentials in jobs.	No effect expected; no effect found.
1964	Civil Rights Act: Title VII prohibits employment discrimination based on race, sex, national origin, or religion. Title VI prohibits public access discrimination, leading to school desegregation. Title VIII is the original "federal fair housing law," amended in 1988.	Significant rise in the level of violence.
1965	Executive Order 11246: Affirmative action requirements of government contractors and subcontractors.	Significant rise in the level of violence.
1967	ADEA prohibits age discrimination for 40- to 65-year-olds, amended in 1986 to remove the 65-year-old age cap.	No effect expected; no effect found.
1968	Architectural Barriers Act: requires accessibility for disabled in buildings and facilities financed with federal funds.	No effect expected; no effect found.

(continued)

1968	Gun control legislation in 1968: prohibits transfers to minors and mail-order sales; requires that guns carry serial numbers; implements a tracking system to determine the purchaser of a gun whose make, model, and serial number are known; prohibits gun ownership by convicted felons.	No effect found.
1968	In *Jones v. Alfred H. Mayer Co.*, the Supreme Court holds that the Civil Rights Act of 1866 bans racial discrimination in housing by private and governmental housing providers.	No effect found.
1971	In *Griggs v. Duke Power Co.*, the Supreme Court rules that Title VII of the 1964 Civil Rights Act prohibits not only intentional job discrimination but also employment practices that have a discriminatory effect on minorities and women. The court holds that tests and other employment practices that disproportionately screened out African American job applicants at the Duke Power Company were prohibited when the tests were not shown to be job related.	No effect found.
1973	In *Roe v. Wade*, the Supreme Court rules that a right to privacy under the Due Process Clause of the Fourteenth Amendment extended to a woman's decision to have an abortion but that the right must be balanced against the state's two legitimate interests in regulating abortions: protecting prenatal life and protecting women's health. Arguing that these state interests became stronger over the course of a pregnancy, the court resolves this balancing test by tying state regulation of abortion to the trimester of pregnancy, so that a person has a right to abortion until viability. The *Roe* decision defines "viable" as being "potentially able to live outside the mother's womb, albeit with artificial aid," adding that viability "is usually placed at about seven months (28 weeks) but may occur earlier, even at 24 weeks."	No effect found.

Table 5.2 Far-right violence and civil rights policy initiatives and Supreme Court rulings (continued)

1973	§504 of the Rehab Act: bars federal contractors or subcontractors from employment discrimination on the basis of disability.	No effect found.
1976	In *Planned Parenthood of Central Missouri v. Danforth*, the court strikes down state laws requiring the consent of spouses and parents of patients under the age of eighteen before an abortion procedure. It ruled the Missouri laws unconstitutional because they "delegated to third parties an absolute veto power which the state does not itself possess."	No effect found.
1978	In *Regents of the University of California v. Bakke*, the Supreme Court rules that the medical school's special admission program setting aside a fixed number of seats for minorities violated Title VI of the 1964 Civil Rights Act. At the same time, however, in an opinion written by Justice Powell, it rules that race could lawfully be considered as one of several factors in making admissions decisions. Justice Powell notes that lawful affirmative action programs may be based on reasons other than redressing past discrimination; in particular, a university's educational interest in attaining a diverse student body could justify appropriate affirmative action programs.	No effect found.
1987	In *United States v. Paradise*, the Supreme Court upholds a one-for-one promotion requirement—i.e., for every white candidate promoted, a qualified African American would also be promoted—in the Alabama Department of Public Safety.	No effect found.
1988	Fair Housing Amendments Act: disabled access required for multifamily housing intended for the first occupancy after March 13, 1991.	No effect expected; no effect found.

(continued)

1989	Air Carriers Access Act: disabled access required in the construction of terminal facilities owned or operated by an air carrier.	No effect expected; no effect found.
1990	Americans with Disabilities Act: Title I prohibits disability discrimination by employers. Titles II and III require disability access in all places of public accommodation and business for the first occupancy after January 26, 1993, or for occupancy for new alterations, and in all state and local government facilities after January 26, 1992.	No effect expected; mild increase from the previous year.
1989–1992	Series of pro-life Supreme Court decisions (*Webster v. Reproductive Health Services, Rust v. Sullivan, and Planned Parenthood v. Casey*), in which state laws regarding the provision of increased state supervision of abortion procedures are upheld.	Increase in the number of attacks, especially antiabortion-related attacks.
1991	Civil Rights Act: adds provisions to Title VII protections, including the right to jury trial.	No effect expected; no effect found.
1993–1994	The Brady Handgun Violence Prevention Act institutes a federal background check on firearms purchases in the United States.	Increase in the level of violence starting in 1994; the rise of the militia movement.
1993–1994	Violent Crime Control and Law Enforcement Act: prevents purchases of specific firearms with specific characteristics	Increase in the level of violence starting in 1994; the rise of the militia movement.
2010	In *McDonald v. Chicago* the Supreme Court holds that the right of an individual to "keep and bear arms" protected by the Second Amendment is incorporated by the Due Process Clause of the Fourteenth Amendment and applies to the states. This resolves the uncertainty left in the wake of *District of Columbia v. Heller* as to the scope of gun rights in regard to the states.	No effect expected; a decrease in the level of violence.

Table 5.2 Far-right violence and civil rights policy initiatives
and Supreme Court rulings (continued)

2014	In *Schuette v. Coalition to Defend Affirmative Action*, the Supreme Court concludes that a Michigan State constitutional amendment that bans affirmative action does not violate the Equal Protection Clause.	No effect expected; no effect found.
2015	In *Obergefell v. Hodges*, the Supreme Court holds that the Fourteenth Amendment requires a state to license a marriage between two people of the same sex with all the accompanying rights and responsibilities and to recognize a marriage between two people of the same sex when their marriage was lawfully licensed and performed out of state.	A significant rise in the level of violence, including against members of the LGBTQ community.
2016	In *Whole Woman's Health v. Hellerstedt*, the Supreme Court rules that both the admitting privileges and the surgical-center requirements place a substantial obstacle in the path of women seeking a previability abortion, constitute an undue burden on abortion access, and thus violate the Constitution.	No effect found.

federal legislation, Supreme Court decisions, and executive orders related to civil rights, abortion policies, and gun control. In each case, the table attempts to provide information on the visible impact on the level of far-right violence.

Three clusters of events seem to facilitate a rise in far-right violence: the Supreme Court decisions against segregation in educational systems, the Civil Rights Acts of 1964, and the antigun legislation of 1993–1994. Most of the other pieces of legislation and Supreme Court decisions focused mainly on disability rights and affirmative action and therefore had a limited impact on trends of far-right violence. More specifically, it can be concluded that legislation or decisions that directly affect the normative fabric of communities and leads to changes in behavioral practices are more likely to trigger a violent counter-response. Additionally, in all cases, there was a vociferous local leadership that framed the legislation as almost an "existential threat" to the community's way of life. Both aspects—catastrophic framing by leadership and challenging policies—correspond with findings of previous studies that analyzed political violence within counterculture communities.[23]

Another important insight is the linkage between the level of violence and Supreme Court decisions on abortion issues. The initial Supreme Court decisions that set the foundations for the legality of abortion in the United States during the 1970s met with limited response from the far right; that is, no abortion-related attacks could be identified from 1973 through 1976, and in general these years were characterized by limited violence. However, a series of pro-life decisions in 1989 and the early 1990s facilitated a significant rise in far-right violence, in particular, abortion-related attacks. To illustrate, while in 1988 and 1989 there were seven and eight abortion-related attacks respectively, during 1990 through 1992, no fewer than seventy-five attacks on abortion-related targets were documented. These findings generally correspond with the results presented earlier, that far-right groups and individuals appear to be empowered by what could be perceived as growing support for their values within the political and judicial systems (that is, a political opportunity for advancing their ideological agenda).

To test the relative impact of all the factors discussed so far (composition of the legislature, presidency's partisan affiliation, executive/SCOTUS decisions) on the level of far-right violence, they were included in a Poisson regression model, with the yearly number of attacks as the dependent variable (which is appropriate when the dependent variable is count data). The results of the model are further supportive of Political Opportunity Structure theory. All variables and the entire model are statistically significant. Empowering executive/judicial decisions had the most direct impact on the level of violence, followed by the composition of the Senate and House, and then the partisan identity of the president. (A full statistical account of these effects can be found in the appendix.)

It is important to note, however, that Political Opportunity Structure theories have attracted significant criticism, mainly because of the subjective and unclear usage of the concept of "opportunity," the mixed results of empirical attempts to confirm the theory, and their sometimes limited utility for comparative analysis. Yet the consistency of the findings with regard to the American case and the fact that they encompass both opportunities associated with actions of the executive and judicial branches as well as those related to electoral dynamics seem to provide strong support for the notion that perceptions related to opportunities to promote specific policies play a role in the fluctuation in the volume of far-right violence.

Social Breakdown Theories and Geographical Distribution of Far-Right Violence

Social breakdown and status theories (see table 5.1) see the growing support in far-right ideology as a response to significant demographic and economic changes that result in a decline in the status and economic power of segments of the population that in the past used to be located at the upper middle of the socioeconomic strata. Moreover, such theories also tend to emphasize related normative and societal changes that can further facilitate sentiments of animosity and hostility toward those perceived as the agents of such changes (in many cases minorities and immigrants). The United States represents an effective laboratory for an examination of the validity of such theories, especially since we can compare demographic and economic changes in different states and test their potential correlation with changes in the level of far-right violence. At the first stage, it is useful to look at the distribution of attacks over the last twenty-seven years by state (see table 5.3).

The first clear conclusion is that what is known as the "Deep South," considered the birthplace of American white supremacy and racist practices, especially during the 1950s, 1960s, and 1970s, is no longer today the natural habitat of the violent American far right. North Carolina, the southern state with the highest level of far-right violence, is ranked only twelfth among all states. If we include Texas, we can find only two southern states in the top fifteen. Furthermore, the states that were mostly associated with the American far right in the past are mostly ranked in the middle or the lower third in terms of number of attacks, including Mississippi (ranked 36), West Virginia (42), Kansas (39), Alabama (31), South Carolina (29), Kentucky (28), Tennessee (25), Georgia (23), Louisiana (22), and Missouri (16). This clearly represents a different situation from earlier

Table 5.3 Far-right violence and minority demographics by state

	STATE	ATTACKS SINCE 1990	MINORITY POPULATION IN 2000 (%)	MINORITY POPULATION IN 2014 (%)
1	California	992	50	58.1
2	New York	657	36.5	41.5
3	Florida	323	33.1	42.4
4	Texas	245	46.2	54.7
5	Illinois	222	30.8	36.1
6	Washington	211	16.2	23.9
7	Pennsylvania	190	15	20.5
8	Massachusetts	188	16	23.8
9	New Jersey	174	32.6	41.5
10	Oregon	158	12.6	18.4
11	Maryland	124	36.2	44.9
12	North Carolina	112	27.7	33
13	Arizona	109	30.2	37.6
14	Ohio	108	14.6	17.8
15	Michigan	107	19.3	21.5
16	Missouri	107	14.4	17.5
17	Virginia	98	28	34.1
18	Wisconsin	97	11	15.4
19	Colorado	95	23.1	28.1
20	Minnesota	95	9.3	15.4
21	Indiana	90	12.9	17.8
22	Louisiana	90	36.1	38.6
23	Georgia	82	36.1	43.8
24	Connecticut	81	20.9	29.3
25	Tennessee	80	19.6	23.5
26	Washington, DC	64	70.6	61.7

Table 5.3 Far-right violence and minority demographics by state (continued)

	STATE	ATTACKS SINCE 1990	MINORITY POPULATION IN 2000 (%)	MINORITY POPULATION IN 2014 (%)
27	Iowa	60	6.2	11.1
28	Kentucky	54	9.5	12.7
29	South Carolina	53	32.8	34.2
30	Oklahoma	47	14.2	19.2
31	Alabama	45	28.4	31.8
32	Idaho	44	9.2	14
33	Utah	41	11.5	16.9
34	Maine	40	1.9	4.1
35	New Hampshire	37	2.7	7.1
36	Mississippi	33	38.4	41.2
37	Arkansas	32	19.7	23.8
38	New Mexico	32	45.1	51
39	Kansas	31	14.4	20
40	Nebraska	30	10.8	16.9
41	Montana	28	2.8	4.8
42	West Virginia	23	4.4	5.8
43	Nevada	22	31	43.9
44	North Dakota	22	2.4	6.4
45	Rhode Island	22	15.5	23
46	Vermont	18	2.3	4.4
47	Delaware	15	26.1	33.8
48	Alaska	10	11.6	16.3
49	South Dakota	10	2.6	6.6
50	Wyoming	9	7.8	12.1
51	Hawaii	3	50.6	48.7

decades, in which these states were engraved in the American collective mindset as hotbeds of racist, antiabortion, and religiously driven violence. Additional findings are that the top five states are what can be considered politically left-leaning states with a minority population that exceeds one-third of the state's population, and that eight of the top ten states in terms of the size of the Jewish population are also in the top ten in terms of the number of attacks.

These findings hint at an association between the proportion of the minority population and the level of violence, a trend also supported by more rigorous analysis. To begin with, the number of attacks is positively correlated with the proportional size of minority populations (African Americans, Hispanics, and Asians) in each state. When looking at the proportions of the minority groups separately, the level of violence is correlated with the proportion of Hispanics and Asians in the overall population.

However, since most social breakdown and status theories emphasize changes in the demographics as the main facilitator of violence, it is important to examine how changes in the proportion of minorities in the population are correlated with the level of violence. Here again, the findings provide strong support that demographic changes are correlated with rising violence. First, the size of the increase in the Hispanic and Asian proportion of the state's population (between 2000 and 2014) is strongly correlated with the number of attacks. Second, the increase in the Hispanic and Asian proportion of the state's population is also strongly correlated with the increase in the number of attacks, specifically between 2010 and 2017. The correlation between the overall general increase in the proportion of minority groups of the state's population (between 2000 and 2014) is close to being statistically significant with the increase in the number of attacks between 2010 and 2017.

While these findings may be persuasive, the strong correlation between the level of violence and state population size requires the use of a procedure that will control for this variable, as well as provide an assessment of the relative importance of the various demographic factors. Therefore, a Poisson regression model (with the number of attacks per state as the dependent variable) was conducted. The analysis again is supportive of the findings presented here (see the statistical appendix). While the population size has an effect on the level of violence in the different states, the other demographics also are statistically significant. The relative sizes of the Hispanic and Asian populations, as well as their growth rate, are strongly correlated with the level of far-right violence. With regard to African Americans, while their relative size is not directly correlated with the level of violence, the growth rate of their population does affect the levels of violence. It appears that anti-immigration sentiments and narratives that are still emphasized and dominant within the ideological frameworks of most far-right streams provide a breeding ground in which diversification of the population leads to rises in far-right violence. Locations undergoing demographic diversification related to "other" racial categories results in the socially and economically marginalized to feel strain regarding their present social and economic status and thus become more open to express their frustration via violent attacks against the agents of change.

Social and Political Changes as Facilitators of Far-Right Violence

The various analyses in this chapter provide support to a couple of major schools of thought regarding the rise of far-right activism and violence. The first identifies a clear association between changes in the political environment—and the interpretations given to these changes by some segments of the population—and levels of far-right violence. Electoral results and related judicial and executive policies that seem to support conservative values and practices intensify rather than reduce the tendency to engage in illegal and violent political activism. These perceived opportunities empower potential ideological perpetrators, whether because they feel that the environment is more permissible for such acts or because they believe they have more public legitimacy to express their radical far-right views. These findings reflect the great responsibility of decision makers, especially from the conservative side of the political spectrum, to help their political supporters, or those in their political camp, develop a more balanced understanding of the meaning of electoral results and how exactly they reflect the public will.

Demographic changes are also clearly correlated with the increase in the level of far-right violence. Those states that experience population growth, mainly via immigration to the United States or the arrival of minority groups, are becoming the centers of far-right violence. Members of communities that are experiencing changes in their social, cultural, and political characteristics as a result of the population's diversification tend to use militant activism to express their dissatisfaction with the breaking of the traditional social and economic communal fabric. Hence it is important to develop mechanisms that will provide support for those who find it challenging to adapt to such rapid changes in their community and proximate environment.

Both the demographic and political dynamics associated with the rise of far-right violence seem to be further intensified by the growing polarization of the American political system and discourse. Therefore, developing a marketplace of ideas inclusive enough to offer policies and ideologies that adopt a middle-ground approach and avoid the complete delegitimization of political adversaries seems to be crucial in countering the impact of facilitators of far-right violence. However, can this approach also help undermine the attempts of far-right groups to convince potential recruits to engage in militant activism by providing them with an absolutist and contentious framework of the political landscape? In order to answer this question and to gain a better understanding of the motivations of the individuals who join far-right groups, the next chapter will dive into the sociological profile of perpetrators of far-right violence.

6

Perpetrators of Far-Right Violence

Students of political violence have always been fascinated with what can be termed the "perpetrator's personality." This fascination was fueled for many years by a couple of common assumptions:[1] First, perpetrators of political violence, especially terrorists, have specific personality features that differentiate them from those who do not engage in ideological violence. Second, these features are common across ideological, geographical, and cultural settings. Four primary reasons seem to convince experts about the validity of these two assumptions. The first is what can be described as the high-risk and high-cost nature of terrorism and similar acts of political militancy. An individual who decides to take part in an ideologically violent activity sacrifices significant personal resources and takes a very high risk. For example, in terms of giving up personal resources, in many cases he needs to cut off his relationships with his family and friends, leave behind much of his property/material possessions, and possibly become a pariah within his community. Naturally, joining a militant group also carries the possibility of incarceration or death. The overall assumption of many experts is that only people with a particular personality or background would be willing to engage in an activity that demands such high levels of sacrifice and risk.[2] Many professions demand some level of risk, but rarely do they also demand such a significant sacrifice of personal resources, as is the case with joining a violent political group.

Second, what puzzles many students of political violence is not just that the members of violent political groups are willing to take significant risks and to make substantial sacrifices but that they do so not for their personal benefit but for a perceived altruistic goal.[3] After all, the great majority of the perpetrators of ideological violence seem not to gain significant material or financial benefits from their acts; they are instead motivated by some political goal related to their desire to promote specific policies/values/social processes. Thus, using conventional cost-benefit analyses, it seems difficult to explain the decision of an individual to engage in politically motivated violence. If this is the case, many experts argue, we can assume that some specific personality traits or biographical background should explain this "irrational" decision to join a violent political group.

Third, one of the trademarks of some forms of political violence, especially modern terrorism, is the use of extreme violent tactics. For example, acts of beheading became the operational symbol of groups such as ISIS, and suicide attacks against civilian targets became one of the more popular methods used by many terrorist organizations, such as the LTTE, Hamas, and al-Qaeda.[4] Such manifestations of brutal violence convinced many that people who are willingly engaged in such acts must be "different," hence have some specific personality profile. Fourth, many experts argue that the puzzle of why people join terrorist groups is further complicated by the fact that so few terrorist groups are successful. Most terrorist groups do not survive for long.[5] Why are people still interested in joining what can be described as very likely to be a failed enterprise and in risking so much for such a limited prospect of success? The answer to this question may be rooted in the distinctive psychological and/or demographic profile of members of terrorist groups.

It is important first to clarify that not all experts agree that terrorists are different from regular people (those who do not join terrorist groups). In fact, many experts believe that almost anyone can be convinced or pressured to join a violent group under specific conditions. Nonetheless, over the last fifty years, two major approaches for profiling perpetrators of political violence have evolved. These two approaches focus on different types of characteristics to distinguish between the perpetrators and the general population. The first is the sociological approach, which appeared in the mid- to late 1970s and includes studies that have attempted to identify specific sociological characteristics of perpetrators of political violence, such as age, education, marital status, immigration status, and income.[6] After several decades of study, the results can be described as ambiguous at best,[7] but at least two conclusions can be drawn with high confidence: no consensual sociological profile can fit all types of perpetrators, and it is possible, in specific cases, to identify a sociological profile of individuals who are affiliated with a specific ideological stream or fulfill a specific role within a militant organization.[8]

The second approach assumes that people who join militant groups have specific mental pathologies or psychological conditions.[9] This approach attempts to identify the mental and psychological processes that drive, enable, or permit individuals to take part in violent activities. Most scholars who adopt this approach are engaged in a psychological diagnosis of activists and leaders of militant groups from afar (using their biographies) or via interviews, in order to understand how their psychological condition facilitates a rationalization of the violence (or makes them feel emotionally compelled to exercise violence). As with the case of the sociological approach, psychological profiling seems to fail to provide satisfactory results, leading many to argue that it is not really feasible to develop a compelling psychological profile.[10] Nonetheless, recent studies seem to adopt a more narrow approach and to identify mental conditions that can facilitate specific dynamics related to radical and violent activities.[11]

Why Do People Join Terrorist Groups?

The efforts to develop a sociological or psychological profile of members of militant groups are directly related to the question of motivating factors. In other words, by identifying common characteristics among perpetrators of political violence, we also hope to gain better insight into the motivations that drive their militant behavior. Studies that aimed to identify such motivating factors usually focused on one of several theoretical paradigms. A common perception is that people join violent political groups, especially in developing countries, because they want access to material or financial resources. In other words, for poor people, joining a terrorist or insurgency group represents a path to improve their economic status or that of their families.[12] For example, some Chechen organizations used the difficult economic situation of widows of Chechen fighters to convince the widows to engage in suicide attacks. In return, the organizations would provide the widows' families and remaining offspring with significant financial assistance.[13]

Another way to explain the linkage between low economic status and motivation to join violent groups was provided by the political scientist Ted Gurr and other scholars who focused on the concept of "relative deprivation." They argue that political violence is an expression of frustration resulting from the gap between reality and peoples' or community expectations. Simply put, people have some expectations from their government and leaders (for example, that they will provide public goods such as security, employment, or education). When these expectations are not met for a long time, the people will become frustrated and eventually willing to use violence to coerce the government to respond to their demands and needs.[14] Hence, individuals with limited human capital and material resources will be more vulnerable to such frustrations (since they are more likely to feel that the government does not provide them with the expected material or social goods) and therefore more inclined to support violent means to improve their situation. It is important to note that some scholars, such as Charles Tilly, argue for a positive correlation between socioeconomic status and the tendency to join violent groups. He and others assert that financial wealth provides individual resources (such as free time or education) that facilitate better understanding and internalization of political issues and public policies, which motivate people to become involved in political struggles.[15]

A different paradigm asserts that ideology and identity play a crucial role in an individual's tendency to become engaged in political violence. The violent act helps them solidify their values and beliefs and fosters their sense of belonging to a specific ideological collective. Thus, for example, according to this approach the young Muslims who traveled to Syria and Iraq from Western countries in order to join ISIS are doing so because they feel stronger attachment and commitment to their Muslim religious identity and community than to their national identity (whether British, American, French, etc.). The jihadi groups are able to convince these young people that their national identity is meaningless, that they are truly part of a Muslim jihadi community or identity, and that the jihadi groups are the only ones who represent their real interests and values.[16] This "ideological" approach also sees the existence of an emotional connection to a specific set of norms and practices (the group's ideology) and/or what they symbolize as an important precondition for the individual's radicalization process because it allows the individual to relate his personal experiences to the group's (or related constituency) goals and ideological framework. For example, many working-class white Americans who feel politically or socially marginalized tend to see their marginalization as part of a broader narrative of an ongoing clash between traditional American values and a global or universal set of values and political practices.[17] They feel that their marginalization is part of the growing hostility toward (or war against) their culture, values, and way of life and thus become motivated to participate in acts of "resistance." Studies that adopt this approach in the context of jihadi and Jewish Orthodox terrorism emphasize the affiliation of the individual to a dense and homogeneous social network that helps instill and maintain a transnational, religious identity, as well as alienation toward a Western or national identity, which facilitates processes of radicalization.[18] It is also important to emphasize that many in the academic world completely reject the ideological approach, especially its use of "clash of civilizations" terminology. They argue that there is limited empirical evidence to support this approach and that in fact some data reflect that many members of terrorist groups are not attracted to the groups because of a specific ideological orientation.[19]

Finally, a growing number of scholars explain political violence via an instrumental perspective. They assert that people join militant groups because of specific expected benefits (which are not necessarily material), especially in a setting where the costs are fairly low. Similarly, terrorist groups tend to engage in what can be described as "differential recruitment." Thus, for high-skilled positions, the group will recruit more educated individuals, while for positions that demand fewer skills or are short term in nature (for example, suicide bombers), the group will prefer to recruit individuals with limited human capital.[20] This approach shifts the focus to the organizational decision-making process and offers a more symmetric approach to the recruitment process. In other words, it is not just or mainly about the radicalization of the recruits but about the group's ability to identify a particular set of skills that the group needs, locate individuals who possess those skills, and then apply various techniques to recruit the identified individuals. Supporters of this approach, for example, tend to mention 2014's Abu Bakr al-Baghdadi's (the leader of ISIS) "special call" for skilled individuals (such as medical doctors or engineers) to provide services to those who live within the borders of the Islamic State.[21]

In the following sections, I will analyze empirical data in order to assess which of these approaches can best explain the motivation of perpetrators of far-right violence in the United States. The data are based on the database constructed for this book, described in chapter 4 and further detailed in the statistical appendix.

Far-Right Attacks: Groups or Individuals?

Most scholars emphasize that political violence is a phenomenon of collective action. Indeed, the majority of politically motivated violent acts are perpetrated by groups or by individuals who represent a wider operational entity. However, in the case of the American far right, this trend seems to be reversed. Out of the 3,544 incidents in which perpetrators were identified, 57.6 percent were perpetrated by a single person, another 18.1 percent by two perpetrators, and the rest (24.3 percent) by a group. Thus, at least in the case of the American far right, violence is not exclusively a collective action but frequently an individual expression. It seems that the importance of understanding perpetrators' characteristics is no less important than an understanding of organizational dynamics that lead to involvement in far-right violence.

Moreover, the findings may reflect a further, more extreme implementation of the leaderless-resistance doctrine, which has been promoted by various leaders of the American far right during the last couple of decades.[22] It appears that their words have not fallen on deaf ears. The findings may also indicate an interesting operational path that, on the one hand, ensures the survival of far-right organizations and, on the other hand, allows them to engage indirectly in violent activities. While the organizations as a whole cannot afford to be directly involved in sponsoring and perpetrating a violent campaign, since the legal and organizational implications may be costly, especially in the American and Western context of highly qualified and efficient law enforcement, they can still encourage individual members to engage in violent activities that are not directly part of the organizational operational framework. This strategy may not work in cases of extreme manifestations of violence—for example, the loose and previous affiliation of McVeigh with the Michigan Militia, which eventually led to a harsh response against the militia movement after the attack in Oklahoma—but it may be effective in cases of minor attacks. Moreover, considering that one of the most effective countermeasures against far-right groups during the 1980s and the 1990s was civilian lawsuits, the importance of distancing a given group from a direct link to attacks is further evident. Another important explanation for this trend of solo attacks is the spontaneous nature of many of the attacks. This will further be discussed in later sections of this chapter.

From an operational perspective, the fact that most attacks are perpetrated by single individuals loosely affiliated with a group explains the limited level of sophistication of the attacks of the American far right. My analysis has found that there are significant gaps in terms of the number of casualties produced by attacks initiated by one or two people and attacks that are the production of groups (see figure 6.1). Thus, notwithstanding the advantages of the leaderless-resistance doctrine, it seems to incur costs in terms of the lethality of the violence.

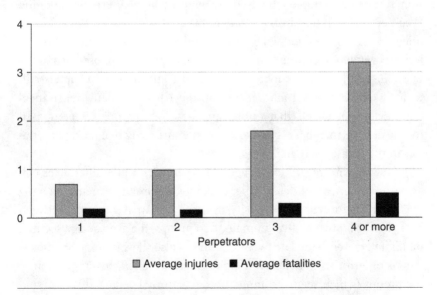

Figure 6.1. Average number of victims per number of perpetrators

It is important to note, however, that the fact that the perpetrators are operating independently does not mean that they do not have connections with some hate groups or that they are not exposed to far-right propaganda. The data collected about the perpetrators show that more than two-thirds of them (72 percent) had some kind of affiliation with a hate group and thus were exposed to the militant discourse of the American far right.

Sociological Characteristics of Perpetrators of Far-Right Violence

Most of the existing data about terrorist attacks suggest that the majority of perpetrators are males. However, a thorough examination will uncover a more complicated reality. For example, in some jihadi terrorist groups, female members are engaged in specific missions, such as intelligence gathering, couriers, and medical assistance, but for ideological reasons are not allowed to participate in combat missions.[23] In contrast, in some left-wing groups in Latin America and Europe, women made up a significant portion of the members (sometimes beyond 50 percent) and filled leadership roles (for example, the Red Army Faction in Germany and the Weather Underground in the United States). It is clear that the equality-oriented ideology of left-wing groups influenced their composition in terms of gender. In contrast, most far-right groups are composed of and led by men. Until the early 1980s, for example, and in some chapters still today, women were not allowed to join the KKK. Similarly, most anecdotal evidence reflects that militia and neo-Nazi groups are composed mostly of male members. Therefore, it is not surprising that most perpetrators in the dataset were male (93.5 percent).

Likewise, with regard to the age of perpetrators, some differences can be observed between different types of groups. For example, many left-wing organizations formed by university students had an average age between twenty-two and twenty-five. In nationalist groups, the average age seems a bit higher, closer to the late twenties. Studies also show that specific populations of terrorists may be even older, such as the leadership echelon of the groups (which seems to range between thirty-five and fifty-five) and contemporary foreign fighters (recent studies show that at least a third of them are above the age of thirty).[24] Overall, it is clear that young people are joining terrorist groups, but there are still some differences between different types of groups, and some roles attract more mature individuals. The age of American far-right perpetrators seems to be in line with these expectations, as almost half of them perpetrated their attack before age twenty-three, and the overall average age is 27.5. Indeed, above the age of forty-five, the likelihood of involvement in violent activities greatly declines.

The concept of biographical availability is usually employed to explain the young age of members of violent groups. It refers to the number of competing commitments the individual is engaged in. Simply put, as people get older, they tend to absorb various financial and social commitments, such as a mortgage, children, a professional career, etc.[25] Hence, the potential costs of being involved in illegal and risky activities rise as a person matures and develops a growing number of competing commitments. In contrast, young people, with a significantly lower number of competing commitments, have less to lose by joining militant groups. The same rationale is usually also employed with regard to other demographic characteristics, for example, the expectation that members of violent groups will be less attached to marital commitment or have a demanding professional career.

While the data collected about marital status and employment was limited, it was still possible to conclude that the findings regarding both traits among far-right perpetrators further support the linkage between biographical availability and violent activism. Less than 45 percent of the perpetrators were married when they perpetrated their violent attack, and just 12.7 percent of them had children. This is significantly lower than the average for the entire U.S. population (by the age of thirty-five, close to 80 percent of Americans were married at least once, and more than 55 percent are married at any point; 69 percent of those married have children). Moreover, the great majority of perpetrators were students (52.6 percent) or unemployed (10.2 percent), and those who were employed were mainly working in the service industry (14 percent) or construction (13 percent). Just 5 percent had a professional career. It is clear that most perpetrators of far-right violence have high levels of biographical availability and, in general, are not part of the upper socioeconomic echelons.

Another important characteristic of far-right perpetrators is the high proportion of those with a prior criminal background. While, again, data on this was difficult to collect, it was possible to identify that between 70 and 80 percent of perpetrators had prior arrests and served some time in a correctional facility. Although data limitations demand caution, there is some indication that many of the perpetrators of the far right are repeat offenders and were already involved in illicit or illegal activities. While it is not clear if far-right groups attract or try actively to recruit individuals with criminal experience, it is clear that they do not try to avoid such individuals participating in their activities. Another strong possibility is that many individuals with criminal tendencies find in far-right groups and ideology a convenient platform to exercise their criminal inclinations and to legitimize their aggressive or violent behavior.

The Environment of Perpetrators of Far-Right Violence

Some characteristics of the perpetrators of ideological violence are difficult to identify and collect. A partial solution for this challenge involves analyzing the features of the close environment of the perpetrator (his/her area of residence and close social networks) and indirectly gaining insight into potential stressors and pull factors that may lead him/her to engage in violent activities. This can help determine if socioeconomic factors had a role in the individual's radicalization process.

The environmental data mostly seems to correspond with previous indicators that emphasize the tendency of mainly (white) working-class Americans to join far-right groups and participate in their activities. For example, while the average family size in the United States stands at 2.53 per household, the average family size in the cities from where far-right perpetrators are coming is over 20 percent higher, at 3.13. Similarly, while the unemployment rate in the United States has fluctuated between 4 and 5.5 percent over the last couple of decades (except for a peak of 10 percent as a result of the 2008 recession), far-right perpetrators usually reside in areas where the average employment rate is 10 to 15 percent higher (6.25 percent). Furthermore, while the median income in the United States usually trends between $55,000 and $65,000, far-right perpetrators tend to reside in districts where the average median income is close to $27,000. Finally, while 32 percent of the U.S. population (above the age of twenty-five) has a bachelor degree, far-right perpetrators tend to come from districts in which the percentage of college-educated individuals among those who are twenty-five years old or older is less than 30 percent, and where the percentage of those with a high school diploma is less than 83 percent (in comparison to 90 percent for the entire U.S. population).

These findings seem to indicate that some socioeconomic factors facilitate involvement in radical activism and work in combination with the demographic and political factors discussed in chapter 5. However, these generalizations miss an important distinction between different types of perpetrators of far-right violence. A closer look at the data reveals that many acts of violence in the name of far-right ideology seem to be abrupt and unplanned, that is, basically spontaneous acts of violence. Hence, we cannot assume a priori that perpetrators of spontaneous and planned attacks share similar characteristics, as it seems they are being motivated by distinct situations. The following section will test the possibility of multiple profiles of perpetrators of far-right violence.

Perpetrators of Spontaneous and Planned Attacks

Spontaneous acts of violence, which are usually against minorities, seem to be both compatible with but also contradictory to some basic notions of criminal theory. While the criminological literature finds that most homicides are relatively spontaneous and a result of an intense emotional state, elements that can be found in most spontaneous acts of far-right violence as well, it also indicates that in many cases homicides are precipitated by the victims (who for the most part are not aware of the fact that their behavior may trigger a violent response) and involve individuals who had familiarity previously.[26] However, spontaneous far-right violence seems rarely to be triggered by the victims' actions, is often interracial, and tends not to include prior familiarity between the perpetrator and the victims.

It is also important to note that spontaneous acts of political violence also contradict common patterns of radicalization and related violent behaviors. Most models of political radicalization include multiple stages and assume a gradual progression toward the acceptance of violence as a legitimate means for promoting political goals and include in many cases a phase of joining a radical group.[27] These parameters are more difficult to observe in many of the perpetrators of spontaneous attacks, which in many cases did not exhibit prior behaviors or attitudes that indicated their radical views and state of mind or were part of a radical political group.

Through the dataset my team and I constructed for this book and related research,[28] it is possible to identify several additional differences between perpetrators of spontaneous and planned attacks. The first group included perpetrators of incidents in which the victim and offender did not have prior familiarity, the violence was not planned (the perpetrator did not make any preparations or was seeking a potential victim), and the perpetrator relied on an immediate context to act (he justified his violence by addressing visible triggers such as the victim's skin color or ethnic affiliation). The second group included incidents in which the perpetrator took specific steps in preparation for the attack and the intent of the act emerged before contact with the victim.

The findings indicate several important distinctions. Spontaneous perpetrators are significantly younger (an eight-year gap on average), less educated, and more likely to be unemployed, in comparison to perpetrators of planned attacks. No less interesting is that spontaneous attacks tend to occur in more affluent areas and in districts with lower minority-population levels.[29] What can we conclude from these differences? First, young people with fewer resources (such as education) naturally are less capable of engaging in sophisticated and planned operations and thus will express their views more in the form of spontaneous attacks. Moreover, it is possible to assume that since "spontaneous perpetrators" have less to lose from being involved in violent acts (exemplified by their higher rates of unemployment), they are less concerned with the consequences and more "trigger happy." Older individuals with more resources and competing commitments will be more inclined to make plans and preparations that will reduce their chances of paying the costs of their involvement in violent acts.

A surprising finding is that spontaneous incidents are more likely to occur in more affluent and less diverse areas.[30] A possible explanation is that the scarcity of potential targets (minority groups) diminishes the motivation to engage in long-term planning and organize as a hate group. The outcome is that if hate crimes do occur in such homogeneous areas, these are almost exclusively spontaneous. This explanation is also in line with the fact that most hate groups are proliferating in poor and middle-class areas with a high or increasing proportion of minorities (see chapter 5).

The Perpetrators of the Far Right: Developing a Sociological Profile

This chapter aimed to provide insights into the sociological profile of violent far-right activists and into the motivating factors that facilitate their slide to violent activities. Before discussing the main theoretical and policy implications of the findings, it is important to note that it is possible to identify several factors that reduce the costs of involvement in far-right violence, which usually are absent in other cases of ideologically motivated violence. To begin with, recent studies emphasize that in comparison to foreign perpetrators of terrorism, far-right perpetrators are less exposed to the public because the popular media tends to cover their actions less. The type of coverage is also fundamentally different. The treatment of media platforms of far-right activists tends not to emphasize their threat to society or dehumanize them; it is also more reluctant to designate them as "homegrown" or "domestic" terrorists.[31] Relatedly, the discourse that legitimizes the perceptions of threat from immigrants and foreign influence, a discourse promoted in some formal political streams, including by people who hold political office, may provide both a sense of legitimacy to potential perpetrators and lead to more lenient treatment of them by the criminal justice system. Finally, the growing diversity of the American population provides increasing opportunities to express violent behavior and sentiments toward out-groups, in many cases, without the need to engage in any long-term preparations and planning.

The findings regarding the perpetrators' socioeconomic characteristics seem to be related to some of the findings of the geographical and social concentrations of attacks (see chapter 5). They suggest that sociodemographic changes (an increase in the diversity of the population) in specific areas of the country do not affect everyone similarly in terms of the tendency to engage in far-right activism. More specifically, those who are the most vulnerable to the economic consequences of diversification, that is, those with limited material and status-related resources, are the ones who are more inclined to join far-right groups and participate in violent activities. It is not surprising, then, that many far-right groups increasingly shape their rhetoric to emphasize the declining status of white Americans and the need to protect that group's rights.

Since none of the sociodemographic processes that are linked to an increase in far-right violence (diversification and restructuring of the ethnic-class relations) are expected to slow or reverse in the foreseeable future, it is imperative to develop policy mechanisms that can curb their potential side effects. But the challenge facing law enforcement and policy makers also stems from the changes in the operational nature of far-right violence. The growing spontaneous nature of far-right violence and the substantial number of individuals who operate without collaboration with others elevate the challenge of countering far-right violence because opportunities to collect preventive intelligence or to identify potential perpetrators become more limited. An associated concern is that spontaneous perpetrators receive significantly shorter correctional sentences than those involved in planned attacks.[32] It appears that the criminal justice system perceives spontaneous violent incidents as a more minor threat in comparison to planned attacks. Beyond the obvious negative consequences of such an approach, it is also problematic, since spontaneous incidents almost always involve an actual victim, while many planned attacks include just a "potential" victim who never actually gets attacked.

Finally, the findings confirm the role of biographical availability in the likelihood to join militant groups or to engage in violent activities. It thus further emphasizes the importance of understanding the relationships between an individual's personal commitments and his/her tendency to take risks, including joining a militant group. Any potential counter-radicalization program can benefit not just from countering the various means of radical indoctrination and related environmental factors but also from helping vulnerable individuals develop skills that will elevate their engagement and investment in their community and other social frameworks. In this context, it is also important to identify the language and rhetorical mechanisms employed by radical groups to create an emotional disconnection between potential recruits and their communities and facilitate their joining alternative ideological and social communities, whether online or in the physical domain. The next chapter will provide an overview of the contemporary discourse of the American far right.

7

Contemporary Discourse of
the American Far Right

An intriguing development of recent years is the growing tendency of far-right perpetrators involved in mass-casualty attacks to provide a comprehensive ideological manifesto that aims to explain the ideological and operational reasoning behind their actions and encourage others to follow in their steps. This practice, which in the past was exclusive to leaders of far-right groups, has become common also among lone wolves. Anders Breivik, who killed seventy-seven people and injured more than three hundred on July 22, 2011, is one of the first, and prime, examples. After detonating a car bomb near the office of the Norwegian prime minister in Oslo, which killed eight people, he traveled to the nearby island of Utoay and began to shoot at attendees of a youth summer camp, killing another sixty-nine people. On the day of the attack, Breivik released an electronic version of his ideological manifesto, titled "2083: A European Declaration of Independence." The text, over 1,500 pages long, provided a detailed overview of his motivation for the attack. Specifically, he identified the supposed consequences of Muslim immigration to Europe and the growing advancement of multiculturalism and foreign values (via practices of political correctness, for example) by the European left as the most significant threats to the survival of European white Christian culture.[1] His arguments were in many ways an echo of similar arguments raised by American far-right activists in the early 1990s, which asserted that diversity policies are a codeword for the "White Genocide."[2]

Breivik's manifesto and the writings of far-right perpetrators who were inspired by his actions and committed similar attacks—such as Patrick Wood Crusius, a white American supremacist who killed twenty-two people in a Walmart store in El Paso, Texas, on August 3, 2019—reflect several important transformations in the discourse of the racist far right in many corners of the globe. While far-right discourse has always emphasized the superiority of Western culture and the need for segregation between racial groups, in the last few years it seems that a growing number of far-right ideologists prefer to focus on cultural and normative differences between communities rather than on primordial attributes such as race and ethnic origin. The rhetoric now more often includes justifications mainly based on the need to preserve specific cultural-religious norms and practices, rather than the genetic purity of the white race. Breivik writes specifically that:

the root of Europe's problems is the lack of cultural self-confidence (nationalism). Most people are still terrified of nationalistic political doctrines thinking that if we ever embrace these principles again, new "Hitler's" will suddenly pop up and initiate global Armageddon. . . . This irrational fear of nationalistic doctrines is preventing us from stopping our own national/cultural suicide as the Islamic colonization is increasing annually.

Similarly, Kyle Chapman, the founder of the U.S.-based Fraternal Order of Alt-Knights (FOAK), declared that the world, particularly Western nations, must protect itself and fight to rid itself of Islam, neo-Marxism, and globalization. He added that the fight against Antifa and BAMN (By Any Means Necessary, a minority support group) reflects "a resurgence of a warrior spirit to Western Society and re-institution of our constitutional republic and traditional western values."[3] An even more direct call to a shared (white) European resistance and identity is manifested by a member of the National Socialist Movement, who explains in an online post from 2006 that "white American" is an identity like any other, such as African American or Jewish American, and that all whites should come together with knowledge and weapons in order to halt the non-Europeans from pushing their secular agenda via the use of government and media. That is, all Europeans must come together to defeat evil.[4]

Breivik also addresses an additional theme that, while traditionally part of the far-right discourse, was rarely foregrounded: the concern that the left's cultural influence paves a path to the collapse of the patriarchal order. "Politically correct" terminology, which is becoming more prevalent in the West, according to Breivik, intends to "deny the intrinsic worth of native Christian European heterosexual males," who are being reduced to "emasculate[d] . . . touchy-feely subspecies." Masculine exclusiveness, which was always part of the far-right subculture, seems to be becoming a prime motivating factor for violence.

The consequence of the declining emphasis on traditional aspects of nationalism led to the embrace of a transnational racial cultural-religious identity. More specifically, while racial identity was always a primary component of the identity of far-right activists, it was usually constructed in the context of local political frameworks. Hence, whereas collaborations and coordination existed between similar far-right groups from different countries, they still emphasized local nationalist sentiments and rarely discussed transnational racial issues. In contrast, Breivik and a growing number of other far-right ideologists seem increasingly to embrace a more regional if not global perspective in the way they define "their" constituencies and the overall struggles and threats facing the white race.[5] In this context, it seems also that popular past distinctions between different types of white nations and Christian traditions are less important in the face of the growing importance of the global "cultural clash."

These dynamics are not completely unrelated to recent stylistic changes in the discourse of the far right; these changes aim to provide far-right parties and organizations with a more legitimate, mainstream image. For example, studies identified the increased use of equivocation in the messaging of far-right parties and movements. That is, they tend to employ ambiguous, contradictory, tangential, obscure, or even evasive language in order to portray their ideological agenda in a more moderate and less offensive manner.[6] The "rights" of white people are emphasized, rather than the desire for the discrimination or marginalization of out-groups; activists frame themselves as "white nationalists" or "alt-right" rather than as white supremacists. The Brotherhood of the Klan went even further by designating itself a "Racial Awareness Group."[7] Similarly, many European far-right parties are engaged in what scholars describe as the recalibration of fascism, shifting their rhetorical focus to the scarcity of resources channeled to white communities, which is caused by (according to far-right ideologists) growing state support for ethnic minorities.[8]

The current chapter provides a contemporary overview of the discourse of the American violent far right. But before delving into the main themes that form that discourse, it is necessary to discuss developments in the methodology of discourse analysis and how they are reflected in the current chapter.

The Logic of Discourse Analysis

In academic research, discourse analysis refers to the process of analyzing social interactions that are conducted via writing, speech, or various artistic platforms or means of communication. Such exploration aims to provide insights into the relationships between texts/communications and context. The analysis of the historical and social context of communications facilitates comprehension of the evolution and solidification of the meaning of social or political constructions and how they are legitimized and experienced by individuals and collectives.[9] The utility of discourse analysis stems from the understanding that discourse creates, reproduces, and changes social reality and is influenced by the changes in the political, social, and economic environment. Therefore, to understand society or parts of it, we also need to look into discursive dynamics.

As in many fields of the social sciences, the area of discourse analysis experienced the growth of a critical approach. Similar to the orientation of critical approaches in areas such as sociology, political science, and terrorism studies, critical discourse analysis emphasizes the role of power distribution. Language cannot be analyzed in a vacuum or considered neutral; rather, discourse analysis needs to expose how linguistic mechanisms play a role in shaping instruments of power and control and how they frame political reality in accordance with specific agendas and interests. The logic of critical discourse analysis is that political and social actors are utilizing and disseminating discourse that helps them legitimize specific knowledge, social roles, identities, and political perceptions.[10]

The discourse-historical approach (DHA) is in many ways an extension of critical discourse analysis. It evolved over the last thirty years, initially in

Europe and then spreading to other regions. While it has a strong historical emphasis, as its name suggests, today it is also being used in studies focusing on more contemporary historical and social processes. At its core, DHA stresses the need to understand both the intentions of the speakers/ writers and extralinguistic factors (the status of the participants, timing and place, personal characteristics, etc.).[11] Thus sociopsychological, cognitive, and linguistic elements play an even larger role in the exploration of meaning and linguistic constructions.[12]

DHA is especially appropriate for the study of far-right language, propaganda, and social interactions because it strongly emphasizes power relations in their historical context. More specifically, it is concerned with the way national and ethnic identities and related social frameworks are created through discourse and especially how "others" are presented as threats to a specific collective or elites. It is not surprising that DHA is used extensively in the study of discrimination (racism, nationalism, xenophobia, Islamophobia, sexism) and of particularistic political dynamics such as past political commemorations, nation building, migration, and cultural policies.[13]

Discourse Analysis and the Violent American Far Right

The traumatic consequences of the rise of fascist regimes in Europe in the early 1930s and the growing popularity of far-right parties since the early 1980s has led many social scientists to examine the mechanisms that have contributed to the persuasive rhetoric and propaganda of this political stream. In the 1950s, Victor Klemperer and Rolf Sternberger published seminal works that endeavored to understand the language of far-right politics (particularly German National Socialism).[14] They were followed by many who have focused primarily on analyzing the rhetoric of contemporary far-right parties and the countering "healing" rhetoric used by European governments. In this tradition, this chapter will provide an overview of the rhetoric of the contemporary American far right groups.

Four major themes will be at the center of the analysis:

1. Rhetoric related to the justification and exercising of violence
2. The depiction and framing of the "enemy" or "threat," with special emphasis on out-groups commonly victimized by the far right
3. Interpretive rhetoric that addresses historical and contemporary global and domestic events and processes
4. Interpretive rhetoric that addresses future global and domestic events and processes, with special attention to the apocalyptic visions and narratives being formulated by many far-right groups

To collect primary sources that discuss these issues, I reviewed multiple communication platforms, including organizational and independent websites promoting a far-right ideology, relevant social media platforms, and personal accounts, as well as publications, some disseminated electronically and some as hard copies. Finally, an effort was made to ensure sufficient coverage of each stream of the American far right (racial, antigovernment, and fundamentalist).

The Rhetoric of the Racist Stream

An examination of the ideological discourse of America's white supremacy groups reveals that the rhetorical modifications that were initiated with the resurgence of the "Klean Klan" in the 1980s have resurfaced and further gained momentum in the last few years. From a movement focusing on the oppression of other races and minority groups and on the preservation of white privileges, it has expanded its objectives to include a series of issues that, while related to the social and economic status of America's white working class, are not necessarily exclusive to them. For example, the United Northern & Southern Knights of the KKK (UNSKKK) and the National Alliance separately released new sets of organizational goals in the mid- to late 2010s. Whereas they still embrace their commitment to the Fifteen Words doctrine ("We must secure an existence for ourselves and the future of our white Christian children") and the end of (what they perceive as) white discrimination, the other points in their strategic documents mostly use terminology that could probably be found in many

mainstream political parties and movements. There is a focus on restrict-
ing immigration, free trade, and ending or limiting foreign aid (since these
are perceived as contributing to the collapse of the U.S. economy and
middle class), as well as on providing protection to small businesses, agricultural workers, and gun owners. This broad ideological framework also
spilled over to some skinhead organizations. Volkfront, for example,
declares in its online mission statement that beyond white nationalism,
the organization will fight for environmental conservation, economic
issues, states' rights, crime reduction, and labor rights.[15]

Consequently, it is not surprising to see that such issues eventually
shape the day-to-day propaganda efforts of far-right organizations. For
example, the KKK Knight Party released a pamphlet in 2017 that, while
not including any racist or hate terminology, argues that 1,880,000 American workers are displaced from their jobs every year by immigrants and
that the cost of providing welfare assistance to these Americans is surpass-
ing $15 billion a year.[16] Similarly, Hammerskin Nations activists repeatedly
posted on the organization's website forums opinion messages that emphasize that antigun legislation is intended to strip white people of their ability
to protect themselves.[17] Some of the propaganda concerning the discrimination of whites tries to touch on perceived institutional discrimination
from a more legal perspective. Of note is a publication by Keystone United,
which discusses the (alleged) double standard between blacks and whites in
the military. It states that underqualified blacks go up for promotion while
whites are passed over and that while NAAWP (National Association for
the Advancement of White People) members are being discharged, members of the NAACP are able to conduct meetings and operate freely in military facilities.[18]

The strategic documents of the National Alliance and UNSKKK also
include segments about the necessity to restore order to the streets of
America. Indeed, the attention to issues of law and order, and especially
the implementation of stricter punishments, is echoed in many racist
groups' platforms. This includes calling for an expansion of the death penalty (which interestingly became an important point of discussion mainly
on skinhead message boards) and providing harsher punishments to sexual offenses. It is important to note that since minorities are overrepre-
sented among the American incarcerated population, these views may be
perceived by far-right activists as an alternative and more "legitimate" way

to "punish" members of minority groups. This rationale was being articulated in a post on a message board affiliated with Keystone United, in which a user calling himself "Steve Smith" highlighted President Trump's tweet from 2013 in which he claimed, "Sadly, the overwhelming amount of violent crime in our major cities is committed by blacks and Hispanics—a tough subject—must be discussed."[19]

This is not the only domain in which there seems to be a growing convergence between mainstream right and racist far-right rhetoric. Another is regarding the concept of "America First," or the need of the United States to disengage from world politics and primarily focus on the welfare of Americans. The user "38 Florida" emphasized in his post on the Hammerskin Nation message board that he felt that the country should "Pull all US assets out and let S. Korea fight its own battle."[20] He then provides a quote from one of Adolf Hitler's speeches in which he emphasizes his complete disinterest in how other nations perceive Nazi Germany. As this quote reflects, the far right's criticism of the executive branch is not necessarily restricted to Democratic presidents. For example, a repeated point in contemporary far-right discourse is a criticism of the ongoing support of President Trump for Israel and his close relationships with Jewish donors. Such criticism aligns not just with the concept of "America First" but also with traditional conspiracy theories linking Jews with manipulating political regimes via control of the financial markets. For example, the user "BMX racist" posted on a Hammerskins message board that "The Real Donald Trump has emerged as a dedicated supporter of the most hardline elements in Israel, whose aspirations are fueled by the money flowing from American Jewish Billionaires."[21] An additional popular line of criticism against the government focuses on perceived sociocultural attacks against whites. Thomas Robb, the national director of the National Knights of the Ku Klux Klan, stated in 2002 that "Anti-White discrimination is official government policy through affirmative action schemes such as minority scholarship, minority business grants . . . we demand an end to all government enforced race mixing."[22] Such ideas are being echoed in numerous similar texts produced by far-right activists.

An additional current-affairs issue that became popular in U.S. far-right discourse and that in many ways can be linked to the ongoing concerns of the far right about the proliferation of "leftist" values and concepts (such as multiculturalism and political correctness) is the rise of left-wing movements such as Black Lives Matter, Occupation Wall Street, and Antifa. These groups are perceived in many cases as antiwhite. The Brotherhood of the Klans, for example, explains in its new mission statement that the organization is aiming to "regain the courage and pride that has been systematically stripped from them [whites] by the liberals in the name of political correctness,"[23] and the National Socialist Movement and Federal Order of Alt-Knights (FAOK) advocate designating Antifa as a terrorist group in their online publications.[24] Similarly, users on the Rise Above Movement (RAM) message board emphasize in numerous posts the substantial impact and importance of counterprotest of white nationalists against the demonstrations of Antifa and similar groups. Rise Above Movement even directly criticizes on its "gab" (a social media platform used by extreme political groups) page those "keyboard warriors" who do not directly and physically confront Antifa members: "The day we got our start. Not many altrighters can say they Not only stood and fought antifa but actually chased them out of rallies and keep fellow patriots safe."[25]

In some instances, left-wing groups are perceived as an actual and direct threat, a context that helps legitimize violence against them. The user "Mojocat27" clarified in a Hammerskin Nations' message board post that the proper response against left-wing activists is "Protect myself, my family and my brothers and sisters by any and all means possible!!"[26] What helps further legitimize violent response against left-wing activist groups is the inclination to define the perceived cultural attack from the left as an attack against the Christian nature of America or against core symbols of the far-right ethos. An online post by James Rafferty, Imperial Kludd of Brothers of the Klan, states: "Religion in this country has been under constant attacks from all fronts. The removal of prayer from our schools, the removal of nativity scenes from our government property, the removal of crosses or any religious symbols from many municipal flags and logotypes . . . we need to fight to regain the religious fundamentals that this country was founded upon."[27] Similarly, when voices were raised to eliminate the Confederate flag's emblem from the flags of several southern states, the KKK released a call to fight against such reforms— "Save the Flag. The flag of the South is now the flag of Worldwide Unity . . . the battle to save the Confederate flag is raging . . . the effort is being manifested to STEAL the flag away from those who still cherish it's memory."[28]

The discourse of American white supremacists also proves to be fairly innovative and productive in the formulation and dissemination of alternative historical narratives. While some narratives are based on somewhat legitimate academic debates, such as if the Civil War was indeed driven by issues related to the expansion of slavery,[29] others are clearly based on false facts. For instance, some white supremacist activists will quote an erroneous historical narrative that President Lincoln was planning to send African Americans back to Africa and had no interest in producing political and social equality, usually quoting from Lincoln's debates with Douglas to substantiate such claims, despite the fact that Lincoln's views changed dramatically in subsequent years. Another prominent conspiracy theory in this vein is that the 2012 mass shooting event at Sandy Hook Elementary School, which led to the death of twenty students and six teachers, was a government-staged operation in order to legitimize attacks against gun owners. Sometimes these conspiracy narratives are more general, but they nonetheless still clearly lack factual support. The Atom Waffen Division stated in a 2017 publication that the world is collapsing because of corruption and that democracy and capitalism have been failures and run by the Jews, who are engaged in the cultural and racial displacement of the white race. The group writes, "National Socialism is the only solution to reclaim dominion over what belongs to us. The west cannot be saved, but it can be rebuilt and even stronger without the burdens of the past."[30] A similar idea was expressed in a post published by the user "Hillbilly" in July 2018 on a Hammerskin Nation forum: "They are pushing white genocide by race mixing by turning our children [gay] and sterilizing our girls with those dam shots plus they plan on flooding all white 3world trash to replace us."[31] In both cases, and in many similar publications,[32] the revisionist historical narratives aim to provide an apocalyptic framework (society is failing) and instill the notion that only neo-Nazi organizations can rebuild a better socialist nation when the inevitable collapse occurs. It is also clear from such publications what will be the destiny of those who oppose the new order. A neo-Nazi propaganda flyer released in 2018 depicts a person being hanged and reads, "Race Traitors face capital punishment on the day of reckoning";[33] another flyer's caption reads, "Once the seeds of revolution are sown the kikes are all done."[34]

The unique or alternative interpretations of historical and contemporary events also lead to the rise of those who can be described as unpredictable "heroes" of the racism-driven wing of the far right. For example, during the high-profile trial of George Zimmerman, who claimed self-defense following his deadly shooting of the unarmed African American teenager Trayvon Martin, far-right forums saw a dramatic spike in messages supportive of and legitimizing Zimmerman's actions. A post by "Junior member" from June 2013 is a representative example: "A White man shoots a nigger in self-defense, and all the other niggers scream hate crime. But earlier this year 2 niggers shoot a newborn white baby dead and then take 2 shots at the childs mother and its just treated like annother murder."[35] Likewise, a Discord chat survey used by the Patriot Front group published an image of Dylann Roof, who shot to death nine African American congregants at the Emanuel African Methodist Episcopal Church in Charleston, South Carolina, in June 2015, that depicted him as a holy saint holding a paper with the slogan "We must secure the existence of our people and a future for our white children." Along with the image, the user includes an excerpt from Dylann Roof's journal that references Hitler, the tyrannical system of the U.S. government, and how "the White people" are the target of society.[36]

Alongside the mainstreaming of some discursive elements, there are also some areas in which there is growing overlap between the different streams of the American far right, and the white supremacist stream is no exception. Some neo-Nazi groups adopt a fundamentalist religious rhetoric, which is usually the domain of the Christian Identity movement. A 2016 publication of the Atom Waffen Division asserts that both the government and the entertainment industry are under Satanic influence.[37] A different flyer, also disseminated by the Atom Waffen Division, adopts more militia-style rhetoric. Its caption states, "Strew the streets with the bodies of bureaucrats!" while showing men in suits and ties hanging and awaiting execution.[38] Similarly, several factions of the KKK increasingly engage in pro-life propaganda. A publication by the Knights, one of the KKK's media arms, is an info sheet that tries to convince women that abortion is a dangerous, life-threatening procedure.[39] But even more surprising is the tendency to use Islamic concepts in some of the racist groups' propaganda efforts. An Aryan Nations publication, for example, calls for an "Aryan Jihad" against the "Judaic Tyrannical System,"[40] and an Atom Waffen Division publication released online depicts an AWD soldier with the hashtag #WhiteJihad.[41]

The Internal Rhetoric of the Racist Stream

Naturally, activists of white supremacy groups do not exclusively focus on outside groups and policies but also engage in various internal debates related to the practices and organization of their groups. One of the more interesting developments within the skinhead subculture is the growing reluctance to endorse violent behaviors and other criminal acts. For example, after an incident in Avalon, Pennsylvania, in which two members of Keystone United were arrested after a bar fight allegedly triggered by their racist attitudes, the movement released a formal clarification, reemphasizing that it is against any violence except in cases of self-defense and that it opposes attacks based on race.[42] Similarly, in a post on the Hammerskin Nation message board, one of the supposed leaders explains: "The club here is drug-free and I know of no one who looks down on any respectable crew who doesn't share that viewpoint . . . if you allow too much freedom on the issue you could end up like the Aryan Brotherhood." Finally, an official release on the Blood and Honor website in 2018 indicates that the group will not recruit drug dealers and sexual predators.[43] It is clear that there is a concentrated effort to rebrand these organizations and distance them from criminal practices.

Internal debates are also highly focused on suitable propaganda practices and organizational structure. For example, some skinheads argue that the movement must adopt more sexually oriented propaganda in order to continue to attract young males. The user "CaseofPride" posted on the Hammerskin Nations message board a post that refers to White Power music and claims that "this movement has become so boring and PC. bring back angry Aryans and boot parties haha. Young men want sex violence and partying."[44] He then suggests that like in rap music, there is a need to focus more on sex and violence in the movement's propaganda. Similar ideas are also reflected in a post on the same message board by "Odessa 14," who explains: "Now, what teenage male doesn't like boobs? . . . As a Movement, we should really push the sex appeal. If a teenage kid sees hot chicks on our posters, CD covers, or websites, it will immediately grab their attention. Through that, we can convey our message. We gotta present our movement that if you are a skinhead, you will get the hottest girls."[45]

Likewise, one can find debates about how the movement can enhance its political influence. An Aryan Nation essay published in March 2018 on the Screwdriver website focuses on the future of the movement and the different paths it can choose while elaborating on the pros and cons of operating within the legal democratic system via a pure national socialist party, in contrast to employing other methods of power-grabbing.[46] It also warns about chasing solutions that promise quick progress but are just illusions. In another post on the same website, there is a call for employing the tactic of direct action, which was popularized by environmental groups. Thus, each member of the movement (or local cell) is expected to engage in various acts of political activism, mostly locally, in order to create a political momentum that will force the government to change its policies.[47]

Some internal debates focus on the importance of the members' own professional development. For example, the National Socialist Movement emphasized in its online publication that it is important for the members to maintain consistent employment and that if they are unemployed they will be unable to get elected to political offices, and the judges, officers, and lawyers will continue to be corrupted and stall the movement's ability to advance its goals.[48] Another publication of the movement also calls for donations so the movement can help pay the tuition of members interested in enrolling in law school.[49]

To conclude, one of the more interesting trends in the far-right racist discourse is the emergence of different variations of the idea of creating segregated political communities. Order 15, a far-right ideological movement, promotes the creation of communities on the "periphery of the old (world)" and depicts in its publications the life in "decentralized national communities."[50] Its rationale is that this is a way white nationalists can promote and protect their culture with only limited confrontation with the government. Likewise, the National Alliance emphasizes in its propaganda the importance of "White Living Space" for the survival of the white race while providing elaborate plans on how such spaces should be organized and structured.[51] Even some skinhead groups embrace the concept of white autonomy. Volksfront in its mission statement indicates that it "has long been at the forefront of the struggle for White autonomy, White self-determination and the issues of the White Working Class."[52] Does this reflect ideological fatigue and growing comprehension within the far right about its limited ability to mobilize sufficient support to lead to political and policy changes? Is it now focusing efforts on maintaining the existing constituency of the far right, rather than expanding it? If this is the case, it is possible to argue that while most far-right leaders understand that imposing the ideology of the U.S. far right as the national status quo is not really attainable, they differ in their proposed solutions. While some advocate isolation and separation, others promote the continued attempt to mainstream far-right rhetoric. At least for now, the latter seems to be the more popular solution.

The Discourse of the Antigovernment Stream

The election of Barack Obama, the first African American president of the United States, did not just lead to a violent backlash from the far right, as described in chapter 5, but also seems to have facilitated a new wave of antigovernment groups, which were able to mobilize support also from the moderate right and forge a more moderate and legitimate image (see also chapter 3). While part of their success in gaining relative popular legitimacy is related to the fact that many of their members are veterans or former members of law enforcement organizations, it is also important to identify if and how their discourse may contribute to their growth.

One of the most important mechanisms that allow antigovernment groups to form a more legitimate posture is the practice of extending their "services" to a community or parts of it. For example, following several active-shooter incidents in schools between 2017 and 2019, the Oath Keepers expressed their willingness to deploy in order to protect schools all over the country.[53] Likewise, the III Percenters created an organizational national disaster relief team, whose goal is to provide assistance in cases of natural or manmade crises.[54] Many of the new militia groups consistently rush to join and support communities or groups of citizens who are engaged in a confrontation with federal agencies. For example, when a conflict between Cliven Bundy, a rancher from Nevada, and the Bureau of Land Management (BLM) escalated over the latter's attempt to seize Bundy's cattle in lieu of $1 million, which Bundy owed the federal government in unpaid grazing fees, heavily armed militiamen arrived to support Bundy and deployed in his Bunkerville ranch. The BLM agents had no choice but to retreat.[55] While many saw these events as acts of vigilantism, members of Bundy's community and of other rural communities perceived him as a hero and supported the militiamen. Thus, for the militias, joining Bundy gained them further legitimacy and support from rural communities all over the country. Even some of the recruiting language of the organizations emphasizes elements of service. The leadership of the Constitutional Sheriffs and Peace Officers of America (CSPOA) "calls for volunteers to join the organization and perform different positions and tasks across the great republic."[56]

But the new militias' involvement in mainstream politics goes beyond providing security or military "services." They also in many cases promote mainstream, nonviolent political activism. On April 12, 2018, the Oath Keepers called for all their members to attend Second Amendment rallies (which were to be held in all capital cities two days later), and when Democratic congresswoman Maxine Waters expressed her support for harassing Trump administration employees in public places (following the news that children of undocumented immigrants were being detained separately from their parents along the Mexican border), the Oath Keepers encouraged their members to protest against her, tweeting on their official account: "Oath Keepers Call For Action: Protest Terrorist Inciter Maxine Waters Thursday, July 19. Oath Keepers stand against Terrorism, Stand for Freedom of Speech and Association in support for ICE/Border Patrol as they Enforce Constitutional Immigration."[57] Similarly, when the National Football League (NFL) announced a new policy permitting players to stay in the locker room while the National Anthem is performed before games, the Oath Keepers' founding leader, Stewart Rhodes, called on its members to boycott NFL games and stop watching them.[58]

Expectedly, the involvement of militias in mainstream political discourse also led them to adopt some of the relatively new cultural/political trends proliferating within the American right, such as the notion that institutions of higher education are engaged in indoctrinating young Americans in left-wing liberal ideas, as well as the resentment toward globalism. Before the 2018 midterm elections, members of the III Percenters warned about an anti-Trump alliance between Democratic and Republican globalists, and the Oath Keepers website published multiple videos aiming to convince young members to engage in private entrepreneurial initiatives rather than enroll in colleges, since the latter are a "Center for

Globalism."[59] Similarly, the right-wing criticism of the mainstream media is being echoed in the discourse of the militia groups. A III Percenters member, Matthew Bishop, stated blatantly in a post that he published on the organization's message board that "As we get closer to the November Elections, the Mainstream Media (MSM) and the Globalists . . . are attacking Trump relentlessly . . . Internet Platforms are suspending, or canceling accounts of Conservative and Libertarian Pundits." A fellow member, Charles Cole, responded, "They are acting like a wounded animal backed into a corner, and that can be a dangerous thing."[60]

Despite these interesting rhetorical trends, the two topics that still seem to drive much militia discourse are the public disputes regarding the Second Amendment and immigration. By far these are the two most prominent rallying cries of such groups, and in some cases these issues lead them to overreach and directly challenge federal authorities' sovereignty. In April 2017, the CSPOA called for law officers to refuse to enforce gun controls that (in their view) infringe on the Second Amendment.[61] The issue of immigration seems to generate an even more active approach from militia groups. During 2019, as conservative pundits intensely discussed illegal immigrants crossing the Mexican border, including caravans arriving from Central America, groups such as the United Constitutional Patriots, Patriots of the Constitution, and Mountain Minutemen collaborated to engage in vigilant operations along the border. On October 19, 2018, they issued a press release claiming:

> The Invaders are now being trucked to the border. Several thousand expected. We do understand that Trump is deploying troops but, in the meantime, it is imperative that we have boots on the ground. We are working with the border patrol and their orders are above in the update from Robert Crooks [the Mountain Minutemen's leader]. Not only are the Invaders being trucked, they [are] coming by boat to San Diego and they are also coming from Africa then up through South America to our border.[62]

In this context, some of the members of these groups were willing to state their extreme views about what needed to be done. Armando Gonzalez, a member of United Constitutional Patriots, was quoted in a police report from April 24, 2019: "Why are we just apprehending them and not lining them up and shooting them . . . we have to go back to Hitler days and put them all in a gas chamber."[63]

At least one of the reasons for the growing activism of militias in the Mexican border region seems to be related to the link that many of them make between (what they perceive as) inclusive and soft immigration policies and conspiracy theories related to the "true" interest of the federal government. In other words, they see illegal immigration as a tool used by globalists and anti-American elements within the federal government to further erode American values and constitutional principles. Chuck Davis, a member of United Constitutional Patriots, reflected this mindset when he stated in a YouTube video that "these people [migrants] obviously are being paid to come here and crash the system. Why? Because that's the only way the deep state can still win."[64]

To conclude, similar to the tendencies observed in the racist stream, the rhetoric of the antigovernment stream now engages in a discussion of more contemporary political issues and events, not just in the traditional conspiracy theories that were the trademark of the movement in the 1990s and early 2000s and focused more on the hijacking of the government by foreign agents and the merging of the United States with an international government as part of the New World Order. In many ways, these conspiracy theories were reshaped in order to make them easier to internalize and legitimize. Thus, instead of a discussion about the hijacking of the government, the discourse shifted to the role of bureaucratic forces (the Deep State) within the government in oppressing constitutional rights. Similarly, the theories about the merging of the United States into a global government were modified into a discourse about the need to oppose globalism and especially globalist policies, which represent a threat to the preservation of American culture, ethos, and foundational principles.

By embracing ideological issues that represent major disputes within the American public, such as gun control, immigration policies, and state sovereignty, the militias portray themselves as legitimate partisan political actors and mobilize support from the increasing margins of the political divide in the United States. Thus, the intensified polarization of the American political electorate provides an instrumental advantage to the mobilization efforts of the antigovernment groups. This unique dynamic will be further discussed in the concluding chapter of the book, and it reflects the growing political sophistication of contemporary far-right groups and their ability to push their ideological ideas into mainstream political discourse.

The Discourse of the Christian Identity Movement

Reliance on a unique interpretation of religious texts is still the primary feature of the discourse of the Christian Identity movement. But an equally powerful tendency over the last few years is the association of contemporary events with the movement's overall ideological framework and biblical interpretations. It reflects ideological "creativity," which aims essentially to point out "signs" of the upcoming apocalypse. A recent illustration can be found in a newsletter America's Promise Ministries published in April 2018, in which the organization argues that the fires that spread all over California at that time and caused substantial damage are probably depictions of God's punishment: "Could these flames be flames of Divine Judgment? Considering all the fires the state of California has been subject to over the past several months and the fact that California has turned into one of the most corrupt states in America, would it be unthinkable to Bible-believing people to assume that God Almighty is visiting them with fires of judgment?" In the following passages, the author lists all of California's sins: "California has become more and more perverted and corrupt . . . become a sanctuary for hoards [sic] of aliens who hate America, it has become a bastion for homosexual activity and politics."[65]

In other cases, references to current events aim to solidify the identity of the movement's enemies. In these cases, usually, the nativist and racist nature of the movement is in full view. A newsletter published in July 2018, also by America's Promise Ministries, explains that Russia's president Vladimir Putin's involvement in Syria is actually a positive development because "Obama has done nothing but spread Islamism by destabilizing the Middle-East which has caused hoards [sic] of Syrian, Iraqi, Libyan and other into Europe and the United States. . . . Obama hates Christian Western nations and everything White Christian nations stand for, though such 'Christianity' is a very muddied picture in today's dumbed down society."[66] Similarly, an online essay published by the Christian Identity Church website challenges Trump's commitment to Christianity by criticizing his support of Israel and the LGBTQ community, as well as the fact that he "allowed his daughter to marry a Jew and allowed his son, Eric, to marry a Jewess. . . . If Donald Trump raised his Children to be Christians and really knew the Bible, his children would not even consider marrying Jews."[67] Interestingly but not surprisingly, the same website supports Trump's description of African nations as "shithole countries." In September 2018, it stated: "But the Fact is when people had too much, sugar coated words go out the window. The fact is that the countries that Trump was referring to are just that. They are the pits and anyone who has lived in an African country can tell you of the corruption. It's really money thrown down a rat hole. Perhaps this word should be used."[68]

Another important dynamic that can be observed in the Christian Identity discourse, which is also clearly visible in the previous streams discussed in this chapter, is the growing ideological overlap with other groups on the far right. This is evident especially when an issue such as immigration is being discussed. Christian Identity church leaders, for example, emphasized that "the Muslim numbers are growing throughout the continent of Europe. They are rapidly transforming Europe into conclaves of Sharia-law strongholds. London has closed 500 Christian Churches and open 423 new Mosques. 'London is more Islamic than many Muslim countries put together' according to Maulana Syed Raza Rizvi, one of the Islamic Preachers who now lead 'Londonistan.'"[69]

Yet, probably the more surprising adoption of other groups' ideas is what seems to be an embrace of the rhetoric usually used by the Sovereign Citizens. America's Promise Ministries (APM) warned its followers about the Federal Reserve and its manipulation of measures of wealth and money—"The Federal Reserve's phony money is and always has been a lying, cheating standard of weights and measures. Almost all the presidents, Congress, Senate, Supreme Court, all political parties, certainly both the Republicans and Democrats, have not spoken boldly about the problem,"[70] and in a different newsletter it declared that the government, DOJ, FBI, and BLM are all corrupt and acting like tyrants.[71] This language almost exactly echoes the popular Sovereign Citizens theory that asserts that the current U.S. monetary system is a hoax and an instrument exploited by the government to pay foreign debts.

The discourse of the Identity movement resembles the language of other groups also in its manifestation of the growing concerns about the rise of militant socialist left-wing groups and in the defensive tone it employs, focusing on the protection of the rights of the white race. America's Promise Ministries directly warns its members about the growing hate against white people. "Think of Barack Obama's eight-year atrocious reign. Think of all the riots, militant negro out of control violent displays, lawlessness and anarchy. The rise of hate against White people and for all practical purposes, neither Obama, or any of his Washington swamp staff, political insiders, or hacks did a thing about that."[72]

Despite these new developments in its discourse, it is still important to mention the Identity movement's ongoing practice of employing the interpretation of religious texts to justify various xenophobic, nativist, and racist ideas. In many Identity group websites, one can find a long list of biblical verses that are supposed to support the movement's ideological convictions. Usually, these verses can be divided into at least three categories. The first are verses that are used to support racial segregation. Popular ones are a verse from Joshua 23:12–13, "If you do in any way go back and cleave unto the remnants of these Nations, even these that remain among you, and shall make marriages with them, and go in unto them and they unto you: Know for a certainty that there shall be snares and traps unto you, and scourges in your side and thornes in your eyes. Until ye perish off from this good land which the Lord your God has given you," and a verse from Deuteronomy 7:3–4, "Do not intermarry with them. Do not give your daughters to their sons or take their daughters for your sons, for they will turn your children away from following me to serve other gods, and the Lord's anger will burn against you and will quickly destroy you."[73]

The second category of verses is used to illustrate the immorality of homosexuality and transgenderism. Some of the more common verses are from Leviticus 20:13, "If a man also lie with mankind as he lieth with a woman, both of them have committed an abomination, they shall surely be put to death, their blood shall be upon them," and from Deuteronomy 22:5, "A woman shall not wear that pertaineth unto a man, neither shall a man put on a woman's garment. For all that do are an abomination unto the Lord thy God."

Finally, there are verses that are used explicitly to provide moral legitimacy to doctrines of white supremacy and anti-Semitism. Interestingly, in this category, the verses seem to be less effective or at least need more imaginative interpretation in order to be associated with racist and nativist notions. A verse used frequently is from John 15:22–25: "If I had not come and spoken to them, they would not be guilty of sin; but now they have no excuse for their sin. Whoever hates me hates my Father as well. If I had not done among them the works no one else did, they would not be guilty of sin. As it is, they have seen, and yet they have hated both me and my Father. But this is to fulfill what is written in their Law: 'They hated me without reason.'" In this verse, the Christian Identity interpretation is that "them" means "the Jews." Another verse used frequently is from Deuteronomy 15:6: "For the Lord your God will bless you as he has promised, and you will lend to many nations but will borrow from none. You will rule over many nations but none will rule over you." This verse, according to Identity followers, supposedly confirms God's promise to maintain the superiority of the white race by ensuring that other races will never rule it.

Overall, such verses are employed by the Christian Identity movement to legitimize and popularize their views by asserting that they are based on religious practices and principles rooted in the texts of the New and Old Testaments. In this sense, their rhetorical techniques are not dissimilar from the ones that in many cases are being used by other, non-Christian, religious militant groups.

Mainstreaming and Competition

Examination of the evolving rhetoric of the American far right provides insights about the main themes and ideas that inspire its members and helps identify some of the reasons for its resurgence in the second decade of the twenty-first century. The capacity of contemporary far-right groups to inject their ideas into contemporary public debates about, for example, the Second Amendment, immigration, and U.S. foreign aid and involvement in foreign conflicts allows them to assume relevance in the current political environment. In addition, the increasing sophistication of their use of a defensive, protectionist, and civil rights jargon enables them to gain more legitimacy and acceptance within growing segments of the American populace.

No less important for the process of legitimization of the far right was the understanding that in order to appear and be embraced as a legitimate political force, it needed also to engage in some adaptation of its practices, including the conduct of its individual supporters. Thus, many far-right leaders and organizations promote, at least publicly, policies that denounce unprovoked violence and that revoke membership from individuals who are engaged in criminal activities. Although many if not most far-right groups are still engaged in extreme violent practices and in criminal enterprises, the trend of "rehabilitation" within the contemporary far right is substantial. Related to that is the dramatic change in the composition of many contemporary far-right groups. Their strong emphasis on the recruitment of former law enforcement and veterans gives them an aura of legitimacy and helps them further portray themselves as the true followers of the historical American patriots and their ideals.

The discourse analysis conducted in this chapter also reveals that there is mutual ideological influence and convergence, as well as collaboration, between the various streams of the American far right. This is not a new trend within the American far right, but it has intensified over the last few years. Nonetheless, it is important to note that competition and internal critique is still very much present within the rhetorical landscape of the far right. In 2007, one of the more important skinhead organizations, the Vinlanders Social Club (VSC), abruptly disengaged from the White Power movement, stating:

We are no longer in competition with anyone to "change" or "control" the white racialist movement. Others such as the NSM, Bill White, Volksfront, etc . . . can have it. We will no longer be regarded as "white power skinheads", racialists, or members of the movement or old scene. We will simply be Vinlanders, modern tribalists, and followers of an older and better way. . . . We created this group because we were disappointed with the movement that we dedicated our young lives to. Several different types of pro-white activists and fraternal order members came together in 2003 to create a new organization. It was to be something that was going to replace and surpass the old guard in the skinhead scene. Even by force if necessary.[74]

Contemporary critical rhetoric does not usually match the language and dramatic organizational policy changes that the VSC exercised in 2007, but it nevertheless illustrates that the far right is still far from being able to consolidate its various fragments into a more coordinated organizational nationwide apparatus. For example, Clifford Herrington, one of the prominent National Socialist Movement's leaders, warned in 2009 about the risk of members wanting to embrace Identity principles. To prevent this trend, which in his eyes may have caused the collapse of the American Nazi movement, he sent emails to former chairmen of NSM chapters, urging them to come out of retirement to save the American Nazi Party and fight "the vile Christian plague infecting society."[75]

Herrington's response to the growing appeal of Identity ideology to members of the NSM reflects a broader propensity within American neo-Nazi organizations, which is the perception that other white supremacy groups, especially the KKK, are a more primitive, out-of-date version of white nationalism, which today causes more harm than good. To illustrate, Jeff Heuremann, another NSM leader, stated in an email from 2009 to William Herring (a member of the NSM staff corps) that other far-right organizations are "dinosaur" organizations that don't actively try to carry out their goals.[76] Some other conflicts are more mundane and reflect a natural gap emerging between regional chapters of the same organization. An email from Maine's branch leader of the Aryan Nations, James Lynch, which was sent to the Aryan Nations council in 2010, expresses his objection to the council's decision to change the name of the Aryan Nations to the Church of Jesus Christ Christian. His main concern was that this would probably lead to the termination of the collaboration of the Maine chapter with the local chapter of the NSM.[77]

To conclude, it seems that the current interactions between far-right groups are what Moghadam identified as "low-end cooperation."[78] In other words, cooperation is restricted to single, one-time events and does not include usually resource sharing and joint violent operations. Moreover, cases of mergers are extremely rare. Thus, for the foreseeable future, it seems that the American far right will maintain its ideologically and organizationally fragmented nature. Nonetheless, if political polarization and population diversification continue to intensify, this may present important opportunities for the American far right to expand its reach and further mobilize support from additional segments of the American population. Under such conditions, some of the more prominent far-right groups may be able eventually to construct more comprehensive nationwide organizational infrastructure, similar to the processes that allowed the Hammerskin Nation to unify the skinhead groups in the 1990s or that facilitated the national expansion of the KKK in the 1920s.

8

The Future of the Violent American Far Right

In late May 2019, German prime minister Angela Merkel warned that dark forces are on the rise in Europe, referring to the growing support on that continent for populist far-right parties.[1] This support led to the emergence of regimes that embrace nationalist authoritarian tendencies in several countries, including Hungary, Poland, and Italy. Coincidentally, roughly at the same time, a senior FBI official announced that the first few months of 2019 had seen a significant rise in the number of domestic terrorist cases involving white supremacists.[2] These are just two examples of the growing awareness of and concerns about radicalization and violence emanating from the far right of the political spectrum in many Western countries. Such concerns also witnessed calls to apply the powerful legal and policy mechanisms constructed to fight terrorism after 9/11 to violence from the far right. Unlike with international terrorism, in the United States there is no legal definition of domestic terrorism, and thus government agencies do not have a procedure that allows domestic groups to be designated as terrorist organizations. The consequence is that perpetrators of domestic acts of political violence are usually charged for violations of laws related to guns or other similar charges.

However, before addressing the policy question, if hate crimes should be dealt with as acts of terrorism (that is, if antiterrorism laws should be applied against organizations and individuals engaged in hate crimes), it is useful first to identify if indeed there are any qualitative gaps between these two concepts. At its essence, terrorism is a form of psychological warfare in which substate groups use violent campaigns to manipulate public opinion in an effort to influence policy change. In some cases, the violence is intended to instill fear or anxiety in a target population;[3] in other instances, terrorist groups engage in a violent campaign to enhance public awareness of their grievances and facilitate public empathy and support for their demands. Whether the violence is to instill anxiety or enhance empathy, its symbolic and psychological impact is used to generate public pressure on policy makers to meet the terrorists' demands.[4] Since terrorist violence is a medium that allows groups to communicate a political message to the public and policy makers and (hopefully) create mass support for political change, most experts agree that it includes four major elements: (1) the exercise of violence (2) against noncombatants (3) to promote political ideas/policies. In order for the violent act to be effective, terrorists shape their attacks to (4) maximize their psychological and symbolic influence (via specific target or weapon selection), which in turn allows them to enhance the reach and impact of the violence on policy makers and the public.[5]

Examination of the rationale of hate crimes reveals an identical logic. For the most part, they include the use of violence against a symbolic target (representatives of a specific ethnic or religious group) in order to convey a political message to a wider audience. As with most terrorist attacks, the victims and violence serve as an instrument for promoting a specific ideological narrative and clarifying the costs for those who challenge the ideological practices the perpetrators want to promote.

In 2009, Travis Ricci started to shout racist comments at an interracial couple walking in a park in Phoenix, Arizona. After a few minutes, Ricci went back to his home, picked up a shotgun, and returned in a sedan driven by a fellow neo-Nazi. When they found the couple, he leaned out of the car and fired two shots, missing the African American man but killing his girlfriend.[6] This was a violent attack motivated by political ideology and carrying a wider message about which social practices are accepted and what the consequences for those who dare to violate them are. The couple was chosen because of their symbolic meaning and the psychological impact that attacking an interracial couple can generate. Thus, hate crimes follow the same logic, and include similar components, as terrorist attacks. In both cases, violence is employed to convey or force a political narrative or ideas, and there are important symbolic and psychological dimensions, which are in many ways what makes such attacks effective.

If hate crimes are a form of terrorism, there is at least a basic rationale to support the argument that the same legal and operational tools used against terrorist organizations also should be used against groups perpetrating hate crimes. If this is the case, why do we still see a significant reluctance among policy makers to designate hate crimes as acts of terrorism and thus implement more harsh measures to combat them? Most answers to this question are related to the desire of politicians to limit the political costs of their policies. But before addressing these reasons and other related aspects of countering far-right violence, it is important to place the findings of this book in a wider context, in order to understand the broad processes that are facilitating the rise of far-right violence in the United States.

Diversification and Political Polarization

The analyses from chapter 5 illustrate two important dynamics that seem to facilitate far-right violence. The first is a contentious political environment, which may lead to a sense of empowerment among more radical members of the political camps. The second is the diversification of the population, combined with related economic and social changes. The United States in the second decade of the twenty-first century (and probably in the near future) is experiencing both dynamics. The American political system is characterized by increasing political polarization, which intensifies political animosity and the sense that every political competition is a zero-sum game. It also undermines the ability to promote more bipartisan policies that can be appealing to broader segments of the population and thus reduce the toxicity of the political discourse. At the same time, the United States is becoming more ethnically and religiously diverse, a process most demographers believe will intensify over the next couple of decades.

The further solidification of these two processes means that we are not likely to see a decline in far-right violence in the foreseeable future—probably the opposite. Moreover, it is important to note that these two processes are related in a way that probably enhances the effects they have on the rise of far-right violence. The diversification of the American populace is for the moment also reflected in the growing overlap between ethnic and religious affiliation and political attitudes. Simply put, minorities in the United States, at least in the early twenty-first century, are consistently more supportive of the American left, while Christian white Americans are more inclined to support the American right. For example, more than 70 percent of American Jews tend to support Democratic candidates for the presidency. Similarly, consistently more than 80 percent of African Americans tend to vote for Democratic candidates during elections. In the 2018 midterm elections, the number climbed to 90 percent. The trend is less strong, though still consistent, among other minorities. Usually around 60 to 70 percent of Asian Americans and Latinos vote for Democratic candidates, in comparison to 30 to 40 percent of white Americans.[7]

The fact that the divisions between minorities and the American white population are not just cultural and social but also political further intensifies animosity and general negative sentiments toward immigrants and minorities, and these animosities can be exploited effectively by far-right groups. The narrative that immigrants are controlling one of the two major parties helps far-right groups delegitimize the American left and its policies and rationalize why it is justified to operate against the American government when it is controlled by the left and abandoning what they see as American values. Such dynamics create a more permissible environment for attacks against political opponents and their electorates, which indeed we have witnessed in the last decade. The combination of political polarization and diversification of the population also seems to generate more intense political rhetoric, especially during elections. In 2016, it seems that the highly negative rhetoric used by Donald Trump, the Republican candidate, against minorities and immigrants, as well as against government officials from those groups, found a receptive audience, a development that helped him win both the Republican presidential nomination and the presidential election.

The Changing Geography of the American Far Right

I still remember a Saturday in early 2012 when I took my kids for a stroll around a pond in the center of a small town in upstate New York, located an hour's drive from New York City. While my kids played in a nearby playground, I walked to a small gazebo near the pond to sit down. When I entered the gazebo, I saw that all its walls had been sprayed with racial slurs. I was surprised; after all, that town was considered by many as practically a suburb of New York City and located in a fairly upscale socioeconomic area in a state known for its tolerance toward immigrants. This incident was a wakeup call. Apparently, not everyone in town felt comfortable with the arrival in the region of immigrants and minorities.

When I started studying the geographical distribution of far-right attacks, it became clear that what I had witnessed in that small town in upstate New York was not necessarily unique. The geospatial analysis presented in chapter 5 did not just further confirm that increasing population diversity is one of the major triggers of violence but also that to understand the contemporary far-right landscape, we must overcome traditional misconceptions, such as that southern states are the hotbed of hate crimes and that progressive states are safer for ethnic and religious minorities. Most importantly, my analysis points to a deep policy failure that has contributed to the growth of far-right violence. The diversification of entire communities presented substantial challenges to local municipalities, most of which lacked any systematic policy mechanism to help with the effective integration of new immigrants. In many cases, these led to changes in the cultural and social practices of these communities, which unsurprisingly led to a backlash and hostility toward the "newcomers." Simply put, the accelerating upward mobilization of minority groups in the United States allowed them to move to the suburbs and upscale communities outside the big cities, and the resulting changes in the nature of these communities produced frustration and anger among locals, which was effectively exploited by far-right groups.

Countering violent radicalization, especially from the far right, requires not just engaging with individuals who are already members of far-right groups but also developing policies that can facilitate better integration of immigrants or minorities who populate communities that have had little past experience with dealing with ethnic and religious diversity. In other words, a policy should also focus on preventing social situations that will drive people into the open arms of far-right groups, not just on trying to deradicalize those who have already embraced a violent far-right ideology.

"Glocalization" of the Far Right

While European far-right groups for many years opposed the European Union and the erosion of their states' sovereignty, in the last decade anti-globalization sentiments have become a central theme of the rhetoric of the American far right as well. Far-right groups see globalization as an ideology that legitimizes the integration of foreign practices and costumes and eventually erodes national identity. And the more that globalization continues to affect labor markets and economic developments, the more that opposition to it will be increasingly linked to perceived economic deprivation. In the United States, however, antiglobalization sentiments are also fused into traditional perceptions of American exceptionalism. Thus, far-right elements equate adopting global practices with the promotion of the destruction of the United States.

Nevertheless, while American far-right groups may reject globalization, they are perfectly fine with "glocalization." This concept reflects the promotion of a global brand while maintaining local, particular forms of it. American far-right groups collaborate with groups from all over the world and occasionally establish foreign chapters while also embracing and fostering local versions of nativist, racist, and xenophobic tendencies. Thus, despite the growing focus in the far-right rhetoric on the need to protect some kind of transnational white Christian civilization or culture, practices of glocalization ensure that it will not come necessarily at the expense of the local nationalist agenda.

It is important also to consider the possibility that eventually the rise of far-right governments will lead to further collaboration and more resources available to such groups worldwide. State sponsoring of terrorism and militant ideological groups is a phenomenon that has affected global and local conflicts for decades. During the Cold War, both the United States and the USSR sponsored ideological militant groups all over the globe, and many Arab countries sponsored Palestinian violent groups in the 1960s and 1970s. More recently, organizations such as Hezbollah are seen as a branch of existing states (Iran, in the case of Hezbollah). Thus, we cannot ignore the possibility that if far-right governments continue to proliferate, they will eventually sponsor and provide safe havens to groups with similar ideological convictions. A glimpse of such a reality is manifesting in the growing evidence that the Russian Republic is funding and facilitating the operation of far-right groups in Europe and the United States.[8]

The Iceberg Model and the American Alt-Right

It is important to clarify from the start that the usefulness of the concept of the "alt-right" (a shortened version of "alternative right") for analyzing the American far right is questionable. Currently, the term mainly describes movements and organizations that are self-described as white nationalist and that aspire to transform the United States into a white ethnostate. Most experts see the movement as a loose network of associations that oppose liberal values, promote nativist and white identity sentiments, and believe that multicultural and globalist policies are threatening white culture. As part of their antiliberal stance, they adopt isolationist policies, antifeminist rhetoric, and strong hostility toward what they see as agents of liberal values (such as institutions of higher education).

In chapter 5 I discussed the iceberg model, arguing that the violent aspects of the American far right, the visible part of the iceberg, is a product of a much broader supporting constituency, which, since it is mostly nonviolent, is usually ignored. We are neither aware of nor care about most of its activities. The alt-right, which is mostly active online and nonviolent, represents a substantial part of the iceberg, but it recently has become more visible for several reasons. First, the mainstreaming of the far right and the growing public legitimacy of many of its ideas, especially during and after the 2016 elections, has encouraged more people to express their support for those ideas publicly. Most of them have done that online, further fostering the popularity and relevancy of the alt-right discourse. Second, the emergence of social media platforms and the expansion of online political forums has led to a democratization of the American conservative camp, and because of its inability to police its "borders" effectively, it is not surprising that we have witnessed the spillover of extreme far-right rhetoric into more central circles of the conservative discourse. Third, some scholars argue that the alt-right is mainly a counter-response to the growing political presence of far-left organizations in the online landscape and the growing influence of left-wing activism and its aggressive use of identity politics. This is reflected in the use among alt-right activists of such terms as "white privilege" or "male privilege."

I would suggest that the alt-right is a product of two processes. The first is the mainstreaming of far-right ideology, and the second is the efforts of actors from within the far-right camp to adapt and modify both the rhetoric and mobilization practices of the movement in order both to legitimize and expand its constituency. The willingness of some mainstream political actors to embrace some far-right rhetoric further intensified these processes. It is important, however, to acknowledge that the alt-right represents mainly the growing visibility of ideas, attitudes, and practices that have existed on the far right for a long time, not the emergence of a new movement or success in the mobilization of new members.

Nonetheless, the increasing legitimacy of far-right discourse makes the mobilization efforts of far-right groups more effective, since it lowers some of the psychological and social barriers that previously prevented some people from adopting or expressing far-right ideology.

The Far Right and Jihadism: The Utility of Comparison

The rise of far-right terrorism has also prompted a growing effort to adapt practices and concepts that were employed to understand and respond to jihadi terrorism to the new threat on the domestic front. There are some similarities between the jihadi landscape and the far-right ecosystem. In both cases, we can observe a highly fragmented ideological environment and processes of glocalization. Moreover, both jihadists and some far-right groups exploit a literal interpretation of religious texts in order to legitimize their violent practices and mobilize support. Finally, in both cases, groups try to construct alternative sources of identity in order to attract new members. In the case of the jihadists, they emphasize the transnational community of Muslim believers who are committed to jihadi principles, while among the far right we can see growing attempts to shape a transnational white Christian identity that can potentially unite far-right groups under one ideological umbrella and foster collaboration.

At the same time, it is also important to identify fundamental differences. Significant portions of the far right reject religious fundamentalism and actually see it as a potential adversary. More importantly, while the jihadi ideology opposes the essence and rationale of the concept of the nation-state, many far-right associations are motivated precisely because they feel and oppose the erosion of the traditional nation-state. Thus, while jihadism can be perceived as a revolutionary movement whose ultimate goal is the destruction of the Westphalian world order, the far right sees itself as the protector of that order. Indeed, while both ideological movements emphasize their heritage and historical roots, and while on some level both believe they operate to restore a past historical reality, they differ greatly in terms of their attitude toward the basic building blocks of the current political world order.

Utilizing knowledge and insights from the ongoing struggle against jihadi terrorism is important and can be occasionally useful; however, it is important to be aware of the fundamental differences between these two types of violent political movements. That said, it is also clear that each movement has an influence on the other. As discussed in chapter 7, some far-right elements have adopted jihadi-style rhetoric, and there is no reason to assume that we will not also see a reciprocal process. Finally, both movements may also "benefit" from the existence of the other, at least in terms of maintaining their relevancy, especially as some on the far right see jihadism as a product of globalization and multiculturalism and some jihadists see in the rise of the far right a confirmation of the ongoing oppression of Muslims.

No Silver Bullet

While this book has not focused on analyses of the response to radicalization and violence on the far right, several general insights can be suggested based on our discussion of the causes and facilitators of far-right violence in the United States. To devise an effective response, we must understand the deep and corrosive impact of ideological violence, which undermines public trust in the political system and the government, intensifies animosity between ethnic and religious groups, and can lead to the disintegration of shared values and norms. To counter that, we must employ a multitude of measures on the state, communal, and individual levels. The market of political ideas must include significant and competent antidotes to the main arguments of the far right. It is crucial to engage in the online domain and actively undermine the credibility, popularity, and attractiveness of the far right's ideological narratives. The U.S. government needs to facilitate the creation of online enterprises that provide rigorous tools to refute and counter ideologies that promote violence and hostile, illegal practices against segments of the population. In this context, political leaders need to consider the impact of their rhetoric on the legitimization of far-right narratives and what long-term effects it might have on the shared American political culture.

The United States cannot continue to ignore the necessity of developing effective integration policies that will help communities respond productively to the processes of demographic diversification they are experiencing. This is especially true for the rural areas of the Northeast and the West Coast, where we are seeing significant ethnic and religious diversification. At the same time, it is important to invest in slowing the proliferation of White Power gangs in correctional facilities and counteract the mechanisms they use to mobilize recruits. More research needs to be done in order to understand the dynamics and factors that facilitate the emergence of such gangs and how they ensure the ideological loyalty of their members even after they are released from prison.

Additionally, legislation and law enforcement agencies must prioritize the threat from the far right. Ideological violence presents a special threat and thus demands a special response, one that takes into consideration the long-term impact on the American public and political system. Similar to the reforms made in the response to the foreign terrorist threat after the 9/11 attacks, we need to rethink how we can restructure existing institutions and legal mechanisms to ensure Americans will not continue to be victims of far-right violence.

To conclude, this book has illustrated how multiple societal, communal, and political factors are responsible for the rise in far-right violence and the rapid proliferation of its ideological framework. Americans need to acknowledge that a systematic response to the threat from the far right cannot be restricted to relatively short-range responses to slow political polarization, prevent dissemination of militant propaganda, or create better-equipped institutions to manage ethnic and religious diversification. It is also necessary to develop a more comprehensive long-term vision of the

United States, one that will help Americans prepare for a future that will probably include the further democratization of information sources, globalization of political ideas, and an increasing influence of the ongoing environmental crisis, dynamics that together may provide new avenues of growth to far-right ideology. I hope this book is able at least to plant some intellectual seeds in the minds of future leaders regarding the much-needed long-term vision of an America that can be more resilient to militant ideologies that promote racism, xenophobia, exclusionism, and hatred of the other/s.

APPENDIX

Methodology and Statistical Results

Dataset Construction

To decipher the current landscape of the violent American far right, my team and I constructed a dataset that documents all violent attacks perpetrated by groups or individuals affiliated with far-right associations and/or were intended to promote ideas compatible with far-right ideology. Many scholars treat these acts as "terrorism." While there is no consensual definition of terrorism among academics or practitioners, most agree that it consists of violent acts perpetrated to promote specific political goals of a national, religious, or communal collective and aimed against civilians or noncombatants.[1] Most scholars also emphasize the psychological and symbolic nature of terrorism and its ability to exploit violence in order to shape political discourse.[2] Many of the attacks in the dataset are compatible with all of these criteria. However, some of them, while exhibiting a clear political context, lack the instrumental use of violence. In other words, while the political motivation of the act is detectable, how it is supposed to influence the broader political discourse is much less clear; for this reason, the symbolic element identifiable in the majority of terrorist campaigns is absent from a significant number of violent far-right attacks. For this reason, in the current study, the more generalized designation of "political violence" is used to describe far-right violent activities, as this term is broader than "terrorism."

The dataset includes violence against human targets as well as property and contains details regarding (1) the date of the attack, (2) the organizational and ideological affiliation of the perpetrator(s), (3) the target's characteristics, (4) implications of the attack (number of fatalities and injured and whether it was completed successfully), (5) geographical location of the attack, (6) tactical details, and (7) a concise description of the attack.

Data gathering was based on a variety of resources, including the Global Terrorism Dataset; the SPLC hate crime dataset; reports by various relevant organizations, such as SPLC, ADL, and RSCAR; relevant academic texts; and various media source datasets such as Lexis-Nexis. The consolidated dataset includes information on 5,697 violent attacks that occurred between 1990 and 2017 within U.S. borders, which caused 823 fatalities and injured 3,786 people.

While our dataset is probably one of the most comprehensive accumulations of data on far-right violence in the United States, several limitations of the data should be noted. First, since the quality of and accessibility to data on hate crimes and far-right violence has improved during the last couple of decades, it is important to be cautious when interpreting findings relating to fluctuations in levels of violence over time. Second, the differences between states with regard to their cultural norms and legal practices may affect the level of visibility and reporting of hate crimes. Finally, discrepancies may exist between the dataset used in this book and other existing hate crimes datasets. This may be a result of differential or failed categorization, whereby violent incidents involving parties with different racial/ethnic affiliations but lacking clear evidence of far-right ideological motivation or association were not included.

Regressions Model: Political Factors

A Poisson regression model (which is appropriate when the dependent variable is count data) with the yearly number of attacks as the dependent variable was conducted in order to identify the impact of political characteristics on the fluctuation in the level of far-right violence. The model is presented in table A.1. Several elements of the model demand some caution in terms

Table A.1

VARIABLE	WALD CHI-SQUARE (COEFFICIENT)
No. of House Republicans	74.667*** (.177)
No. of House Democrats	58.254*** (−.156)
No. of Senate Republicans	63.219*** (.088)
No. of Senate Democrats	79.291*** (−.103)
Presidents' partisan affiliation	19.906*** (.137)
Empowering political/executive decisions	651.200*** (.812)
Chi square	3620.758***
N	57

*P<.05, **P<.01, ***P<.001 'P<0.1

of its interpretation. First, since the dependent variable is the yearly number of far-right attacks, the overall number of cases included (N=57) is fairly small. Second, the inclusion of a subjective variable (years in which potential empowering executive/judicial decisions were made) may also create potential for internal bias within the model (although will have limited effect on the statistical significance of the other variables).

Regressions Model: Demographic Factors

To provide an assessment of the relative importance of the various demographic factors on the level of far-right violence, a Poisson regression model (which is appropriate when the dependent variable is count data) with the number of attacks per state as the dependent variable was conducted. The model is presented in table A.2. Also, with regard to this model, some caution is necessary in terms of its interpretation: since the dependent variable is the number of far-right attacks per state, the overall number of cases included (N=51) is fairly small.

Table A.2

VARIABLE	WALD CHI-SQUARE (COEFFICIENT)
Portion of African American population	3.446 (−.004)
Portion of Hispanic population	67.193*** (−.032)
Portion of Asian American population	18.520*** (−.045)
Increase rate in African American population	36.430*** (−.062)
Increase rate in Hispanic population	7.342** (.048)
Increase rate in Asian American population	190.053*** (.461)
Population size	905.229*** (9.194)
Chi square	5705.021***
N	51

*P<.05, **P<.01, ***P<.001 ¹P<0.1

Notes

1. The Challenges of Comprehending and Responding to Domestic Terrorism

1. Katie Delong, "Sons Remember Mother Killed in Temple Shooting After Completing Prayers," Fox6 (Milwaukee), last modified August 7, 2012, http://fox6now.com/2012/08/07/sons-remember-mother-killed-in-temple-shooting-after-completing-prayers/.

2. "Police Identify Army Veteran as Wisconsin Temple Shooting Gunman," CNN, August 7, 2012, https://www.cnn.com/2012/08/06/us/wisconsin-temple-shooting/index.html.

3. Neil Shortland, Nader Elias, Nicholas Imperillo, Kyrielle Ross, and Jared Dmello, "The Interaction of Extremist Propaganda and Anger as Predictors of Violent Responses," *Journal of Interpersonal Violence* (2017): 1–21.

4. Marilyn Elias, "Sikh Temple Killer Wade Michael Page Radicalized in Army," Southern Poverty Law Center, November 11, 2012, https://www.splcenter.org/fighting-hate/intelligence-report/2012/sikh-temple-killer-wade-michael-page-radicalized-army.

5. "'Anarchists' Accused of Murder; Broader Plot Against Government," CNN, last modified December 28, 2012, https://www.cnn.com/2012/08/28/justice/georgia-soldiers-plot/index.html.

6. Michael Martinez and Nick Valencia, "5 More Charged in Anti-Government Militia Plot Linked to Fort Stewart," CNN, September 11, 2012, https://www.cnn.com/2012/09/11/us/georgia-soldiers-plot/index.html.

7. The Soufan Center, *White Supremacy Extremism: Transnational Rise of the Violent White Supremacist Movement* (Soufan Center, 2019), https://thesoufancenter.org/wp-content/uploads/2019/09/Report-by-The-Soufan-Center-White-Supremacy-Extremism-The-Transnational-Rise-of-The-Violent-White-Supremacist-Movement.pdf.

8. Richard Abanes, *American Militias: Rebellion, Racism, and Religion* (Downers Grove, IL: Intervarsity Press, 1996); Michael Barkun, *Religion and the Racist Right: The*

Origins of the Christian Identity Movement (Chapel Hill: University of North Carolina Press, 2014); Mark S. Hamm, *American Skinheads: The Criminology and Control of Hate Crime* (Westport, CT: ABC-CLIO, 1994); Rory McVeigh, *The Rise of the Ku Klux Klan: Right-Wing Movements and National Politics* (Minneapolis: University of Minnesota Press, 2009); Arnold S. Rice, *The Ku Klux Klan in American Politics* (1962; repr., London: Forgotten Books, 2017); Charles H. Roberts, *Race Over Grace: The Racialist Religion of the Christian Identity Movement* (New York: iUniverse, 2003); William H. Schmaltz, *Hate: George Lincoln Rockwell and the American Nazi Party* (Washington, DC: Potomac, 2000); Robert L. Snow, *Terrorists Among Us: The Militia Threat* (Cambridge, MA: Da Capo, 2002); Jerome Walters, *One Aryan Nation Under God: Exposing the New Racial Extremists* (Cleveland, OH: Pilgrim, 2000); Susan Canedy, *America's Nazis: A Democratic Dilemma: A History of the German American Bund* (Menlo Park: CA: Markgraf, 1990); and Joshua D. Freilich, *American Militias: State-Level Variations in Militia Activities* (El Paso, TX: LFB Scholarly Publishing, 2003).

9.   Betty A. Dobratz and Stephanie L. Shanks-Meile, *The White Separatist Movement in the United States: "White Power, White Pride!"* (Baltimore, MD: Johns Hopkins University Press, 2000); Chester L. Quarles, *The Ku Klux Klan and Related American Racialist and Antisemitic Organizations: A History and Analysis* (Jefferson, NC: McFarland, 1999); James Ridgeway, *Blood in the Face: The Ku Klux Klan, Aryan Nations, Nazi Skinheads, and the Rise of a New White Culture*, 2nd rev. ed. (New York: Thunder's Mouth, 1995).

10. C. Michael McGarrity and Shivers A. Calvin, "Confronting White Supremacy," Statement Before the House Oversight and Reform Committee, Subcommittee on Civil Rights and Civil Liberties, Washington, DC, June 4, 2019; https://www.fbi.gov /news/testimony/confronting-white-supremacy.

11. Morgan Chalfant, "FBI's Wray Says Most Domestic Terrorism Arrests This Year Involve White Supremacy," *The Hill*, July 23, 2019, https://thehill.com/homenews/administration /454338-fbis-wray-says-majority-of-domestic-terrorism-arrests-this-year.

2. An Ideological Typology of the Violent Far Right

1.   Murphy Doyle, Mark Morales, and Bill Hutchinson, "3 Killed in Shootings at Kansas Jewish Community Center and Senior Home," *New York Daily News*, April 14, 2014, http://www.nydailynews.com/news/national/3-dead-shootings-kansas-jewish -community-center-senior-home-article-1.1755143; "Man Yells 'Heil Hitler' After Fatally Shooting 3 at Jewish Centers," KCTV5 (Kansas City, MO), April 13, 2014, http://www .kctv5.com/story/25235053/shooting-reported-at-overland-park-jewish-community -center.

2.   "Frazier Glenn Miller," Southern Poverty Law Center, n.d., https://www.splcenter.org /fighting-hate/extremist-files/individual/frazier-glenn-miller

3.   "Frazier Glenn Miller."

4.   "Frazier Glenn Miller."

5. "Frazier Glenn Miller."

6. "Frazier Glenn Miller."

7. Doyle, Morales, and Hutchinson, "3 Killed in Shootings at Kansas Jewish Community Center and Senior Home"; "Man Yells 'Heil Hitler' After Fatally Shooting 3 at Jewish Centers."

8. Arie Perliger, *Challengers from the Sidelines: Understanding America's Violent Far-Right* (West Point, NY: Combating Terrorism Center, 2012), https://doi.org/10.21236/ada576380.

9. Jonathan Marcus, "Exorcising Europe's Demons: A Far-Right Resurgence?" *Washington Quarterly* 23, no. 4 (December 1, 2000): 31–40; Paul Hainsworth, "Introduction to the Extreme Right," in *The Politics of the Extreme Right: From the Margins to the Mainstream*, ed. Paul Hainsworth (London: Pinter, 2000), 1–17; Hans-Georg Betz, *Radical Right-Wing Populism in Western Europe* (New York: Palgrave Macmillan, 1994); Sabrina Ramet, "Defining the Radical Right: Values and Behaviors of Organized Intolerance in Post-Communist Central and Eastern Europe," in *Radical Right in Central and Eastern Europe Since 1989*, ed. Sabrina Ramet (University Park: Pennsylvania State University Press, 1999), 3–27.

10. Ulrike M. Vieten and Scott Poynting, "Contemporary Far-Right Racist Populism in Europe," *Journal of Intercultural Studies* 37, no. 6 (November 2016): 533–40; Nigel Copsey, "The Radical Right and Fascism," in *The Oxford Handbook of the Radical Right*, ed. Jens Rydgren (Oxford: Oxford University Press, 2018), 105.

11. Ami Pedahzur and Arie Perliger, "An Alternative Approach for Defining the Boundaries of 'Party Families': Examples from the Israeli Extreme Right-Wing Party Scene," *Australian Journal of Political Science* 39, no. 2 (2004): 285–305.

12. Kenneth D. Wald and Allison Calhoun-Brown, *Religion and Politics in the United States* (Baltimore, MD: Rowman & Littlefield, 2014).

13. Cass Mudde, *Populist Radical Right Parties* (Cambridge: Cambridge University Press, 2007), 11–14.

14. Eric J. Hobsbawm, *Nations and Nationalism Since 1780: Programme, Myth, Reality* (Cambridge: Cambridge University Press, 1990); Ernest Gellner, *Nations and Nationalism* (Ithaca, NY: Cornell University Press, 2008).

15. Koen Koch, "Back to Sarajevo or Beyond Trianon? Some Thoughts on the Problem of Nationalism in Eastern Europe," *Netherlands Journal of Social Sciences* 27, no. 1 (1991): 29–42.

16. Mudde, *Populist Radical Right Parties*, 169; Pedahzur and Perliger, "An Alternative Approach for Defining the Boundaries of 'Party Families.'"

17. John Higham, *Strangers in the Land: Patterns of American Nativism, 1860–1925* (New Brunswick, NJ: Rutgers University Press, 2002).

18. Cass Mudde, *Ideology of the Extreme Right* (Manchester: Manchester University Press, 2000), 169.

19. Cass Mudde, "Right-Wing Extremism Analyzed: A Comparative Analysis of the Ideologies of Three Alleged Right-Wing Extremist Parties (NPD, NDP, CP'86)," *European Journal of Political Research* 27 (1995): 203–24; Mikael Hjerm, "National Identities,

National Pride, and Xenophobia: A Comparison of Four Western Countries," *Acta Sociologica* 41, no. 4 (October 1998): 335–47.

20. Robert Miles and Annie Phizacklea, "Some Introductory Observations on Race and Politics in Britain," in *Racism and Political Action in Britain*, ed. Robert Miles and Annie Phizacklea (London: Routledge and Kegan Paul, 1979), 1–27; J. B. McConahay, "Modern Racism, Ambivalence, and the Modern Racism Scale," in *Prejudice, Discrimination, and Racism*, ed. J. F. Dovidio and S. L. Gaertner (Cambridge, MA: Academic Press, 1986), 91–125.

21. Pedahzur and Perliger, "An Alternative Approach for Defining the Boundaries of 'Party Families.'"

22. Vincent Andrew, *Modern Political Ideologies* (Oxford: Blackwell, 1995), 55–58.

23. Hans-Georg Betz, "Politics of Resentment: Right-Wing Radicalism in West Germany," *Comparative Politics* 23 (1990): 15–60; Hans-Georg Betz, *Radical Right-Wing Populism in Western Europe* (New York: Palgrave Macmillan, 1994).

24. Mudde, "Right-Wing Extremism Analyzed," 216–17; see also discussion in Mudde, *Populist Radical Right Parties*, 21–22.

25. Pedahzur and Perliger, "An Alternative Approach for Defining the Boundaries of 'Party Families.'"

26. Mudde, "Right-Wing Extremism Analyzed."

27. D. John McCarty and N. Mayer Zald, "Resource Mobilization and Social Movements: A Partial Theory," *American Journal of Sociology* 82, no. 6 (1977): 1212–41.

28. Betty A. Dobratz and Stephanie L. Shanks-Meile, *The White Separatist Movement in the United States: "White Power, White Pride!"* (Baltimore, MD: Johns Hopkins University Press, 2000), 36.

29. Dobratz and Shanks-Meile, *The White Separatist Movement in the United States*, 36; Chester Quarles, *Ku Klux Klan and Related American Racialist and Antisemitic Organizations: A History and Analysis* (Jefferson, NC: McFarland, 1999), 40.

30. Stanley Fitzgerald Horn, *Invisible Empire: The Story of the Ku Klux Klan, 1866–1871* (Boston: Houghton Mifflin, 1939), 3–4; Quarles, *Ku Klux Klan*, 31; Rory McVeigh, *Rise of the Ku Klux Klan* (Minneapolis: University of Minnesota Press, 2009), chap. 1; Dobratz and Shanks-Meile, *The White Separatist Movement in the United States*, 39.

31. Susan Canedy, *America's Nazis: A Democratic Dilemma* (Menlo Park, CA: Markgraf, 1990), 191–92.

32. Canedy, *America's Nazis*, 191–92; Joachim Remak, "Friends of the New Germany: The Bund and German-American Relations," *Journal of American History* 29, no. 1 (1957): 38–41; Sander Diamond, *The Nazi Movement in the United States: 1924–1941* (Ithaca, NY: Cornell University Press, 1974).

33. Wyn Craig Wade, *Fiery Cross: The Ku Klux Klan in America* (New York: Simon and Schuster, 1987), 368.

34. Barbara Perry. *Hate and Bias Crime: A Reader* (New York: Routledge, 2012).

35. Susan Willis, "Hardcore: Subculture American Style," *Critical Inquiry* 19, no. 2 (1993): 365–83.

36. Mark S. Hamm, *American Skinheads: The Criminology and Control of Hate Crime* (New York: Praeger, 1993), 23–25.
37. Southern Poverty Law Center, "Brotherhood of the Klan," https://www.splcenter.org /fighting-hate/extremist-files/group/brotherhood-klans.
38. Daniel Levitas, *Terrorist Next Door: The Militia Movement and the Radical Right* (New York: St. Martin's, 2004).
39. Richard Abanes, *American Militias* (Downers Grove, IL: Intervarsity, 1996), 7–20; Joel Dyer, *Harvest of Rage* (Boulder, CO: Westview, 1998), 24–44; Kathlyn Gay, *Militias: Armed and Dangerous* (Springfield, NJ: Enslow, 1997), 36–52.
40. Abanes, *American Militias*, 7–20.
41. Gay, *Militias*, 36–52; Robert L. Snow, *Terrorists Among Us: The Militia Threat* (Cambridge, MA: Da Capo, 1999), 27.
42. Snow, *Terrorists Among Us*, 27.
43. Martin Durham, "American Far Right and 9/11," *Terrorism and Political Violence* 15, no. 2 (2003): 96–111.
44. Mark Koernke, "America in Peril," *Liveleak* (Real World Publication, 1993), http:// www.liveleak.com/view?comments=1&i=be2_1269967024.
45. Neil A. Hamilton, *Militias in America* (Santa Barbara, CA: ABC-CLIO, 1996), 35–37.
46. Darren Mulloy, *American Extremism: History, Politics, and the Militia Movement* (New York: Routledge, 2004).
47. J. M. Berger, "Without Prejudice: What Sovereign Citizens Believe," Program on Extremism at George Washington University, 2016, https://extremism.gwu.edu/sites/g /files/zaxdzs2191/f/downloads/JMB%20Sovereign%20Citizens.pdf.
48. Berger, "Without Prejudice."
49. Berger, "Without Prejudice"; Casey Sanchez, "Sovereign Citizens Movement Resurging," Southern Poverty Law Center, 2009, https://www.splcenter.org/fighting-hate /intelligence-report/2009/sovereign-citizens-movement-resurging.
50. Sanchez. "Sovereign Citizens Movement Resurging."
51. Judith Nagata. "Beyond Theology: Toward an Anthropology of 'Fundamentalism,'" *American Anthropologist* 103, no. 2 (2001): 481–98; Bob Altemeyer and Bruce Hunsberger, "Authoritarianism, Religious Fundamentalism, Quest, and Prejudice," *International Journal for the Psychology of Religion* 2, no. 2 (1992): 113–33.
52. Michael Barkun, *Religion and the Racist Right* (Chapel Hill: University of North Carolina Press, 1994); Robert Charles, *Race Over Grace: The Racialist Religion of the Christian Identity Movement* (Lincoln, NE: iUniverse, 2003); Walter Jerome, *One Aryan Nation Under God: Exposing the New Racial Extremists* (Cleveland, OH: Pilgrim, 2000).
53. Charles, *Race Over Grace*.
54. Dan Gayman, *Do All Races Share in Salvation? For Whom Did Jesus Christ Die?* (Schell City, MO: The Church of Israel, 1995).
55. Jerome, *One Aryan Nation Under God*, 49.
56. Barkun, *Religion and the Racist Right*, 4–15; Charles, *Race Over Grace*.

57. Dan Gayman, *Two Seeds of Genesis*, 3:15 (Schell City, MO: Church of Israel, 1994), 7.

58. Charles, *Race Over Grace*.

59. Willie Martin, "The Assyrians Who Took the Israelites Captive Did Not Call Them by That Name!," part 7 of 32 (chap. 5), in *In Search of Isaac's Children*, http://www.fathersmanifesto.net/wm/wm0170/wm0170g.html.

60. Hans-Georg Betz, *Radical Right-Wing Populism in Western Europe* (New York: Palgrave Macmillan, 1994).

61. Julianna S. Gonen, Jo DeLosSantos, and Tina Vasquez, "Fascists Find Fertile Recruitment Ground in Anti-Choice Movement," *Rewire.News*, December 11, 2018, https://rewire.news/article/2018/12/11/fascists-find-fertile-recruitment-ground-in-anti-choice-movement/.

62. Southern Poverty Law Center, "Matthew Heimbach's Neo-Nazi Group Tries to Co-Opt Anti-Abortion Protest in Tennessee," January 19, 2018, https://www.splcenter.org/hatewatch/2018/01/19/matthew-heimbachs-neo-nazi-group-tries-co-opt-anti-abortion-protest-tennessee.

63. Connie Paige, *Right to Lifers* (New York: Summit, 1983), 60.

64. Patricia Baird-Windle and Eleanor J. Bader, *Targets of Hatred: Anti-Abortion Terrorism* (New York: Palgrave, 2001), 41.

65. Baird-Windle and Bader, *Targets of Hatred*, 41.

66. Frank Schaeffer, "We Who Sowed Hate Share Blame in Killing of Abortion Doctor," *Baltimore Sun*, June 2, 2009, http://articles.baltimoresun.com/2009-06-02/news/0906010039_1_abortion-late-term-roe-v.

67. *Army of God Manual*, 3rd ed., chap. 1, http://www.armyofgod.com/AOGsel3.html.

68. *Army of God Manual*.

3. Historical Pillars of the Violent American Far Right

1. Rutledge M. Dennis, "Socialization and Racism: The White Experience," in *Impacts of Racism on White Americans*, ed. Benjamin P. Bowser and Raymond G. Hunt (Thousand Oaks, CA: Sage, 1981).

2. James M. McPherson, *Battle Cry of Freedom: The Civil War Era* (Oxford: Oxford University Press, 1988).

3. Tyler Anbinder, *Nativism and Slavery: The Northern Know Nothings and the Politics of the 1850s* (Oxford: Oxford University Press, 1992).

4. A. Cheree Carlson, "The Rhetoric of the Know-Nothing Party: Nativism as a Response to the Rhetorical Situation," *Southern Communication Journal* 54, no. 4 (1989): 364–83.

5. Anbinder, *Nativism and Slavery*.

6. Carlson, "The Rhetoric of the Know-Nothing Party"; William J. Bromwell, *History of Immigration to the United States* (Bibliobazaar, 1856).

7. Bruce Levine, "Conservatism, Nativism, and Slavery: Thomas R. Whitney and the Origins of the Know-Nothing Party," *Journal of American History* 88, no. 2 (2001): 455; Carlson, "The Rhetoric of the Know-Nothing Party."

8.   Charles Granville Hamilton, *Lincoln and the Know Nothing Movement* (1954; Forgotten Books, 2018).

9.   Anbinder, *Nativism and Slavery*.

10. Lorraine Boissoneault, "How the 19th-Century Know Nothing Party Reshaped American Politics," *Smithsonian Magazine*, 2017, https://www.smithsonianmag.com/history/immigrants-conspiracies-and-secret-society-launched-american-nativism-180961915/.

11. Richard C. Sinopoli, *From Many, One: Readings in American Political and Social Thought* (Washington, DC: Georgetown University Press, 1996).

12. Sinopoli, *From Many, One*.

13. Anbinder, *Nativism and Slavery*.

14. Marion Mills Miller, U.S. Congress, and Parliament, *Great Debates in American History*, part 1: *Civil Rights* (New York: Current Literature Pub. Co., 1913).

15. Chester Quarles, *Ku Klux Klan and Related American Racialist and Antisemitic Organizations: A History and Analysis* (Jefferson, NC: McFarland, 1999), 16.

16. David Chalmers, *Hooded Americanism* (New York: Doubleday, 1965), 181.

17. Quarles, *Ku Klux Klan*, 43.

18. Susan Lawrence Davis, *Authentic History, 1865–1877* (New York: American Library Service, 1924), 15–16.

19. Martin Gitlin, *The Ku Klux Klan: A Guide to an American Subculture* (Santa Barbara, CA: ABC-CLIO, 2009), 5.

20. "Interview with Nathan Bedford Forrest," Wikisource, The Free Library, http://en.wikisource.org/w/index.php?title=Interview_with_Nathan_Bedford_Forrest&oldid=3853811.

21. William Loren Katz, *The Invisible Empire: The Ku Klux Klan Impact on History* (Washington, DC: Open Hand, 1986).

22. Gitlin, *The Ku Klux Klan*, 7.

23. J. C. Lester and D. L. Wilson, *Ku Klux Klan, Its Origin, Growth, and Disbandment* (Nashville, TN: Walter Lynwood Fleming, 1884).

24. William Pierce Randel, *Ku Klux Klan: A Century of Infamy* (Philadelphia: Chilton, 1965), 181.

25. Randel, *Ku Klux Klan*, 181; Arnold Rice, *The Ku Klux Klan in American Politics* (1962; London: Forgotten Books, 2017), iii.

26. Henry P. Fry, *The Modern Ku Klux Klan* (New York: Negro University Press, 1922), 16; Randel, *Ku Klux Klan*.

27. Fry, *The Modern Ku Klux Klan*, 16.

28. Stanley Frost, *The Challenge of the Klan* (Indianapolis, IN: Bobbs-Merrill, 1924), 238; Southern Poverty Law Center Klanwatch Staff, *Ku Klux Klan: A History of Racism and Violence*, ed. Susan Ballard (Montgomery, AL: SPLC, 1988), 46.

29. Isabel Wilkerson, *The Warmth of Other Suns: The Epic Story of America's Great Migration* (New York: Vintage, 2011).

30. Quarles, *Ku Klux Klan*, 43–53.

31. Rory McVeigh, *The Rise of the Ku Klux Klan: Right-Wing Movements and National Politics* (Minneapolis: University of Minnesota Press, 2009), 5–7.

32. Quarles, *Ku Klux Klan*, 57.

33. Rice, *The Ku Klux Klan in American Politics*, 19.

34. Katz, *The Invisible Empire*.

35. Chalmers, *Hooded Americanism*, 4; Quarles, *Ku Klux Klan*, 74.

36. Quarles, *Ku Klux Klan*, 79–92.

37. Gitlin, *The Ku Klux Klan*, 28.

38. Chalmers, *Hooded Americanism*, 32–33.

39. Robert P. Ingalls, *Hoods: The Story of the Ku Klux Klan* (New York: Putnam, 1979), 81.

40. Quarles, *Ku Klux Klan*, 81–82.

41. Gene Smith, "Bundesfuehrer Kuhn," *American Heritage* 46, no. 5 (1995): 102.

42. Joachim Remak, "Friends of the New Germany: The Bund and German-American Relations," *Journal of American History* 29, no. 1 (1957): 38–41.

43. Betty A. Dobratz and Stephanie L. Shanks-Meile, *The White Separatist Movement in the United States: "White Power, White Pride!"* (Baltimore, MD: Johns Hopkins University Press, 2000), 55–57.

44. Susan Canedy, *America's Nazis: A Democratic Dilemma* (Menlo Park, CA: Markgraf, 1990), 190–91.

45. Leland Bell, "The Failure of Nazism in America," *Political Science Quarterly* 85, no. 4 (1970): 585–99.

46. Bell, "The Failure of Nazism in America."

47. Canedy, *America's Nazis*, 224–25.

48. John George and Laird Wilcox, *Nazis, Communists, Klansmen, and Others on the Fringe* (Buffalo, NY: Prometheus, 1992), 352–54.

49. Christopher Hewitt, *Political Violence and Terrorism in Modern America: A Chronology* (Westport, CT: Praeger, 2005).

50. William H. Schmaltz, *Hate: George Lincoln Rockwell and the American Nazi Party* (Washington, DC: Potomac, 2000).

51. Schmaltz, *Hate*.

52. FBI file on ANP, 18–45, https://vault.fbi.gov/American%20Nazi%20Party%20/American%20Nazi%20Party%20Part%201%20of%202/view.

53. FBI file on ANP, 18–45.

54. FBI file on ANP, 18–45.

55. Schmaltz, *Hate*, 39, 57, 247–49.

56. Schmaltz, *Hate*, 304–5.

57. George and Wilcox, *Nazis, Communists, Klansmen, and Others on the Fringe*, 363–65.

58. George and Wilcox, *Nazis, Communists, Klansmen, and Others on the Fringe*, 359.

59. Anti-Defamation League, *Hate Groups in America: A Record of Bigotry and Violence*, 2nd ed. (New York: ADL, 1988), 49.

60. George and Wilcox, *Nazis, Communists, Klansmen, and Others on the Fringe*, 364–68.

61. Dobratz and Shanks-Meile, *The White Separatist Movement in the United States*, 59–63.

62. George and Wilcox, *Nazis, Communists, Klansmen, and Others on the Fringe*, 360–68.

63. Rice, *The Ku Klux Klan in American Politics*, 118.

64. Gitlin, *The Ku Klux Klan*, 86.

65. Quarles, *Ku Klux Klan*, 99–101.

66. Quarles, *Ku Klux Klan*, 99–101.

67. Hewitt, *Political Violence and Terrorism in Modern America.*

68. U.S. Congress, *House Un-American Activities Committee Report on the Activities of the Ku Klux Klan* (Washington, DC: Government Printing Office, 1967), 73.

69. Gitlin, *The Ku Klux Klan*, 36.

70. Wyn Craig Wade, *Fiery Cross: The Ku Klux Klan in America* (New York: Simon and Schuster, 1987), 368; Dobratz and Shanks-Meile, *The White Separatist Movement in the United States*, 48–49.

71. Dobratz and Shanks-Meile, *The White Separatist Movement in the United States*, 48–49.

72. Quarles, *Ku Klux Klan*, 118–22.

73. Lisa Klobuchar, *Birmingham Church Bombing: The Ku Klux Klan's History of Terror* (Mankato, MN: Compass, 1963), 80; Mark S. Hamm, *American Skinheads: The Criminology and Control of Hate Crime* (New York: Praeger, 1993), 44.

74. Stephen E. Atkins, *Encyclopedia of Right-Wing Extremism in Modern American History* (New York: ABC-CLIO, 2011), 222–23.

75. Gitlin, *The Ku Klux Klan*, 100.

76. Gitlin, *The Ku Klux Klan*, 89.

77. Greensboro Truth and Reconciliation Commission Report, Executive Summary (May 25, 2006), http://www.greensborotrc.org/exec_summary.pdf.

78. George and Wilcox, *Nazis, Communists, Klansmen, and Others on the Fringe*, 364–65.

79. Matt Koehl, *NS Bulletin* (November 1982).

80. FBI file, *Aryan Nation*, parts 1 and 2, http://vault.fbi.gov/Aryan%20Nation.

81. Southern Poverty Law Center Intelligence Project, *Skinheads in America: Racists on the Rampage* (SPLC, 2009), 4.

82. Hamm, *American Skinheads*, 37.

83. John Leo, "A Chilling Wave of Racism," *Time*, January 25, 1988, 57; Irwin Suall, David Lowe, and Tal Recanati, *Young and Violent: The Growing Menace of America's Neo-Nazi Skinheads* (Anti-Defamation League of B'nai B'rith/Civil Rights Division, 1988).

84. Southern Poverty Law Center Intelligence Project, *Skinheads in America*, 17–18.

85. Hamm, *American Skinheads*, 52.

86. Owen Brown, "Know your Enemy . . . Tom Metzger and the American Fascist," *No KKK! No Facist USA!*, Spring/Summer 1989, 5–6; Bill Wallace, "Racist Group Using Computers and TV to Recruit in Bay Area," *SF Chronicle*, March 5, 1985, 1–2.

87. Peter Stills, "Dark Contagion: Bigotry and Violence Online," *PC Computing*, December 1989, 144–49.

88. Hamm, *American Skinheads*, 57.

89. Southern Poverty Law Center Intelligence Project, *Skinheads in America*, 17–18.

90. Pete Simi and Barbara Brents, "An Extreme Response to Globalization: The Case of Racist Skinheads," in *Globalizing the Streets*, ed. Michael Flynn and David C. Brotherton (New York: Columbia University Press, 2008), 196–99; Hamm, *American Skinheads*, 32–35.

91. Simi and Brents, "An Extreme Response to Globalization."

92. Simi and Brents, "An Extreme Response to Globalization."

93   William Tafoya, "Rioting in the Street: Déjà Vu," address before the Office of International Criminal Justice, Chicago, 1990; Hamm, *American Skinheads*, 154.

94. Hamm, *American Skinheads*, 154.

95. Paul M. Barrett, "Hate Crimes Increase and Become More Violent: US Prosecutors Focus on Skinheads Movement," *Wall Street Journal*, July 14, 1989.

96. Mary H. Cooper, "The Growing Danger of Hate Groups," *Editorial Research Report* 18 (1989): 262–75.

97. Floyd Clarke, "Hate Violence in the United States," *FBI Law Enforcement Bulletin*, January 1991, 14–17.

98. T. J. Leyden and Bridget M. Cook, *Skinhead Confessions: From Hate to Hope* (Springville, UT: Sweetwater, 2008), 91–98.

99. Anti-Defamation League, "Extremism in America: The Hammerskin Nation," http://www.adl.org/learn/ext_us/hammerskin.asp.

100. Simi and Brents, "An Extreme Response to Globalization," 195–96.

101. Simi and Brents, "An Extreme Response to Globalization"; HSN, "Who We Are/Our History," *Hammerskin Nation*, http://www.hammerskins.net/.

102. Anti-Defamation League, "Extremism in America: The Hammerskin Nation."

103. Southern Poverty Law Center Intelligence Project, *Skinheads in America*, 12–13.

104. Southern Poverty Law Center Intelligence Project, *Skinheads in America*, 5.

105. The most famous of those was probably the Minutemen, a Missouri-based group founded by Robert DePugh in 1960 in order to protect America from the communist threat. For a decade it engaged in paramilitary training and stockpiling of ammunition. While the number of active members reached approximately two thousand at its peak, the group was eventually dissolved in 1970 after DePugh was convicted of violation of gun-control legislation. During the 1980s, several KKK branches engaged in paramilitary activities and in the formation of military-styled camps. For example, in 1981, a KKK "military camp" was established near Birmingham, Alabama.

106. Steve H. Murdock, F. Larry Leistritz, and Rita R. Hamm, "Impacts of the Farm Financial Crisis of the 1980s on Resources and Poverty in Agriculturally Dependent Counties in the United States," *Review of Policy Research* 7, no. 4 (June 1988): 810–27; Lia Bryant, "Social Aspects of the Farm Financial Crisis," in *Agriculture, Environment, and Society*, ed. Geoffrey Lawrence, Frank Vanclay, and Brian Furze (London: Macmillan Education UK, 1992), 157–72.

107. Nella Van Dyke and Sarah A. Soule, "Structural Social Change and the Mobilized Effect of Threat: Explaining Levels of Patriot and Militia Organizing in the United States," *Social Problems* 49, no. 4 (2002): 497–520.

108. Ruby Ridge (near Naples, Idaho) was the place where Randy Weaver, his family, and a family friend spent eleven days under siege by the U.S. Marshals Service and FBI forces, from August 21 until August 31, 1992. Weaver refused to obey a warrant to appear in court for firearms charges. In the first few days of the encounter, a shootout between six U.S. marshals and the Weavers resulted in the deaths of Deputy U.S. Marshal William Francis Degan and the Weavers' son Samuel (Sammy), family dog (Striker), and Weaver's forty-three-year-old wife, Vicki. Waco, Texas, was the location

of a compound owned by a cult named the Branch Davidians, led by the charismatic David Koresh. On February 23, 1993, ATF agents attempted to raid the ranch. In the shootout that erupted, four government agents and six Branch Davidians were killed. After fifty-one days of siege, the FBI assaulted the compound with tear gas. During the attack, a fire broke out, and seventy-six people died, including David Koresh.

109. Lane Crothers, *Race on the Right: The American Militia Movement from Ruby Ridge to Homeland Security* (Lanham, MD: Rowman & Littlefield, 2003), 75–86;

110. Leonard Zeskind, "Armed and Dangerous," *Rolling Stone*, November 1995, http://www.rickross.com/reference/militia/militia7.html.

111. Robert L. Snow, *Terrorists Among Us: The Militia Threat* (Cambridge, MA: Perseus, 1999), 13–14.

112. Morris Dees and James Corcoran, *Gathering Storms: The Story of America's Militia Network* (New York: HarperCollins, 1996), 49–67.

113. The Leaderless Resistance program was published originally by Beam in the 1992 issue of *The Seditionist*. Anti-Defamation League, "Extremists in America: Louis Beam," http://www.adl.org/learn/ext_us/beam.asp?xpicked=2&item=beam; Quarles, *Ku Klux Klan*, 147.

114. "False Patriots: Profiles of 40 Antigovernment Leaders: Church as State—Howard Phillips, 60," *Southern Poverty Law Center Intelligence Report* 102 (Summer 2001), http://www.splcenter.org/get-informed/intelligence-report/browse-all-issues/2001/summer/false-patriots?page=0,8.

115. Anti-Defamation League, "Extremists in America: Militia of Montana," http://www.adl.org/learn/ext_us/mom.asp?xpicked=3&item=mom.

116. Neil A. Hamilton, *Militias in America: A Reference Handbook* (Santa Barbara, CA: ABC-CLIO, 1996), 30–34.

117. ADL, "Extremists in America: Militia of Montana"; Dees and Corcoran, *Gathering Storms*; Beth Hawkins, "Patriot Games," in *Militias in America*, ed. Dani Hazan, L. Smith, and C. Triano (San Francisco, CA: Institute for Alternative Journalism, 1994), 7–12.

118. Joshua D. Freilich, *State-Level Variations in Militia Activities* (El Paso, TX: LFB Scholarly Publishing, 2003).

119. Ami Pedahzur and Arie Perliger, "The Changing Nature of Suicide Attacks—A Social Network Perspective," *Social Forces* 84, no. 4 (2006): 1983–2004.

120. Hawkins, "Patriot Games," 7–12.

121. Berlet and Lyons provide an assessment of between 15,000 and 40,000: Chip Berlet and Matthew N. Lyons, "Militia Nation," *The Progressive* 59, no. 6 (1995): 22.

122. Snow, *Terrorists Among Us*, 14.

123. Anti-Defamation League, "Extremism in America: The Militia Movement," http://www.adl.org/learn/ext_us/militia_m.asp?xpicked=4&item=19.

124. For example, Linda Thompson, one of the more prominent ideologists of the militia movement, asserted that "I definitely believe the government did the bombing. I mean who's got a track record of killing children?" Anti-Defamation League, *Beyond the Bombing: The Militia Menace Grows* (New York: ADL, 1995), 15.

125.   Hamilton, *Militias in America*, 43–44.

126.   See, e.g., Florida, Stat. ch. 870.06 (1994); Georgia, Code ann. § 38-2-277 (Harrison 1995); Iowa, Code § 29A.31 (1995); Kansas, Stat. Ann. § 48-203 (1994); Maine, Rev. Stat. Ann. tit. 37-B, § 342.2 (West 1996); Maryland, Ann. Code, Militia § 35 (1995); Nevada, Rev. Stat. § 203.080 (1995); North Carolina, Gen. Stat. § 127A-151 (1986 and Supp. 1996); West Virginia, Code § 15-1F-7 (1995); Wyoming, Stat. Ann. § 19-1-106.

127.   Norman Olson, "The Militia and Y2K" (1999); Virginian Citizens Militia, Y2K *Policy Statement*, March 6.

128.   "Meet the Former Militiaman Behind the Fast and Furious Scandal," *Mother Jones*, December 2011, https://www.motherjones.com/politics/2011/12/fast-and-furious-scandal -mike-vanderboegh/.

129.   "'Online Novel' Allegedly Inspired Georgia Terrorism Suspects," *Los Angeles Times*, Nov. 3, 2011, http://latimesblogs.latimes.com/jacketcopy/2011/11/online-novel-inspired -georgia-terrorism-suspects.html.

130.   The attack occurred on December 14, 2012, in Newtown, Connecticut. A twenty-year-old Adam Lanza fatally shot twenty elementary school students and six adult staff members from Sandy Hook Elementary School. Before driving to the school, he shot and killed his mother at their Newtown home.

131.   Kim Paxton and Gordan Runyan, "Addresses of CT Legislators Who Voted in Favor of Gun Registration Posted by Patriot Activist," *Freedom Outpost*, February 28, 2014.

132.   Chris Gentilviso "Cliven Bundy Supporter Threatens to Rip Harry Reid's Balls Off," *Huffington Post*, May 1, 2014, https://www.huffingtonpost.com/2014/05/01/cliven-bundy -militia-harry-reid_n_5246085.html.

133.   "Oath Keepers and the Age of Treason," *Mother Jones*, February 2010, https://www .motherjones.com/politics/2010/02/oath-keepers/; Dylan DeCarlo, "Patriots or Problematic? The Media Can't Decide: A Critical Discourse Analysis of the Oath Keepers in Popular Media," PhD diss., Northern Arizona University, 2016.

134.   Amanda Sakuma and Bradley J. Rayford, "'Oath Keepers' Armed with Guns Roam Streets of Ferguson," MSNBC, August 11, 2015, http://www.msnbc.com/msnbc/oath -keepers-armed-guns-roam-streets-ferguson; Terrence McCoy, "The Oath Keepers: The Little-Known Militia Now Roaming the Streets of Ferguson," *Washington Post*, December 1, 2014. During summer 2014, clashes erupted between law enforcement and parts of the city's population. The latter were protesting the killing of the eighteen-year-old African American man Michael Brown Jr. by a white police officer, who fatally shot him on August 9 of that year.

135.   "Tension Between BLM and Mining Operation, Oath Keepers Set Up Camp," *Conservative News & Right Wing News | Gun Laws & Rights News Site*, April 18, 2015, https://rightedition.com/2015/04/18/tension-between-blm-and-mining-operation-oath -keepers-set-up-camp/.

136.   Mayer N. Zald and Bert Useem, "Movements and Counter Movements Interactions: Mobilization, Tactics, and State Development," in *Social Movements in an Organizational Society*, ed. Mayer N. Zald and John D. McCarthy (New Brunswick, NJ:

Transaction, 1987); Arie Perliger and Ami Pedahzur, "Counter Cultures, Group Dynamics, and Religious Terrorism," *Political Studies* 64, no. 2 (June 1, 2016): 297–314.

137. Michael Barkun, *Religion and the Racist Right* (Chapel Hill: University of North Carolina Press, 1994), 17–18.

138. Alexander B. Grimaldy, *Memoirs, and a Selection of Letters from the Correspondence of Eduard Hine* (London: Robert Banks and Son, 1909), 20–50.

139. Charles A. Totten, *Our Race: Its Origins and Destiny, a Series of Studies on the Saxon Riddle* (New Haven, CT: Our Race Publishing Company, 1891); Frank F. Gosset, *Race: The History of an Idea in America* (New York: Schocken, 1987), 191–92.

140. Sawyer was also a KKK member during the early 1920s: this is of little surprise considering that these were the heydays of the second Klan. For his articles, see, e.g., Reuben H. Sawyer, "The American Idea," *Watchman of Israel* 3 (April 1921): 114–15; Reuben H. Sawyer, "Who Are the Americans?" *Watchman of Israel* 3 (August 1921): 182–85.

141. Chester L. Quarles, *Christian Identity: The Aryan American Bloodline Religion* (Jefferson, NC: McFarland, 2004), 54–55.

142. Barkun, *Religion and the Racist Right*, 30–32.

143. Probably the most popular platform for the dissemination of anti-Semitic ideas was the *Independent*, which achieved infamy when it was sued for its International Jew series of publications. David A. Gerber, "Anti-Semitism and Jewish-Gentile Relations in American Historiography and the American Past," in *Anti-Semitism in American History*, ed. David A. Gerber (Urbana: University of Illinois Press, 1986), 20–22.

144. Barkun, *Religion and the Racist Right*, 40–41.

145. Alma M. Hertherington, *70 Years Old! An Outline History of Our Work Since 1909* (Burnaby, BC: Association of Covenant People, 1979), 1–10, 20.

146. Quarles, *Christian Identity*.

147. Glen Jeanstone, *Gerald K. Smith: Minister of Hate* (New Haven, CT: Yale University Press, 1988), 99–100, 105–6.

148. Barkun, *Religion and the Racist Right*, 54–55.

149. Daniel Levitas, *Terrorist Next Door: The Militia Movement and the Radical Right* (New York: St. Martin's, 2004), 25.

150. Jeffrey Kaplan, ed., *Encyclopedia of White Power* (Walnut Creek, CA: Altamira, 2000), 49.

151. Levitas, *Terrorist Next Door*, 97–98.

152. William Porter Gale, "Enemy Within," *Identity* 5, no. 1 (1969): 6.

153. The Minutemen was a paramilitary organization founded by Robert Depugh, a biochemist from Missouri. The organization was engaged mainly in military training and stockpiling of weapons in order to fight what its members believed was an imminent communist invasion. The organization also embraced survivalist and antifederal sentiments.

154. Levitas, *Terrorist Next Door*, 108–10.

155. Levitas, *Terrorist Next Door*, 139–53.

156. Quarles, *Christian Identity*, 133.

157. Anti-Defamation League, "Extremism in America: Aryan Nations/Church of Jesus Christ Christian," http://www.adl.org/learn/ext_us/aryan_nations.asp?xpicked=3&item=an.

158. Evelyn Schlatter, *Aryan Cowboys: White Supremacists and the Search for a New Frontier, 1970–2000* (Austin: University of Texas Press, 2006), 66.

159. G. Gordon Liddy, CDR James G. Liddy, J. Michael Barrett, and Joel Selanikio, *Fight Back: Tackling Terrorism, Liddy Style* (New York: St. Martin's Griffin, 2006), 75.

160. Quarles, *Christian Identity*, 133–34.

161. George Michael, *Confronting Right-Wing Extremism and Terrorism in the USA* (New York: Routledge, 2003), 46; Kaplan, ed., *Encyclopedia of White Power*, 18.

162. Barkun, *Religion and the Racist Right*, 231–34.

163. Quarles, *Christian Identity*, 134.

164. "Furrow Pleads Guilty to Shootings, Will Avoid Death Penalty, Get Life Without Parole," CNN Justice, January 24, 2001, http://articles.cnn.com/2001-01-24/justice/furrow.plea.crim_1_furrow-shooting-rampage-ileto?_s=PM:LAW.

165. Dobratz and Shanks-Meile, *The White Separatist Movement in the United States*, 192.

166. Kevin Flynn and Gary Gerhardt, *The Silent Brotherhood: Inside America's Racist Underground* (New York: Free Press, 1995), 442–46.

167. Jessica Stern, "The Covenant, the Sword, and the Arm of the Lord," in *Toxic Terror*, ed. Jonathan Tucker (Cambridge, MA: MIT Press, 2000), 139–57; Quarles, *Christian Identity*, 135–38.

168. For the verdict summary, see Southern Poverty Law Center, "Case Docket: Keenan v. Aryan Nations," July 9, 2000, http://www.splcenter.org/get-informed/case-docket/keenan-v-aryan-nations.

169. Dobratz and Shanks-Meile, *The White Separatist Movement in the United States*, 80; Anti-Defamation League, "Extremism in America: Peter J. 'Pete' Peters," http://www.adl.org/learn/ext_us/peters.asp?learn_cat=extremism&learn_subcat=extremism_in_america&xpicked=2&item=8.

4. Tactics of the American Far Right

1. Michel Lue and Dan Herbeck, *American Terrorist* (New York: Avon, 2002), 239–40.

2. Emily M. Bernstein, "Terror in Oklahoma: The Overview; Evidence Linking Suspect to Blast Offered in Court," *New York Times*, April 28, 1995, http://www.nytimes.com/1995/04/28/us/terror-oklahoma-overview-evidence-linking-suspect-blast-offered-court.html; Robert D. McFadden, "Terror in Oklahoma: John Doe No. 1—A Special Report.; A Life of Solitude and Obsessions," *New York Times*, May 4, 1995, http://www.nytimes.com/1995/05/04/us/terror-oklahoma-john-doe-no-1-special-report-life-solitude-obsessions.html.

3. McVeigh's trial proceedings suggest that as many as six people were involved in the operation on some level, including Terry Nichols and Michael and Lori Fortier; in

other words, it was not a "lone-wolf" operation. For more details, see http://law2.umkc
.edu/faculty/projects/ftrials/mcveigh/mcveightranscript.html.

4. Douglas O. Linder, "The Trial Transcript (Excerpts) from the Trial of Timothy
    McVeigh," http://law2.umkc.edu/faculty/projects/ftrials/mcveigh/mcveightranscript
    .html; Lue and Herbeck, *American Terrorist*, 223–32; John Kifner, "Oklahoma Blast: A
    Tale in 2 Books?" *New York Times*, August 21, 1995, http://www.nytimes.com/1995/08
    /21/us/oklahoma-blast-a-tale-in-2-books.html.

5. Arie Perliger, "How Democracies Respond to Terrorism: Regime Characteristics,
    Symbolic Power, and Counterterrorism," *Security Studies* 21, no. 3 (July 1, 2012): 490–
    528; Jonathan Matusitz, *Symbolism in Terrorism* (Baltimore, MD: Rowman & Little-
    field, 2014).

6. C. J. M. Drake, "The Role of Ideology in Terrorists' Target Selection," *Terrorism and
    Political Violence* 10, no. 2 (1998): 53–85.

7. Vittorfranco S. Pisano, "A Survey of Terrorism of the Left in Italy: 1970–78," *Terrorism*
    2, no. 3–4 (January 1, 1979): 171–212.

8. Martha Crenshaw, "Causes of Terrorism," *Comparative Politics* 13, no. 4 (1981): 379–99;
    Perliger, "How Democracies Respond to Terrorism."

9. Roger W. Cobb and Marc Howard Ross, *Cultural Strategies of Agenda Denial: Avoid-
    ance, Attack, and Redefinition* (Lawrence: University Press of Kansas, 1997).

10. Attacks against religious sites affiliated with minority groups were coded under the
    category of "religious targets." The great majority of religious sites that were attacked
    were affiliated with minority groups (synagogues, mosques, and African American
    churches).

11. Engy Abdelkader, "When Islamophobia Turns Violent: The 2016 U.S. Presidential
    Elections," Bridge Initiative, Georgetown University, May 2, 2016, https://ssrn.com
    /abstract=2779201; C. Ogan, L. Willnat, R. Pennington, and M. Bashir, "The Rise of
    Anti-Muslim Prejudice: Media and Islamophobia in Europe and the United States,"
    International Communication Gazette 76, no. 1 (2014): 27–46.

12. German Lopez, "The Supreme Court Legalized Same Sex Marriage in the US After
    Years of Legal Battles," *Vox*, March 31, 2015, https://www.vox.com/2015/6/26/17937530
    /supreme-court-same-sex-gay-marriage-obergefell-v-hodges.

13. Kevin Flynn and Gary Gerhardt, *The Silent Brotherhood: Inside America's Racist
    Underground* (New York: Free Press, 1995).

14. James Piazza, "Rooted in Poverty? Terrorism, Poor Economic Development, and
    Social Cleavages," *Terrorism and Political Violence* 18, no. 1 (2006): 159–77.

15. Ehud Sprinzak, "Gush Emunim, the Iceberg Model of Political Extremism," *Medina,
    Mimshal Veyahasim Beinleumiim* 17 (1981).

16. J. O. Mierau, "The Activity and Lethality of Militant Groups: Ideology, Capacity, and
    Environment," *Dynamics of Asymmetric Conflict* 8, no. 1 (2015): 23–37.

17. David Tucker, "What Is New About the New Terrorism," *Terrorism and Political Vio-
    lence* 13 (2001): 1–14; Bruce Hoffman, "Old Madness New Methods," *Rand Review*
    (1998): 12–17.

5. The Rise and Decline of Far-Right Violence
in the United States

1. Southern Poverty Law Center, "Ten Days After: Harassment and Intimidation in the Aftermath of Election," https://www.splcenter.org/20161129/ten-days-after-harassment -and-intimidation-aftermath-election.
2. Anti-Defamation League, "US Antisemitic Incidents Spike 86% So Far in 2017 After Surging Last Year, ADL Finds," https://www.adl.org/news/press-releases/us-anti-semitic -incidents-spike-86-percent-so-far-in-2017.
3. Erica Chenoweth, "Democratic Competition and Terrorist Activity," *Journal of Politics* 72, no. 1 (2010): 16–30.
4. Arie Perliger, "How Democracies Respond to Terrorism: Regime Characteristics, Symbolic Power, and Counterterrorism." *Security Studies* 21, no. 3 (July 1, 2012): 490–528.
5. Perliger, "How Democracies Respond to Terrorism."
6. Steven E. Finkel, "Reciprocal Effects of Participation and Political Efficacy: A Panel Analysis," *American Journal of Political Science* (1985): 891–913.
7. Anne R. Williamson and Michael J. Scicchitano, "Minority Representation and Political Efficacy in Public Meetings," *Social Science Quarterly* 96, no. 2 (2015): 576–87; Marilyn H. Buehler, "Political Efficacy, Political Discontent, and Voting Turnout Among Mexican-Americans in Michigan," PhD diss., University of Notre Dame, 1975; John Merrifield, "The Institutional and Political Factors That Influence Voter Turnout," *Public Choice* 77, no. 3 (1993): 657–67.
8. Leonard Weinberg, "Terrorism and Democracy: Illness and Cure?" *Global Dialogue* 8, nos. 3–4 (2006), http://www.worlddialogue.org/content.php?id=383; Alex P. Schmid, "Terrorism and Democracy," *Terrorism and Political Violence* 4, no. 4 (1992): 14–25.
9. Chenoweth, "Democratic Competition and Terrorist Activity."
10. Paul Ignazi, "The Silent Counter-Revolution: Hypothesis on the Emergence of Extreme- Right Wing Parties in Europe," *European Journal of Political Research* 26, no. 3 (1992): 3–34; Hans Georg Betz, "Conditions Favoring the Success (and Failure) of Radical Right-Wing Populist Parties in Contemporary Democracies," in *Democracies and the Populist Challenge*, ed. Yves Meny and Yves Surel (London: Palgrave Macmillan UK, 2002); Roger Eatwell, "Ten Theories of the Extreme Right," in *Right Wing Extremism in the Twenty First Century*, ed. Peter H. Merkl and Leonard Weinberg (London: Routledge, 2003), 47–73.
11. Bryan Caplan, "Terrorism: The Relevance of the Rational Choice Model," *Public Choice* 128, no. 1 (July 1, 2006): 91–107; William F. Shughart, "Terrorism in Rational Choice Perspective," in *The Handbook on the Political Economy of War*, ed. Christopher Coyne and Rachel L. Mathers (Northampton, MA: Edward Elgar, 2011), 126–53; Claude Berrebi, "The Economics of Terrorism and Counterterrorism: What Matters and Is Rational-Choice Theory Helpful?" in *Social Science for Counterterrorism: Putting the Pieces Together*, ed. Paul K. Davis and Kim Cragin (RAND, 2009), 189–90.

12. Alexander Lee, "Who Becomes a Terrorist? Poverty, Education, and the Origins of Political Violence," *World Politics* 63, no. 2 (April 2011): 203–45; Alan B. Kruger and Jitka Maleckova, "Education, Poverty, and Terrorism," *Journal of Economic Perspectives* 17, no. 4 (2003): 119–44; Jerrold Post, "When Hatred Is Bred in the Bone: Psycho-Cultural Foundations of Contemporary Terrorism," *Political Psychology* 26, no. 4 (2005): 615; Eitan Alimi, "The Israeli Political Arena and Palestinian Contention: The Case of the 'First' Intifada," *British Journal of Political Science* 37, no. 3 (2007): 433–53; David Lehen, "Terrorism, Social Movements, and International Security: How Al Qaeda Affects Southeast Asia," *Japanese Journal of Political Science* 6, no. 1 (2005): 87–109.

13. Jonathan Matusitz and James Olufowote, "Visual Motifs in Islamist Terrorism: Applying Conceptual Metaphor Theory," *Journal of Applied Security Research* 11, no. 1 (2016): 18–32; Catherine Wessinger, "Fighting Words: The Origins of Religious Violence," *Nova Religio* 12, no. 1 (2008): 131–35; David Cook, *Contemporary Muslim Apocalyptic Literature* (Syracuse, NY: Syracuse University Press, 2008); Pippa Norris and Ronald Inglehart, "Islamic Culture and Democracy: Testing the 'Clash of Civilizations' Thesis," in *New Frontiers in Comparative Sociology*, ed. Masamichi Sasaki (Leiden: Brill, 2008), 221–50.

14. Ami Pedahzur and Arie Perliger, "The Changing Nature of Suicide Attacks: A Social Network Perspective," *Social Forces: A Scientific Medium of Social Study and Interpretation* 84, no. 4 (June 1, 2006): 1987–2008; Maxime Bérubé, "Social Networks, Terrorism and Counter-Terrorism, Radical and Connected," *Sécurité et Stratégie* 20, no. 3 (2015): 78; David Knoke, "Social Networks and Terrorism," in *Social Networking and Community Behavior Modeling*, ed. Maytham Safar and Khaled Mahdi (Hershey, PA: IGI Global, 2011), 232–46.

15. Theodor W. Adorno, Else Frenkel-Brunswik, Daniel J. Levinson, et al., "The Authoritarian Personality," 1950, http://www.popflock.com/learn?s=The_Authoritarian_Personality.

16. Arie Perliger, Gabriel Koehler-Derrick, and Ami Pedahzur, "The Gap Between Participation and Violence: Why We Need to Disaggregate Terrorist 'Profiles,'" *International Studies Quarterly* 60, no. 2 (June 1, 2016): 220–29.

17. All these variables will be tested later in a more comprehensive regression model, in order to make a final judgment about their impact on the level of violence in relation to other political variables.

18. Since the current political division between Democrats and Republicans on liberal policies, and thus ideological proximity to the far right, emerged just in the late 1960s, I began the analysis with the presidency of Lyndon B. Johnson.

19. All these variables will be tested later in a more comprehensive regression model, in order to make a final judgment about their impact on the level of violence in relation to other political variables.

20. Doug McAdam, *Political Process and the Development of Black Insurgency, 1930–1970* (Chicago: University of Chicago Press, 2010), xviii.

21. David S. Meyer and Suzanne Staggenborg, "Movements, Countermovements, and the Structure of Political Opportunity," *American Journal of Sociology* 101, no. 6 (1996): 1628–60.

22. Meyer and Staggenborg, "Movements, Countermovements, and the Structure of Political Opportunity"; Eatwell, "Ten Theories of the Extreme Right."

23. Arie Perliger and Ami Pedahzur, "Counter Cultures, Group Dynamics, and Religious Terrorism," *Political Studies* 64, no. 2 (June 1, 2016): 297–314.

6. Perpetrators of Far-Right Violence

1.   John Terraine, "Terrorist Profile," *RUSI Journal*, 122, no. 4 (1977): 72–73; Gavril Cornutiu, "The Profile of the Fanatical Terrorist," *Psychology* 7, no. 4 (2016): 565–71; Charles Russell and Bowman H. Miller, "Profile of a Terrorist," *Terrorism* 1 (1977): 17–34; Jeffrey S. Handler, "Socioeconomic Profile of an American Terrorist: 1960s and 1970s," *Terrorism* 3 (1990): 195–213; Alan B. Kruger and Jitka Maleckova, "Education, Poverty, and Terrorism," *Journal of Economic Perspectives* 17, no. 4 (2003): 119–44.

2.   Jerrold M. Post, *The Mind of the Terrorist: The Psychology of Terrorism from the IRA to al-Qaeda* (New York: St. Martin's, 2007).

3.   Ami Pedahzur, Arie Perliger, and Leonard Weinberg, "Altruism and Fatalism: The Characteristics of Palestinian Suicide Terrorists," *Deviant Behavior* 24, no. 4 (2003): 405–23; Zoey Reeve, "Islamist Terrorism as Parochial Altruism," *Terrorism and Political Violence* 32, no. 1 (2017): 38–56; Robert Pape, "The Strategic Logic of Suicide Terrorism," *American Political Science Review* 97, no. 3 (2003): 1–19.

4.   Pape, "The Strategic Logic of Suicide Terrorism."

5.   Audrey Kurth Cronin, *How Terrorism Ends* (Princeton, NJ: Princeton University Press, 2015).

6.   John Terraine, "Terrorist Profile"; Cornutiu, "The Profile of the Fanatical Terrorist"; Russell and Miller, "Profile of a Terrorist"; Handler, "Socioeconomic Profile of an American Terrorist"; Kruger and Maleckova, "Education, Poverty, and Terrorism."

7.   Jeff Victoroff, "The Mind of the Terrorist: A Review and Critique of Psychological Approaches," *Journal of Conflict Resolution* 49, no. 1 (2005): 3–42.

8.   Arie Perliger, Gabriel Koehler-Derrick, and Ami Pedahzur, "The Gap Between Participation and Violence: Why We Need to Disaggregate Terrorist 'Profiles,'" *International Studies Quarterly* 60, no. 2 (June 1, 2016): 220–29; Post, *The Mind of the Terrorist*; Jessica Stern, *Terror in the Name of God: Why Religious Militants Kill* (New York: Harper Collins, 2009; Scott Atran, "Genesis of Suicide Terrorism," *Science* 299, no. 5612 (March 7, 2003): 1534–39.

9.   Post, *The Mind of the Terrorist*; Stern, *Terror in the Name of God*; Atran, "Genesis of Suicide Terrorism"; John Horgan, *The Psychology of Terrorism* (New York: Routledge, 2004).

10. Horgan, *The Psychology of Terrorism*.

11. Neil Shortland, Nader Elias, Nicholas Imperillo, et al., "The Interaction of Extremist Propaganda and Anger as Predictors of Violent Responses," *Journal of Interpersonal Violence* (2017): 1–21; Samuel T. Hunter, Neil D. Shortland, Matthew P. Crayne, and Gina S. Ligon, "Recruitment and Selection in Violent Extremist Organizations:

Exploring What Industrial and Organizational Psychology Might Contribute," *American Psychologist* 72, no. 3 (April 2017): 242–54.

12. Efraim Benmelech and Claude Berrebi, "Human Capital and the Productivity of Suicide Bombers," *Journal of Economic Perspectives* 21, no. 3 (2007): 223–38; Alexander Lee, "Who Becomes a Terrorist? Poverty, Education, and the Origins of Political Violence," *World Politics* 63, no. 2 (April 2011): 203–45; Pedahzur, Perliger, and Weinberg, "Altruism and Fatalism."

13. Tatyana Dronzina and Vadim Astashin, "Chechen Female Suicide Bombers: Who and Why," *Journal of Human Security* 3, no. 1 (2007): 30–44.

14. Liran Goldman and Michael A. Hogg, "Understanding Terrorism: Effects of Prototypicality and Relative Deprivation on Extreme Behaviors," presentation at the ISPP Thirty-Fourth Annual Scientific Meeting, 2011; Marium Akhtar, "Role of Identity Crisis and Relative Deprivation as Catalysts of Political Violence and Terrorism," *RAIS Journal for Social Sciences* 2, no. 1 (2018): 49–66; Ted Robert Gurr, *Why Men Rebel* (New York: Routledge, 2015).

15. Charles Tilly, "Terror, Terrorism, Terrorists," *Sociological Theory* 22, no. 1 (2004): 5–13.

16. Thomas Hegghammer, "Terrorist Recruitment and Radicalization in Saudi Arabia," *Middle East Policy* 13, no. 4 (2006): 39–60; Assaf Moghadam, *The Globalization of Martyrdom: Al-Qaeda, Salafi Jihad, and the Diffusion of Suicide Attacks* (Baltimore, MD: Johns Hopkins University Press, 2011); Ahmed Reem and Daniela Pisoiu, "Beyond Borders: Subcultural Theory and the Transnational Jihadi Identity in Europe," in *Border Politics: Defining Spaces of Governance and Forms of Transgressions*, ed. Cengiz Günay and Nina Witjes (New York: Springer, 2017).

17. Brenda Major, Alison Blodorn, and Gregory Major Blascovich, "The Threat of Increasing Diversity: Why Many White Americans Support Trump in the 2016 Presidential Election," *Group Processes and Intergroup Relations* 21, no. 6 (2018): 931–40.

18. Jialun Qin, Jennifer J. Xu, Daning Hu, et al., "Analyzing Terrorist Networks: A Case Study of the Global Salafi Jihad Network," in *International Conference on Intelligence and Security Informatics* (Berlin: Springer, 2005), 287–304; Arie Perliger and Ami Pedahzur, "Counter Cultures, Group Dynamics, and Religious Terrorism," *Political Studies* 64, no. 2 (June 1, 2016): 297–314.

19. Arie Perliger and Daniel Milton, *From Cradle to Grave: The Lifecycle of Foreign Fighters in Iraq and Syria* (West Point, NY, Combating Terrorism Center, 2016).

20. Diego Gambetta and Steffen Hertog, "Why Are There So Many Engineers Among Islamic Radicals?" *European Journal of Sociology/Archives Européennes de Sociologie* 50, no. 2 (2009): 201–30; Ethan Bueno de Mesquita, "The Quality of Terror," *American Journal of Political Science* 49, no. 3 (2005): 515–30.

21. "Isis Leader Calls on Muslims to 'Build Islamic State,'" BBC, July 1, 2014, https://www.bbc.com/news/world-middle-east-28116846.

22. Stephen E. Atkins, *Encyclopedia of Right-Wing Extremism in Modern American History* (New York: ABC-CLIO, 2011), 222–23; Aria, "Challengers from the Sidelines: Understanding America's Violent Far-Right," Combating Terrorism Center, West Point, NY, November 2012.

23. "Isis Leader Calls on Muslims to 'Build Islamic State'," BBC, July 1, 2014, https://www
.bbc.com/news/world-middle-east-28116846; Anita Peresin and Alberto Cervone, "The
Western Muhajirat of ISIS," *Studies in Conflict and Terrorism* 38, no. 7 (2015): 495–509.
24. Perliger and Milton, *From Cradle to Grave*.
25. G. L. Wiltfang and Doug McAdam, "The Costs and Risks of Social Activism: A Study
of Sanctuary Movement Activism," *Social Forces* 69, no. 4 (1991): 987–1010; A. Schussman and S. A. Soule, "Process and Protest: Accounting for Individual Protest Participation," *Social Forces* 84, no. 2 (2005): 1083–108.
26. Alexa Cooper and Erica L. Smith, "Homicide Trends in the United States, 1980–
2008," Washington, D.C.: U.S. Department of Justice, 2011.
27. Fathali M. Moghaddam, "The Staircase to Terrorism: A Psychological Exploration,"
American Psychologist 60, no. 2 (February 2005): 161–69; Mitchell D. Silber and Arvin
Bhatt, *Radicalization in the West: The Homegrown Threat* (New York: NYPD Intelligence Division, 2007); Scott Helfstein, *Edges of Radicalization: Ideas, Individuals,
and Networks in Violent Extremism* (West Point, NY: Combating Terrorism Center,
2012).
28. Matthew M. Sweeney and Arie Perliger, "Explaining the Spontaneous Nature of Far-
Right Violence in the United States," *Perspectives on Terrorism* 12, no. 6 (2018): 52–71.
29. Sweeney and Perliger, "Explaining the Spontaneous Nature of Far-Right Violence."
30. Sweeney and Perliger, "Explaining the Spontaneous Nature of Far-Right Violence."
31. Erin M. Kearns, Allison E. Betus, and Anthony F. Lemieux, "Why Do Some Terrorist
Attacks Receive More Media Attention Than Others?" *Justice Quarterly* (2019): 1–24.
32. Sweeney and Perliger, "Explaining the Spontaneous Nature of Far-Right Violence."

7. Contemporary Discourse of the American Far Right

1. Steven Erlanger and Scott Shane, "Norway Shooting and Bomb Attack Leaves at
Least 92 Dead," *New York Times*, July 23, 2011, https://www.nytimes.com/2011/07/24
/world/europe/24oslo.html; Robert Mackey, "Online, Clues to a Suspected Attacker's
Motives," *New York Times*, July 23, 2011.
2. Hammerskin Nation online forum, http://www.crew38.com/forum38/showthread.php
?16250-what-going-on-in-USA/page2; http://www.crew38.com/forum38/showthread
.php?16250-what-going-on-in-USA/page3.
3. https://www.reddit.com/r/The_Donald/duplicates/63bcdi/ama_based_stickman
_kyle_chapman_here_hows_it/. This site provide access to various social media posts of
far-right activists. This post by Kyle Chapman was posted with the title "AMA-Based
Stickman Kyle Chapman here, hows it going The_Donald?" Screenshot available at
author's repository.
4. Post by JG_1488 at NSM forum, nsm88forum.com, January 4, 2006. Screenshot available at author's repository.
5. Rogers Brubaker, "Between Nationalism and Civilizationism: The European Populist
Moment in Comparative Perspective," *Ethnic and Racial Studies* 40, no. 8 (June 21, 2017):

1191–226; Tamir Bar-On, "Fascism to the Nouvelle Droite: The Dream of Pan-European Empire," *Journal of Contemporary European Studies* 16, no. 3 (December 1, 2008): 327–45.

6. Peter Bull and Anne-Marie Simon-Vandenbergen, "Equivocation and Doublespeak in Far Right-Wing Discourse: An Analysis of Nick Griffin's Performance on BBC's Question Time," *Text & Talk* 34, no. 1 (January 1, 2014): 1–22.

7. Published at the Brotherhood of the Klan Website, KnightsofKKK.com:8o/whyBOK .html. Screenshot available at author's repository.

8. Simon Goodman and Andrew J. Johnson, "Strategies Used by the Far Right to Counter Accusations of Racism," *Critical Approaches to Discourse Analysis Across Disciplines* 6, no. 2 (2013): 97–113; Mona Moufahim, Michael Humphreys, Darryn Mitussis, and James Fitchett, "Interpreting Discourse: A Critical Discourse Analysis of the Marketing of an Extreme Right Party," *Journal of Marketing Management* 23, no. 5–6 (2007): 537–58; Sasha Williams and Ian Law, "Legitimizing Racism: An Exploration of the Challenges Posed by the Use of Indigeneity Discourse by the Far-Right," *Sociological Research Online* 17, no. 2 (2012).

9. Norman Fairclough, *Discourse and Social Change* (Cambridge: Polity, 1992); Nelson Phillips and Cynthia Hardy, *Discourse Analysis: Investigating processes of Social Construction* (Thousand Oaks, CA: Sage, 2002).

10. Theo van Leeuwen, "Genre and Field in Critical Discourse Analysis: A Synopsis." *Discourse & Society* 4, no. 2 (April 1, 1993): 193–223; Stefan Titscher, Michael Meyer, Ruth Wodak, and Eva Vetter, *Methods of Text and Discourse Analysis: In Search of Meaning* (Thousand Oaks, CA: Sage, 2000).

11. Martin Reisigl, "The Discourse-Historical Approach," in *Routledge Handbook of Critical Discourse Studies*, ed. John Flowerdew and John E. Richardson (New York: Routledge, 2017), 44–59.

12. Ruth Wodak, "The Discourse-Historical Approach," *Methods of Critical Discourse Analysis* 1 (2001): 63–94.

13. Ruth Wodak and Michael Meyer, "Critical Discourse Analysis: History, Agenda, Theory, and Methodology," *Methods of Critical Discourse Analysis* 2 (2009): 1–33; Titscher et al., *Methods of Text and Discourse Analysis.*

14. David Sternberger, Gerhard Storz, and W. E. Süßkind, *Aus dem Wörterbuch des Unmenschen* (Hamburg: Claassen, 1957); Viktor Klemperer, *The Language of the Third Reich* (London: Continuum, 2005).

15. Post published at volksfrontinternational.com. Screenshot available at author's repository.

16. "Protect our Jobs!" https://kkk.bz/wp-content/uploads/2017/02/Now-protect-jobs-from -illegal-immigration.pdf. Screenshot available at author's repository.

17. Hammerskin Nation online forum, http://www.crew38.com/forum38/showthread.php ?16250-what-going-on-in-USA/page8. Screenshot available at author's repository.

18. Posted March 3, 2018, at http://keystone2001united.wordpress.com. Screenshot available at author's repository.

19. Post by "Steve Smith" (who described himself as member of the Keystone United) on Twitter, August 2, 2018. Screenshot available at author's repository.

20. Posted by 38Florida, March 18, 2013, at HSN forum, http://www.crew38.com/forum38
/showthread.php?12408-North-Korea-missle-crisis. Screenshot available at author's repository.

21. Posted by 38Florida, March 25, 2018, at HSN forum, http://www.crew38.com/forum38
/showthread.php?14938-thoughts-on-donald-trump/pahe10. Screenshot available at
author's repository.

22. http://www.counterextremism.com/content/thomas-robb-national-director-national
-knights-ku-klux-klan-2002. Screenshot available at author's repository.

23. http://www.geocities.ws/itsonlyme53934/index12.html. Screenshot available at
author's repository.

24. https://www.reddit.com/r/The_Donald/duplicates/63bcdi/ama_based_stickman
_kyle_chapman_here_hows_it/. This site provides access to various social media posts
of far-right activists. This post by Kyle Chapman was posted with no specific title as an
extension of previous posts. Screenshot available at author's repository.

25. gab.ai; https://gab.ai/RiseAboveMovement. Screenshot available at author's
repository.

26. Posted by Mojocat27, October 7, 2013, at HSN forum, http://www.crew38.com/forum38
/showthread.php?12877-what-are-you-going-to-do-if-the-niggers-start-rioting. Screenshot available at author's repository.

27. Posted at http://www.geocities.ws/itonlyme53934/index3.html. Screenshot available at
author's repository.

28. "Save the Flag," https://kkk.bz/wp-content/uploads/2017/02/Now-save-the-flag.pdf.
Screenshot available at author's repository.

29. Post by ODIN88, NSM forum, nsm88forum.com, April 16, 2011. Screenshot available
at author's repository.

30. https://web.archive.org/web/20170731075418/https://atomwaffendivision.org/.

31. Post by Hillbilly, July 7, 2018, HSN forum, http://www.crew38.com/forum38/showthread
.php?16552-I-don-t-get-it!!&p=156814#post156814. Screenshot available at author's repository.

32. https://web.archive.org/web/20170829152922/https://atomwaffendivision.org/2017/05/25
/awd-statement/. Screenshot available at author's repository.

33. https://web.archive.org/web/20180303203826/https://atomwaffendivision.org/wp-content
/uploads/2017/12/racetraitorposter.png. Screenshot available at author's repository.

34. https://web.archive.org/web/20180212212724/https://atomwaffendivision.org/wp-con
tent/uploads/2017/12/blindtheeye.png. Screenshot available at author's repository.

35. Post by "Juniormember," June 25, 2018, HSN forum, http://www.crew38.com/forum38
/showthread.php?12808-Zimmerman-trial. Screenshot available at author's repository.

36. https://discordleaks.unicornriot.ninja/discord/view/191951?q=Terrorism+is+a+#msg.
Screenshot available at author's repository.

37. https://web.archive.org/web/20161126005503/http://ironmarch.org/index.php?/topic
/7127-pedophiles-in-govt. Screenshot available at author's repository.

38. https://web.archive.org/web/20180212212727/https://atomwaffendivision.org/wp-content/uploads/2017/12/revolution.png. Screenshot available at author's repository.

39. "Abortion," https://kkk.bz/wp-content/uploads/2017/02/Now-no-to-abortion.pdf. Screenshot available at author's repository.

40. http://web.archive.org/web/20070102064804/http://www.aryan-nations.org/about.htm. Screenshot available at author's repository.

41. https://web.archive.org/web/20180212212724/https://atomwaffendivision.org/wp-content/uploads/2017/12/blindtheeye.png. Screenshot available at author's repository.

42. "Official Statement concerning the incident in Avalon," https://keystone2001united.wordpress.com/2018/07/. Screenshot available at author's repository.

43. http://goldenstateskinheads.org/bloodandhonouramerica. Screenshot available at author's repository.

44. Post by "CaseofPride," September 21, 2013, HSN forum, http://www.crew38.com/forum38/showthread.php?. Screenshot available at author's repository.

45. Post by "Odessa14," September 20, 2013, HSN forum, http://www.crew38.com/forum38/showthread.php?. Screenshot available at author's repository.

46. Essay posted at http://www.skrewdriver.net/fmtwo.html. Screenshot available at author's repository.

47. Essay posted at http://www.skrewdriver.net/covert.html. Screenshot available at author's repository.

48. Post by "8Krieg8," May 9, 2009, NSM forum, http://nsm88forum.com6th; post by "DarkThrone," May 9, 2009, NSM forum, http://nsm88forum.com. Screenshots available at author's repository.

49. Post by "DarkThrone," May 2009, NSM forum, http://nsm88forum.com. Screenshot available at author's repository.

50. http://www.order15.com/the-break-away-community/. Screenshot available at author's repository.

51. "White Biocentrism Forum," https://whitebiocentrism.com/viewtopic.php?f=23&t=3038&start=10. Screenshot available at author's repository.

52. https://web.archive.org/web/20110414111458/http://volksfrontinternational.com/index1.htm. Screenshot available at author's repository.

53. Post by @Oathkeepers, May 18, 2018, 7:12 p.m., https://twitter.com/Oathkeepers/status/997661339332984832. Screenshot available at author's repository.

54. https://docs.wixstatic.com/ugd/6ecfe6_e09e89120cd94270a746dac3ff6d23bf.pdf. Screenshot available at author's repository.

55. Tom Porter, "How Nevada Rancher Cliven Bundy Became an Icon for the Far-Right Militia Movement," Newsweek, January 11, 2018, https://www.newsweek.com/cliven-bundy-mistrial-how-nevada-rancher-became-icon-far-right-militia-776727.

56. https://cspoa.org/sop/. Screenshot available at author's repository.

57. Post by @Oathkeepers, July 17, 2018, 4:23 p.m., https://twitter.com/Oathkeepers/status/1019361977800388608. Screenshot available at author's repository.

58. Post by @Oathkeepers, July 17, 2018, 4:23 p.m.

59. "Do Not Go To College," https://oathkeepers.org/2018/08/do-not-go-to-college/. Screen-shot available at author's repository.

60. Posts on the Three Percenters forum, https://forum/thethreepercenters.org/index.php?r=dashboard%2Fdashboard. Screenshot available at author's repository.

61. Tom Jackmon, "National Sherriff's' Group, Opposed to Federal Laws on Guns and Taxes, Calls for Defiance," *Washington Post*, April 28, 2016, https://www.washingtonpost.com/news/true-crime/wp/2016/04/28/national-group-of-sheriffs-opposed-to-federal-government-overreach-gains-size-momentum/.

62. Southern Poverty Law Center, "United Constitutional Patriots," https://www.splcenter.org/fighting-hate/extremist-files/group/united-constitutional-patriots.

63. "'Put Them All in a Gas Chamber,' Said Border Militia Member: Report," *TYT Network*, https://app.tyt.com/stories/4vZLCHuQrYE4uKagyooyMA/55ZimtgirWgUh9ZgMSPirI.

64. SPLC, "United Constitutional Patriots."

65. APM newsletter, July 20, 2018, http://docs.wixstatic.com/ugd/c16941_74b3938473a1486 2a88a8d28b77f12c5.pdf. Screenshot available at author's repository.

66. APM newsletter, July 31, 2018, http://docs.wixstatic.com/ugd/c16941_e9b2122b06b8 .pdf. Screenshot available at author's repository.

67. https://christianidentitychurch.wordpress.com/2017/04/30/donald-trump-body-language-and-. Screenshot available at author's repository.

68. https://christianidentitychurch.wordpress.com/2018/01/12/trumps-sthole-nations/. Screenshot available at author's repository.

69. https://christianidentitychurch.wordpress.com/2018/05/27/muslim-power-is-growing-in-europe. Screenshot available at author's repository.

70. "Bible Law on Money by Sheldon Emry," https://docs.wixstatic.com/ugd/c16941_37a7 2ee8659c4d0985f9fb2cccc83a37.pdf. Screenshot available at author's repository.

71. APM newsletter, https://docs.wixstatic.com/ugd/c16941_d3cb3ab31f794308999e8b321 61454bc.pdf. Screenshot available at author's repository.

72. APM newsletter, http://docs.wixstatic.com/ugd/c16941_aac636ade69c453baa33625dbc 80a2d5.pdf. Screenshot available at author's repository.

73. All translations of the verses are based on New King James version; for examples of the use of these and other verses, see the websites of the following groups: Anglo-Saxon Israel (http://anglo-saxonisrael.com/), Kingdom Identity Ministry (http://www.king identity.com/doctrine.htm), and Christian Identity Ministers (http://www.christian identityministries.com/more.html).

74. Published February 20, 2007, https://web.archive.org/web/20110414011336/http://vin landers.com:80/modules.php?name=Content&pa=showpage&pid=4.

75. Email communication from Clifford Herrington (nsmchairmanherrington@hotmail .com) to various NSM chapters, December 1, 2007. Screenshot available at author's repository.

76. Email communication from stormwolf98@hotmail.com to nsmfargo@hotmail.com, October 29, 2008. Screenshot available at author's repository.

77. Email communication from aryannationspa@hotmail.com to BMXTRIX88@aol .com, January 31, 2007. Screenshot available at author's repository.

78. Assaf Moghadam, *Nexus of Global Jihad: Understanding Cooperation Among Terrorist Actors* (New York: Columbia University Press, 2017).

8. The Future of the Violent American Far Right

1. Luke McGee, "Angela Merkel Warns Against Dark Forces on the Rise in Europe," CNN, May 28, 2019, https://www.cnn.com/2019/05/28/europe/angela-merkel-interview -amanpour-intl-grm/index.html.
2. Evan Perez, "FBI Has Seen Significant Rise in White Supremacist Domestic Terror- ism in Recent Months," CNN, May 23, 2019, https://www.cnn.com/2019/05/23/politics /fbi-white-supremacist-domestic-terror/index.html.
3. Martha Crenshaw, "Causes of Terrorism," *Comparative Politics* 13, no. 4 (1981): 379– 99; Arie Perliger, "How Democracies Respond to Terrorism: Regime Characteristics, Symbolic Power, and Counterterrorism," *Security Studies* 21, no. 3 (July 1, 2012): 490– 528.
4. Bruce Hoffman, *Inside Terrorism*, rev. and exp. ed. (New York: Columbia University Press, 2006), 1–41.
5. Hoffman, *Inside Terrorism*.
6. "Fatal Attack on Interracial Couple in Arizona Heads to Trial," Associated Press, May 6, 2018, https://apnews.com/1012d7b5af684a569343647010363c78.
7. "The 2018 Midterm Vote: Divisions by Race, Gender, Education," Pew Research Cen- ter, https://www.pewresearch.org/fact-tank/2018/11/08/the-2018-midterm-vote-divisions -by-race-gender-education/.
8. Jo Becker, "The Global Machine Behind the Rise of Far-Right Nationalism," *New York Times*, August 10, 2019, https://www.nytimes.com/2019/08/10/world/europe/sweden -immigration-nationalism.html.

Appendix: Methodology and Statistical Results

1. A useful review of the relevant literature can be found in Bruce Hoffman, *Inside Ter- rorism*, rev. and exp. ed. (New York: Columbia University Press, 2006), 1–41; Leonard Weinberg, Ami Pedahzur, and Sivan Hirsch, "The Challenges of Conceptualizing Terrorism," *Terrorism and Political Violence* 17, no. 1 (2004): 1–17; Peter A. Schmid and Albert Jongman, *Political Terrorism* (Amsterdam: North Holland Publishing, 1988), 1–38.
2. Arie Perliger, "How Democracies Respond to Terrorism: Regime Characteristics, Symbolic Power, and Counterterrorism," *Security Studies* 21, no. 3 (July 1, 2012): 490–528.

Bibliography

Abanes, Richard. *American Militias: Rebellion, Racism, & Religion*. Downers Grove, IL: Intervarsity, 1996.

Abdelkader, Engy. "When Islamophobia Turns Violent: The 2016 U.S. Presidential Elections." The Bridge Initiative, Georgetown University, 2016. https://papers.ssrn.com/abstract =2779201.

Adorno, Theodor W., Else Frenkel-Brunswik, Daniel J. Levinson, R. Nevitt Sanford, et al. "The Authoritarian Personality." 1950. http://www.popflock.com/learn?s=The_Authori tarian_Personality.

Ahmed, Reem, and Daniela Pisoiu. "Beyond Borders: Subcultural Theory and the Transnational Jihadi Identity in Europe." In *Border Politics: Defining Spaces of Governance and Forms of Transgressions*, ed. Cengiz Günay and Nina Witjes. New York: Springer, 2017.

Akhtar, Marium. "Role of Identity Crisis and Relative Deprivation as Catalysts of Political Violence and Terrorism." *SSRN Electronic Journal*, March 28, 2018.

Alimi, Eitan Y. "The Israeli Political Arena and Palestinian Contention: The Case of the 'First' Intifada." *British Journal of Political Science* 37, no. 3 (2007): 433–53.

Altemeyer, Bob, and Bruce Hunsberger. "Authoritarianism, Religious Fundamentalism, Quest, and Prejudice." *International Journal for the Psychology of Religion* 2 (1992): 113–33.

Anbinder, Tyler. *Nativism and Slavery: The Northern Know Nothings and the Politics of the 1850s*. Oxford: Oxford University Press, 1992.

Anti-Defamation League. *Beyond the Bombing: The Militia Menace Grows*. New York: ADL, 1995.

——. *Hate Groups in America: A Record of Bigotry and Violence*. 2nd ed. New York: ADL, 1988.

Arzheimer, Kai, and Elisabeth Carter. "Political Opportunity Structures and Right-Wing Extremist Party Success." *European Journal of Political Research* 45, no. 3 (2006): 419–43.

Atkins, Stephen F. *Encyclopedia of Right-Wing Extremism in Modern American History*. New York: ABC-CLIO, 2011.

Atran, Scott. "Genesis of Suicide Terrorism." *Science* 299, no. 5612 (2003): 1534–39.

Atton, Chris. "Far-Right Media on the Internet: Culture, Discourse, and Power." *New Media & Society* 8, no. 4 (2006): 573–87.

Back, Les. "Aryans Reading Adorno: Cyber-Culture and Twenty-First-Century Racism." *Ethnic and Racial Studies* 25, no. 4 (2002): 628–51.

Bader, Eleanor J., and Patricia Baird-Windle. *Targets of Hatred: Anti-Abortion Terrorism*. New York: St. Martin's, 2015.

Barkun, Michael. *Religion and the Racist Right: The Origins of the Christian Identity Movement*. Chapel Hill: University of North Carolina Press, 2014.

Bar-On, Tamir. "Fascism to the Nouvelle Droite: The Dream of Pan-European Empire." *Journal of Contemporary European Studies* 16, no. 3 (2008): 327–45.

Bell, Leland V. "The Failure of Nazism in America: The German American Bund, 1936–1941." *Political Science Quarterly* 85, no. 4 (1970): 585.

Benmelech, Efraim, and Claude Berrebi. "Attack Assignments in Terror Organizations and the Productivity of Suicide Bombers." NBER Working Paper No. 12910. February 2007.

Berger, J. M. "Without Prejudice: What Sovereign Citizens Believe." Program on Extremism at George Washington University. 2016. https://extremism.gwu.edu/sites/g/files/zaxdzs2191/f/downloads/JMB%20Sovereign%20Citizens.pdf.

Berlet, Chip, and Matthew N. Lyons. "Militia Nation." *The Progressive* 59, no. 6 (1995): 22–25.

Berrebi, Claude. "The Economics of Terrorism and Counterterrorism: What Matters and Is Rational-Choice Theory Helpful?" In *Social Science for Counterterrorism: Putting the Pieces Together*, ed. Paul K. Davis and Kim Cragin. RAND, 2009.

Bérubé, Maxime. "Social Networks, Terrorism, and Counter-Terrorism, Radical and Connected." *Sécurité et Stratégie* 20, no. 3 (2015): 78.

Betz, Hans-Georg. *Radical Right-Wing Populism in Western Europe*. Springer, 1994.

——. "Conditions Favouring the Success and Failure of Radical Right-Wing Populist Parties in Contemporary Democracies." In *Democracies and the Populist Challenge*, ed. Yves Mény and Yves Surel, 197–213. London: Palgrave Macmillan UK, 2002.

Bloom, Mia. *Bombshell: The Many Faces of Women Terrorists*. Hurst, 2011.

Boissoneault, Lorraine. "How the Nineteenth-Century Know Nothing Party Reshaped American Politics." *Smithsonian Magazine*. 2017. https://www.smithsonianmag.com/history/immigrants-conspiracies-and-secret-society-launched-american-nativism-180961915/.

Bromwell, William J. *History of Immigration to the United States*. 1856.

Brubaker, Rogers. "Between Nationalism and Civilizationism: The European Populist Moment in Comparative Perspective." *Ethnic and Racial Studies* 40, no. 8 (2017): 1191–226.

Bryant, Lia. "Social Aspects of the Farm Financial Crisis." In *Agriculture, Environment, and Society*, ed. Geoffrey Lawrence, Frank Vanclay, and Brian Furze, 157–72. London: Macmillan Education UK, 1992.

Buehler, Marilyn H. "Political Efficacy, Political Discontent, and Voting Turnout Among Mexican-Americans in Michigan." PhD diss., University of Notre Dame, 1975.

Bull, Peter, and Anne-Marie Simon-Vandenbergen. "Equivocation and Doublespeak in Far Right-Wing Discourse: An Analysis of Nick Griffin's Performance on BBC's Question Time." *Text & Talk* 34, no. 1 (2014): 1–22.

Canedy, Susan. *America's Nazis: A Democratic Dilemma: A History of the German American Bund.* Menlo Park: CA: Markgraf, 1990.

Caplan, Bryan. "Terrorism: The Relevance of the Rational Choice Model." *Public Choice* 128, no. 1 (2006): 91–107.

Carlson, A. Cheree. "The Rhetoric of the Know-Nothing Party: Nativism as a Response to the Rhetorical Situation." *Southern Communication Journal* 54, no. 4 (1989): 364–83.

Chalmers, David M. *Hooded Americanism.* New York: Doubleday, 1965.

Chenoweth, Erica. "Democratic Competition and Terrorist Activity." *Journal of Politics* 72, no. 1 (2010): 16–30.

Chermak, Steven M., and Jeffrey Gruenewald. "The Media's Coverage of Domestic Terrorism." *Justice Quarterly* 23, no. 4 (2006): 428–61.

Clarke, Floyd I. "Hate Violence in the United States." *FBI Law Enforcement Bulletin* 60 (1991): 14.

Cobb, Roger W., and Marc Howard Ross. *Cultural Strategies of Agenda Denial: Avoidance, Attack, and Redefinition.* Lawrence: University Press of Kansas, 1997.

Cook, David. *Contemporary Muslim Apocalyptic Literature.* Syracuse, NY: Syracuse University Press, 2008.

——. "*Dying to Kill: The Allure of Suicide Terror,* by Mia Bloom." *The Historian* 69, no. 3 (2007).

Cooper, Alexia, Erica L. Smith, and United States Bureau of Justice Statistics. *Homicide Trends in the United States, 1980–2008: Annual Rates for 2009 and 2010.* 2011.

Cooper, Mary H. "The Growing Danger of Hate Groups." *Editorial Research Report* 18 (1989): 262–75.

Copsey, Nigel. "The Radical Right and Fascism." In *The Oxford Handbook of the Radical Right,* ed. Jens Rydgren, 105. Oxford: Oxford University Press, 2018.

Cornutiu, Gavril. "The Profile of the Fanatical Terrorist." *Psychology* 7, no. 4 (2016): 565–71.

Crenshaw, Martha. "The Causes of Terrorism." *Comparative Politics* 13, no. 4 (1981): 379–99.

——. "Reading 8.1: The Strategic Logic of Terrorism." In *Conflict After the Cold War,* 5th ed., ed. Richard K. Betts. New York: Routledge, 2017.

Cronin, Audrey Kurth. "How and Why Do Terrorist Campaigns End?" In *Illusions of Terrorism and Counter-Terrorism,* ed. Richard English. Oxford: Oxford University Press for the British Academy, 2015.

——. *How Terrorism Ends.* Princeton, NJ: Princeton University Press, 2015.

Crothers, Lane. *Rage on the Right: The American Militia Movement from Ruby Ridge to Homeland Security.* Baltimore, MD: Rowman & Littlefield, 2003.

Davis, Susan Lawrence. *Authentic History, Ku Klux Klan, 1865–1877.* New York: American Library Service, 1924.

DeCarlo, Dylan, "Patriots or Problematic? The Media Can't Decide: A Critical Discourse Analysis of the Oath Keepers in Popular Media." PhD diss., Northern Arizona University, 2016. http://search.proquest.com/openview/b2d79270429674bfe4f196c35d4562a7/1?pq-origs ite=gscholar&cbl=18750&diss=y.

Dees, Morris. *Gathering Storm: America's Militia Threat*. New York: HarperCollins, 1997.

Dees, Morris, and James Corcoran. *Gathering Storm: The Story of America's Militia Network*. New York: HarperCollins, 1996.

Dennis, Rutledge M. "Socialization and Racism: The White Experience." In *Impacts of Racism on White Americans*, ed. Benjamin P. Bowser and Raymond G. Hunt. Thousand Oaks, CA: Sage, 1981.

Diamond, Sander A. *The Nazi Movement in the United States, 1924–1941*. Ithaca, NY: Cornell University Press, 2018.

Dobratz, Betty A., and Stephanie L. Shanks-Meile. *"White Power, White Pride!": The White Separatist Movement in the United States*. New York: Twayne, 1997.

——.*The White Separatist Movement in the United States: "White Power, White Pride!"* Baltimore, MD: Johns Hopkins University Press, 2000.

Drake, Charles J. M. "The Role of Ideology in Terrorists' Target Selection." *Terrorism and Political Violence* 10, no. 2 (1998): 53–85.

Dronzina, Tatyana, and Vadim Astashin. "Chechen Female Suicide Bombers: Who and Why." *Journal of Human Security* 3, no. 1 (2007).

Durham, Martin. "The American Far Right and 9/11." *Terrorism and Political Violence* 15, no. 2 (2003): 96–111.

Dyer, Joel, et al. *Harvest of Rage: Why Oklahoma City Is Only the Beginning*. Boulder, CO: Westview, 1997.

Eisenman, Russell. "Review of *Encyclopedia of White Power: A Sourcebook on the Radical Racist Right*, ed. Jeffrey Kaplan." *Journal of Church and State* 43, no. 3 (2001): 626–27.

Fairclough, Norman. *Discourse and Social Change*. Cambridge: Polity, 1992.

Flynn, Kevin, and Gary Gerhardt. *The Silent Brotherhood: Inside America's Racist Underground*. New York: Free Press, 1995.

Freilich, Joshua D. *American Militias: State-Level Variations in Militia Activities*. El Paso, TX: LFB Scholarly Publishing, 2003.

Frost, Stanley. *The Challenge of the Klan*. Indianapolis, IN: Bobbs-Merrill, 1924.

Fry, Henry Peck. *The Modern Ku Klux Klan*. New York: Negro University Press, 1922.

Gambetta, Diego, and Steffen Hertog. "Why Are There So Many Engineers Among Islamic Radicals?" *European Journal of Sociology* 50, no. 2 (2009).

Gay, Kathlyn. *Militias: Armed and Dangerous*. Enslow, 1997.

Gayman, Dan. *Do All Races Share in Salvation?* D. Gayman, 1985.

——. *Two Seeds of Genesis*, 3:15. Schell City, MO: Church of Israel, 1994.

Gellner, Ernest. *Nations and Nationalism*. Ithaca, NY: Cornell University Press, 2008.

George, John, and Laird M. Wilcox. *Nazis, Communists, Klansmen, and Others on the Fringe*. Buffalo, NY: Prometheus, 1992.

Gerber, David A. "Anti-Semitism and Jewish-Gentile Relations in American Historiography and the American Past." *Anti-Semitism in American History* (1986): 3–54.

Gitlin, Martin. *The Ku Klux Klan: A Guide to an American Subculture.* ABC-CLIO. 2009.

Goldman, Liran, and Michael A. Hogg. "Understanding Terrorism: Effects of Prototypicality and Relative Deprivation on Extreme Behaviors." PsycEXTRA Dataset. 2011.

Goodman, Simon, and Andrew J. Johnson. "Strategies Used by the Far Right to Counter Accusations of Racism." *Critical Approaches to Discourse Analysis Across Disciplines* 6, no. 2 (2013): 97–113.

Gordon Liddy, G., Cdr. James G. Liddy, J. Michael Barrett, and Joel Selanikio. *Fight Back: Tackling Terrorism, Liddy Style.* New York: St. Martin's Griffin, 2006.

Gossett, Thomas F. *Race: The History of an Idea in America.* Oxford: Oxford University Press, 1997.

Grimaldy, Alexander B. *Memoirs, and a Selection of Letters from the Correspondence of Eduard Hine.* London: Robert Banks and Son, 1909.

Gurr, Ted Robert. *Why Men Rebel.* New York: Routledge, 2015.

Hainsworth, Paul. *The Politics of the Extreme Right: From the Margins to the Mainstream.* London: Bloomsbury, 2016.

Halebsky, Sandor. *Mass Society and Political Conflict: Toward a Reconstruction of Theory.* Cambridge: Cambridge University Press, 1976.

Hamilton, Charles Granville. *Lincoln and the Know Nothing Movement.* Reprint ed. Forgotten Books, 2018.

Hamilton, Neil A. 1996. *Militias in America: A Reference Handbook.* Santa Barbara, CA: ABC-CLIO, 1996.

Hamm, Mark S. *American Skinheads: The Criminology and Control of Hate Crime.* New York: Praeger, 1993.

Handler, Jeffrey S. "Socioeconomic Profile of an American Terrorist: 1960s and 1970s." *Terrorism* 13 (1990).

Hegghammer, Thomas. "Terrorist Recruitment and Radicalization in Saudi Arabia." *Middle East Policy* 13, no 4. (2006).

Helfstein, Scott. *Edges of Radicalization: Ideas, Individuals, and Networks in Violent Extremism.* West Point, NY: Combating Terrorism Center, 2012.

Hertherington, Alma M. *70 Years Old! An Outline History of Our Work Since 1909.* Burnaby, BC: Association of Covenant People, 1979.

Hewitt, Christopher. *Political Violence and Terrorism in Modern America: A Chronology.* Westport, CT: Praeger, 2005.

Higham, John. *Strangers in the Land: Patterns of American Nativism, 1860–1925.* New Brunswick, NJ: Rutgers University Press, 2002.

Hjerm, Mikael. "National Identities, National Pride, and Xenophobia: A Comparison of Four Western Countries." *Acta Sociologica* 41, no. 4 (1998): 335–47.

Hobsbawm, E. J. *Nations and Nationalism Since 1780.* 2nd ed. Cambridge: Cambridge University Press, 2012.

Hoffman, Bruce. *Inside Terrorism.* New York: Columbia University Press, 2006.

——. "Old Madness New Methods." *Rand Review* (1998): 12–17.

Horgan, John. *The Psychology of Terrorism.* New York: Routledge, 2004.

—— ."The Search for the Terrorist Personality." In *Terrorists, Victims, and Society: Psychological Perspectives on Terrorism and Its Consequences.* New York. Wiley, 2003

Horn, Stanley Fitzgerald. *Invisible Empire: The Story of the Ku Klux Klan, 1866–1871.* Patterson Smith, 1969.

Hunter, Samuel T., Neil D. Shortland, Matthew P. Crayne, and Gina S. Ligon. "Recruitment and Selection in Violent Extremist Organizations: Exploring What Industrial and Organizational Psychology Might Contribute." *American Psychologist* 72, no. 3 (2017): 242–54.

Hu, Xiaoyi, and Illinois State University Department of Politics and Government. *The Effects of Political Participation on Political Efficacy: An Analysis of China's 2005 Survey on Self-Governance at the Village Level.* Illinois State University Department of Politics and Government, 2012.

Ignazi, Piero. "The Silent Counter-Revolution: Hypotheses on the Emergence of Extreme Right-Wing Parties in Europe." *European Journal of Political Research* 22, no. 1 (1992): 3–34.

Ingalls, Robert P. *Hoods, the Story of the Ku Klux Klan.* New York: Putnam, 1979.

Jeansonne, Glen. *Gerald L. K. Smith, Minister of Hate.* New Haven, CT: Yale University Press, 1988.

Jeffrey Kaplan, ed., *Encyclopedia of White Power.* Walnut Creek, CA: Altamira, 2000.

Katz, William Loren. *The Invisible Empire: The Ku Klux Klan Impact on History.* Washington, DC: Open Hand, 1986.

Kearns, Erin, Allison Betus, and Anthony Lemieux. "Why Do Some Terrorist Attacks Receive More Media Attention Than Others?" *SSRN Electronic Journal,* April 2, 2018.

Kepel, Gilles. *Die Rache Gottes: Radikale Moslems, Christen und Juden auf dem Vormarsch.* 2001.

Kitschelt, Herbert P. "Political Opportunity Structures and Political Protest: Anti-Nuclear Movements in Four Democracies." *British Journal of Political Science* 16, no. 1 (1986): 57–85.

Klemperer, Victor. *Language of the Third Reich.* A&C Black, 2006.

Klobuchar, Lisa. *1963 Birmingham Church Bombing: The Ku Klux Klan's History of Terror.* Mankato, MN: Compass, 1963.

Kluch, Sofia Pinero, and Alan Vaux. "Culture and Terrorism: The Role of Cultural Factors in Worldwide Terrorism (1970–2013)." *Terrorism and Political Violence* 29, no. 2 (2015): 323–41.

Knigge, Pia. "The Ecological Correlates of Right-Wing Extremism in Western Europe." *European Journal of Political Research* 34, no. 2 (1998): 249–79.

Knoke, David. n.d. "Social Networks and Terrorism." In *Social Networking and Community Behavior Modeling,* ed. Maytham Safar and Khaled Mahdi, 232–46. Hershey, PA: IGI Global, 2011.

Knowles, Eric, and Linda Tropp. "The Racial and Economic Context of Trump Support: Evidence for Threat, Identity, and Contact Effects in the 2016 Presidential Election." *Social Psychological and Personality Science* 9, no. 3 (2018).

Koch, Koen. "Back to Sarajevo or Beyond Trianon—Some Thoughts on the Problem of Nationalism in Eastern-Europe." *Netherlands Journal of Social Sciences* 27, no. 1 (1991): 29–42.

Koernke, Mark. *America in Peril.* Topeka, KS: Prophecy Club, 1993.

Kornhauser, William. *The Politics of Mass Society.* New York: Routledge, 2017.

Krueger, Alan B., and Jitka Malečková. "Education, Poverty, and Terrorism: Is There a Causal Connection?" *Journal of Economic Perspectives: A Journal of the American Economic Association* 17, no. 4 (2003): 119–44.

Lee, Alexander. "Who Becomes a Terrorist? Poverty, Education, and the Origins of Political Violence." *World Politics* 63, no. 2 (2011): 203–45.

Leeuwen, Theo van. "Genre and Field in Critical Discourse Analysis: A Synopsis." *Discourse & Society* 4, no. 2 (1993): 193–223.

Lehen, David. "Terrorism, Social Movements, and International Security: How Al Qaeda Affects Southeast Asia." *Japanese Journal of Political Science* 6, no. 1 (2005): 87–109.

Leo, John. "A Chilling Wave of Racism." *Time,* January 25, 1988, 57.

Lester, J. C., and D. L. Wilson. *Ku Klux Klan: Its Origin, Growth, and Disbandment.* Neale Publishing Company, 1905.

Levine, Bruce. "Conservatism, Nativism, and Slavery: Thomas R. Whitney and the Origins of the Know-Nothing Party." *Journal of American History* 88, no. 2 (2001): 455.

Levitas, Daniel. *The Terrorist Next Door: The Militia Movement and the Radical Right.* New York: St. Martin's, 2004.

Leyden, T. J. *Skinhead Confessions: From Hate to Hope.* Springville, UT: Sweetwater, 2008.

Lipset, Seymour Martin, and Earl Raab. *The Politics of Unreason: Right Wing Extremism in America, 1790–1970.* Vol. 5. New York: Harper & Row, 1970.

Major, Brenda, Alison Blodorn, and Gregory Major Blascovich. "The Threat of Increasing Diversity: Why Many White Americans Support Trump in the 2016 Presidential Election." *Group Processes & Intergroup Relations* 21, no. 6 (2018): 931–40.

Marcus, Jonathan. "Exorcising Europe's Demons: A Far-Right Resurgence?" *Washington Quarterly* 23, no. 4 (2000): 31–40.

Matusitz, Jonathan. *Symbolism in Terrorism: Motivation, Communication, and Behavior.* Baltimore, MD: Rowman & Littlefield, 2014.

Matusitz, Jonathan, and James Olufowote. "Visual Motifs in Islamist Terrorism: Applying Conceptual Metaphor Theory." *Journal of Applied Security Research* 11, no. 1 (2016): 18–32.

McAdam, Doug. *Political Process and the Development of Black Insurgency, 1930–1970.* Chicago: University of Chicago Press, 2010.

McCarthy, John D., and Mayer N. Zald. "Resource Mobilization and Social Movements: A Partial Theory." *American Journal of Sociology* 82, no. 6 (1977): 1212–41.

McConahay, J. B. "Modern Racism, Ambivalence, and the Modern Racism Scale." In *Prejudice, Discrimination, and Racism,* ed. J. F. Dovidio and S. L. Gaertner, 91–125. Cambridge, MA: Academic Press, 1986.

McPherson, James M. *Battle Cry of Freedom: The Civil War Era.* Oxford: Oxford University Press, 1988.

McVeigh, Rory. 2009. *The Rise of the Ku Klux Klan: Right-Wing Movements and National Politics.* Minneapolis: University of Minnesota Press.

Merrifield, John. "The Institutional and Political Factors That Influence Voter Turnout." *Public Choice* 77, no. 3 (1993): 657–67.

Mesquita, Ethan Bueno de. "The Quality of Terror." *American Journal of Political Science* 49, no. 3 (July 2005): 515–30.

Metzger, Tobias. "Social Movement Theory and Terrorism: Explaining the Development of Al-Qaeda." *Student Pulse* 6, no. 9 (2014).

Meyer, David S., and Suzanne Staggenborg. "Movements, Countermovements, and the Structure of Political Opportunity." *American Journal of Sociology* 101, no. 6 (1996): 1628–60.

Michael, George. *Confronting Right Wing Extremism and Terrorism in the USA.* New York: Routledge, 2003.

Michel, Lou, and Dan Herbeck. *American Terrorist: Timothy McVeigh and the Tragedy at Oklahoma City.* New York: Avon, 2002.

Mierau, Jochen O. "The Activity and Lethality of Militant Groups: Ideology, Capacity, and Environment." *Dynamics of Asymmetric Conflict* 8, no. 1 (2015): 23–37.

Miles, Robert, and Annie Phizacklea. "Some Introductory Observations on Race and Politics in Britain." In *Racism and Political Action in Britain,* ed. Robert Miles and Annie Phizacklea, 1–27. London: Routledge and Kegan Paul, 1979.

Moghadam, Assaf. *The Globalization of Martyrdom: Al Qaeda, Salafi Jihad, and the Diffusion of Suicide Attacks.* Baltimore, MD: Johns Hopkins University Press, 2011.

——. *Nexus of Global Jihad: Understanding Cooperation Among Terrorist Actors.* New York: Columbia University Press, 2017.

Moghaddam, Fathali M. "The Staircase to Terrorism: A Psychological Exploration." *American Psychologist* 60, no. 2 (2005): 161–69.

Moufahim, Mona, Michael Humphreys, Darryn Mitussis, and James Fitchett. "Interpreting Discourse: A Critical Discourse Analysis of the Marketing of an Extreme Right Party." *Journal of Marketing Management* 23, no. 5–6 (2007): 537–58.

Mudde, Cas. *Populist Radical Right Parties in Europe.* Cambridge: Cambridge University Press, 2007.

——. "Right-Wing Extremism Analyzed: A Comparative Analysis of the Ideologies of Three Alleged Right-Wing Extremist Parties (NPD, NDP, CP'86)." *European Journal of Political Research* 27, no. 2 (1995): 203–24.

Mulloy, Darren. *American Extremism: History, Politics, and the Militia Movement.* New York: Routledge, 2004.

Murdock, Steve H., F. Larry Leistritz, and Rita R. Hamm. "Impacts of the Farm Financial Crisis of the 1980s on Resources and Poverty in Agriculturally Dependent Counties in the United States." *Review of Policy Research* 7, no. 4 (1988): 810–27.

Nagata, Judith. "Beyond Theology: Toward an Anthropology of 'Fundamentalism.'" *American Anthropologist* 103, no. 2 (2001): 481–98.

Norris, Pippa, and Ronald Inglehart. "Islamic Culture and Democracy: Testing the 'Clash of Civilizations' Thesis." In *New Frontiers in Comparative Sociology*, ed. Masamichi Sasaki, 221–50. Leiden: Brill, 2008.

Oberschall, Anthony. "Explaining Terrorism: The Contribution of Collective Action Theory." *Sociological Theory* 22, no. 1 (2004): 26–37.

Ogan, Christine, Lars Willnat, Rosemary Pennington, and Manaf Bashir. "The Rise of Anti-Muslim Prejudice: Media and Islamophobia in Europe and the United States." *International Communication Gazette* 76, no. 1 (2014): 27–46.

Paige, Connie. *The Right to Lifers: Who They Are, How They Operate, Where They Get Their Money*. New York: Summit, 1983.

Pape, Robert. *Dying to Win: The Strategic Logic of Suicide Terrorism*. New York: Random House, 2005.

Pedahzur, Ami, and Arie Perliger. "An Alternative Approach for Defining the Boundaries of 'Party Families': Examples from the Israeli Extreme Right-Wing Party Scene." *Australian Journal of Political Science* 39, no. 2 (2004): 285–305.

——. "The Changing Nature of Suicide Attacks: A Social Network Perspective." *Social Forces: A Scientific Medium of Social Study and Interpretation* 84, no. 4 (2006): 1987–2008.

Pedahzur, Ami, Arie Perliger, and Leonard Weinberg. "Altruism and Fatalism: The Characteristics of Palestinian Suicide Terrorists." *Deviant Behavior* 24, no. 4 (2003): 405–23.

Peresin, Anita, and Alberto Cervone. "The Western Muhajirat of ISIS." *Studies in Conflict & Terrorism* 38, no. 7 (2015): 495–509.

Perliger, Arie. "Challengers from the Sidelines: Understanding America's Violent Far-Right." Combating Terrorism Center, West Point, NY, November 2012.

——. "How Democracies Respond to Terrorism: Regime Characteristics, Symbolic Power, and Counterterrorism." *Security Studies* 21, no. 3 (2012): 490–528.

Perliger, Arie, and Ami Pedahzur. "Counter Cultures, Group Dynamics, and Religious Terrorism." *Political Studies* 64, no. 2 (2016): 297–314.

Perliger, Arie, and Daniel Milton. *From Cradle to Grave: The Lifecycle of Foreign Fighters in Iraq and Syria*. West Point, NY: Combating Terrorism Center, 2016.

Perliger, Arie, Gabriel Koehler-Derrick, and Ami Pedahzur. "The Gap Between Participation and Violence: Why We Need to Disaggregate Terrorist 'Profiles.'" *International Studies Quarterly* 60, no. 2 (2016): 220–29.

Perry, Barbara. *Hate and Bias Crime: A Reader*. New York: Routledge, 2012.

Phillips, Nelson, and Cynthia Hardy. 2002. *Discourse Analysis: Investigating Processes of Social Construction*. Thousand Oaks, CA: Sage, 2002.

Piazza, James A. "Rooted in Poverty? Terrorism, Poor Economic Development, and Social Cleavages." *Terrorism and Political Violence* 18, no. 1 (2006): 159–77.

Pisano, Vittorfranco S. "A Survey of Terrorism of the Left in Italy: 1970–78." *Terrorism* 2, no. 3–4 (1979): 171–212.

Porta, Donatella Della. "Institutional Responses to Terrorism: The Italian Case." *Terrorism and Political Violence* 4, no. 4 (1992): 151–70.

Post, Jerrold M. *The Mind of the Terrorist: The Psychology of Terrorism from the IRA to Al-Qaeda*. New York: St. Martin's, 2007.

——. "When Hatred Is Bred in the Bone: Psycho-Cultural Foundations of Contemporary Terrorism." *Political Psychology* 26, no. 4 (2005): 615.

Qin, Jialun, Jennifer J. Xu, Daning Hu, et al. "Analyzing Terrorist Networks: A Case Study of the Global Salafi Jihad Network." In *International Conference on Intelligence and Security Informatics*, 284–304. Berlin: Springer, 2005.

Quarles, Chester L. *Christian Identity: The Aryan American Bloodline Religion*. Jefferson, NC: McFarland, 2004.

——. *The Ku Klux Klan and Related American Racialist and Antisemitic Organizations: A History and Analysis*. Jefferson, NC: McFarland, 1999.

Rae, Jonathan A. "Will It Ever Be Possible to Profile the Terrorist?" *Journal of Terrorism Research* 3, no. 2 (2012).

Ramet, Sabrina. "Defining the Radical Right: Values and Behaviors of Organized Intolerance in Post-Communist Central and Eastern Europe." In *The Radical Right in Central and Eastern Europe Since 1989*, ed. Sabrina Ramet, 3–27. University Park: Pennsylvania State University Press, 1999.

Randel, William Peirce. *The Ku Klux Klan: A Century of Infamy*. Philadelphia: Chilton, 1965.

Reeve, Zoey. "Islamist Terrorism as Parochial Altruism." *Terrorism and Political Violence* 32, no. 1 (2017): 38–56.

Reisigl, Martin. "The Discourse-Historical Approach." In *The Routledge Handbook of Critical Discourse Studies*, ed. John Flowerdew and John E. Richardson, 44–59. New York: Routledge, 2017.

Remak, Joachim. " 'Friends of the New Germany': The Bund and German-American Relations." *Journal of Modern History* 29, no. 1 (1957): 38–41.

Rice, Arnold S. *The Ku Klux Klan in American Politics*. 1962. Reprint ed. London: Forgotten Books, 2017.

Ridgeway, James. *Blood in the Face: The Ku Klux Klan, Aryan Nations, Nazi Skinheads, and the Rise of a New White Culture*. 2nd rev. ed. New York: Thunder's Mouth, 1995.

Roberts, Charles H. *Race Over Grace: The Racialist Religion of the Christian Identity Movement*. New York: iUniverse, 2003.

Roger, Eatwell. "Ten Theories of the Extreme Right." In *Right-Wing Extremism in the Twenty-First Century*, ed. Peter Merkl and Leonard Weinberg, 47–73. London: Routledge, 2003.

Russell, Charles A., and Bowman H. Miller. "Profile of a Terrorist." *Terrorism* 1, no. 1 (1977): 17–34.

Sageman, Marc. "Understanding Terror Networks." *International Journal of Emergency Mental Health* 7, no. 1 (2005): 5–8.

Scaife, Laura. *Social Networks as the New Frontier of Terrorism*. London: Routledge, 2017.

Schlatter, Evelyn A. *Aryan Cowboys: White Supremacists and the Search for a New Frontier, 1970–2000*. Austin: University of Texas Press, 2006.

Schmaltz, William H. *Hate: George Lincoln Rockwell and the American Nazi Party*. Washington, DC: Potomac, 2000.

Schmid, Alex P. "Terrorism and Democracy." *Terrorism and Political Violence* 4, no. 4 (1992): 14–25.

Schussman, A., and S. A. Soule. "Process and Protest: Accounting for Individual Protest Participation." *Social Forces* 84, no. 2 (2005): 1083–108.

Shortland, Neil, Elias Nader, Nicholas Imperillo, et al. "The Interaction of Extremist Propaganda and Anger as Predictors of Violent Responses." *Journal of Interpersonal Violence* (December 2017).

Shughart, William F., II. "Terrorism in Rational Choice Perspective." In *The Handbook on the Political Economy of War*, ed. Christopher J. Coyne and Rachel L. Mathers, 126–53. Northampton, MA: Edward Elgar, 2011.

Silber, Mitchell D., and Arvin Bhatt. *Radicalization in the West: The Homegrown Threat.* New York: NYPD, 2007.

Simi, Pete, and Barbara G. Brents. "An Extreme Response to Globalization: The Case of Racist Skinhead Youth." In *Globalizing the Streets: Cross-Cultural Perspectives on Youth, Social Control, and Empowerment*, ed. David Brotherton and Michael Flynn, 185–202. New York: Columbia University Press, 2008.

Sinopoli, Richard C. *From Many, One: Readings in American Political and Social Thought.* Washington, DC: Georgetown University Press, 1996.

Smith, Gene. "Bundesfuehrer Kuhn." *American Heritage* 46, no. 5 (1995).

Snow, Robert L. 2000. "The Militia Threat: Terrorists Among Us." *Choice Reviews Online* 37, no. 7: 4166.

——. 2002. *Terrorists Among Us: The Militia Threat.* Cambridge, MA: Perseus, 1999.

Southern Poverty Law Center. "False Patriots." *Intelligence Report* 83 (1996): 58–68.

Southern Poverty Law Center Intelligence Project. *Skinheads in America: Racists on the Rampage.* SPLC, 2009.

Southern Poverty Law Center Klanwatch Staff. *Ku Klux Klan: A History of Racism and Violence*, ed. Susan Ballard. Montgomery, AL: SPLC, 1988.

Sprinzak, Ehud. "The Iceberg Model of Political Extremism." In *The Impact of Gush Emunim: Politics and Settlement in the West Bank*, ed. David Newman27–45. London: Croom Helm, 1985.

Stern, Jessica Eve. "The Covenant, the Sword, and the Arm of the Lord." In *Toxic Terror: Assessing Terrorist Use of Chemical and Biological Weapons*, ed. Jonathan B. Tucker. Cambridge, MA: MIT Press, 2000.

——. *Terror in the Name of God: Why Religious Militants Kill.* New York: Harper Collins, 2009.

Sternberger, Dolf, Gerhard Storz, and Wilhelm Emanuel Süskind. *Aus dem Wörterbuch des Unmenschen.* Vol. 48. Ullstein, 1957.

Stills, Peter. "Dark Contagion: Bigotry and Violence Online." *PC Computing*, December 1989, 144–49.

Suall, Irwin, David Lowe, and Tal Recanati. *Young and Violent: The Growing Menace of America's Neo-Nazi Skinheads.* Anti-Defamation League of B'nai B'rith/Civil Rights Division, 1988.

Taegun Yoo. "Relations Among the Types of Political Efficacy and Political Participation." *21st Century Political Science Review* 21, no. 3 (2011): 383–416.

Tafoya, William L. "Rioting in the Streets: Déjà Vu?" *C. J. the Americas* 2 (1989): 6.

Terraine, John. "Terrorist Profile." *RUSI Journal* (1977).

Tilly, Charles. "Terror, Terrorism, Terrorists." In *Collective Violence, Contentious Politics, and Social Change: A Charles Tilly Reader*, ed. Ernesto Castañeda and Cathy Lisa Schneider. New York: Routledge, 2017.

Titscher, Stefan, Michael Meyer, Ruth Wodak, and Eva Vetter. *Methods of Text and Discourse Analysis: In Search of Meaning*. Thousand Oaks, CA: Sage, 2000.

Totten, Charles Adiel Lewis. *Our Race; Its Origin and Its Destiny: The Philosophy of History.* "Our Race" Publishing Co., 1891.

Tucker, D. "What Is New About the New Terrorism and How Dangerous Is It?" *Terrorism and Political Violence* 13, no. 3 (2001): 1–14.

U.S. Congress. *House Un-American Activities Committee Report on the Activities of the Ku Klux Klan*. Washington, DC: Government Printing Office, 1967.

van Dyke, Nella, and Sarah A. Soule. "Structural Social Change and the Mobilizing Effect of Threat: Explaining Levels of Patriot and Militia Organizing in the United States." *Social Problems* 49, no 4 (2002): 497–520.

Vertelyte, Mante. "Review—Alsultany, Evelyn. *Arabs and Muslims in the Media: Race and Representation After 9/11*. 219 Pp. New York: New York University Press, 2012." *Anthropology of the Contemporary Middle East and Central Eurasia* 3, no. 1 (2015).

Victoroff, Jeff. "The Mind of the Terrorist." *Journal of Conflict Resolution* 49, no. 1 (2005).

Vieten, Ulrike M., and Scott Poynting. "Contemporary Far-Right Racist Populism in Europe." *Journal of Intercultural Studies* 37, no. 6 (2016): 533–40.

Vincent, Andrew. *Modern Political Ideologies*. New York: John Wiley & Sons, 2009.

Wade, Wyn Craig. *The Fiery Cross: The Ku Klux Klan in America*. New York: Simon and Schuster, 1987.

Wald, Kenneth D., and Allison Calhoun-Brown. *Religion and Politics in the United States*. Baltimore, MD: Rowman & Littlefield, 2014.

Walters, Jerome. *One Aryan Nation Under God: Exposing the New Racial Extremists*. Cleveland, OH: Pilgrim, 2000.

——. *One Aryan Nation Under God: How Religious Extremists Use the Bible to Justify Their Actions*. Naperville, IL: Sourcebooks, 2001.

Weinberg, Leonard. "Terrorism and Democracy: Illness and Cure?" *Global Dialogue* 8, no. 3–4 (2006): 51.

Weinberg, Leonard, Ami Pedahzur, and Sivan Hirsch-Hoefler. "The Challenges of Conceptualizing Terrorism." *Terrorism and Political Violence* 16, no. 4 (2004): 777–94.

Wessinger, Catherine. "Fighting Words: The Origins of Religious Violence." *Nova Religio* 12, no. 1 (2008): 131–35.

Wilkerson, Isabel. *The Warmth of Other Suns: The Epic Story of America's Great Migration*. New York: Vintage, 2011.

Williamson, Anne R., and Michael J. Scicchitano. "Minority Representation and Political Efficacy in Public Meetings." *Social Science Quarterly* 96, no. 2 (2015): 576–87.

Williams, Sasha, and Ian Law. "Legitimising Racism: An Exploration of the Challenges Posed by the Use of Indigeneity Discourses by the Far Right." *Sociological Research Online* 17, no. 2 (2012): 1–12.

Willis, Susan. "Hardcore: Subculture American Style." *Critical Inquiry* 19, no. 2 (1993): 365–83.

Wiltfang, G. L., and D. McAdam. "The Costs and Risks of Social Activism: A Study of Sanctuary Movement Activism." *Social Forces* 69, no. 4 (June 1991): 987–1010.

Wodak, Ruth. "The Discourse-Historical Approach." *Methods of Critical Discourse Analysis* 1 (2001): 63–94.

Wodak, Ruth, and Michael Meyer. "Critical Discourse Analysis: History, Agenda, Theory, and Methodology." *Methods of Critical Discourse Analysis* 2 (2009): 1–33.

Young, John Wesley. "From LTI to LQI: Victor Klemperer on Totalitarian Language." *German Studies Review* 28, no. 1 (2005): 45–64.

Zeskind, Leonard. "Armed and Dangerous." *Rolling Stone*, September 2, 1995, 54–63.

Index

abortion, 26–28, 85, 86–87, 102, 106
activism: elections and, 111; by far right, 54–55, 95, 130; for leadership, 45; for liberalism, 157–158; politics and, 12–14; propaganda for, 66–67; radical, 123, 126–127, 155; for segregation, 65–66; violence in, 92, 98–99, 155
ADL. See Anti-Defamation League
Admiralty Law, 23–24
Adorno, Theodor, 95
affirmative action, 101, 105
affluence, 125
African Americans: demographics of, 37–38; Emanuel African Methodist Episcopal Church shooting, 138; Jews and, 44, 129; Obama election for, 99; racism against, 48; street gang subculture, 53; in United States, 137; violence against, 36, 47; for white supremacy, 11
age, 120–121, 124
age discrimination, 101
Air Carriers Access Act, 104
Alfred B. Murrah Federal Building, 57, 70–71
al-Qaeda, 114
alt-right, 157–158

alt-right groups, 17
American far right. See far right
American Front, 49
American fundamentalism, 59–68
American nativism, 31–34
American Nazi Party (ANP), 41–43, 47, 149–150
Americans with Disabilities Act, 104
America's Promise Ministries (APM), 146
Anglo-Saxon Christian Congregation, 62–63
Anglo-Saxon Federation of America, 61
anonymity, 133–138
ANP. See American Nazi Party
antiabortion violence, 26–28, 85, 86–87
Anti-Defamation League (ADL), 47, 57, 90
Antifa, 129
antigovernment sentiments, 21–24, 54, 86, 86–87, 177n124; discourse of, 141–144; racism and, 60
anti-Semitism, 25–26, 41–42; in Christian Identity Movement, 62, 147–148; in Independent, 179n143; racism and, 64–66; violence from, 63
AOG. See Army of God

APM. *See* America's Promise Ministries

Architectural Barriers Act, *101*

Army of God (AOG), 27–28

Aryan Brotherhood, 139

Aryan Nations, 52, 63–68, 79, 138, 140, 150

Aryan Youth Movement (AYM), 49

Asians, 111, 154

Atom Waffen Division, 3, 137

attacks: data for, *91*, 91–92; far right, 118–120, 119; ideology for, 93–95; 9/11 attacks, 95; perpetrators of, 123–125; racism in, 123–124, 139; on religion, 181n10. *See also specific attacks*

authoritarian personality, 95

AYM. *See* Aryan Youth Movement

Baghdadi, Abu Bakr al-, 118

BAMN. *See* By Any Means Necessary

Beam, Louis, 45–46, 65

Beauchamp, A. A., 61

Berg, Alan, 66

Bishop, Matthew, 143

Black, Donald, 45

BLM. *See* Bureau of Land Management

Blue Book, 55

Booth, John Wilkes, 70

Border Watch, 46

Brady Handgun Violence Prevention Act, *104*

Branch Davidians, 176n108

Breivik, Anders, 128–130

British Israelite ideology, 60–62

Brotherhood of the Klan, 130, 136

Brown, Michael, Jr., 178n134

Brown v. Board of Education, 101

Bund (German-American Bund), 40

Bundy, Cliven, 59, 141–142

Bureau of Land Management (BLM), 59, 141–142

Burkin, Peter, 27

Butler, Richard, 63–65, 67

By Any Means Necessary (BAMN), 129

California Knights, 45

Cameron, William J., 61–62

CASH. *See* Chicago Area Skinheads

Catholics, 31–32. *See also* religion

CDL. *See* Christian Defense League

CEC. *See* Criminal Extremist Coalition

Chapman, Kyle, 129, 186n3, 188n24

Chechen organizations, 115–116

Chicago Area Skinheads (CASH), 49

Christian Defense League (CDL), 63

Christian Identity movement, 3, 11–12, 64–68, 86–87, 89; ANP and, 42–43; anti-Semitism in, 62, 147–148; discourse of, 145–148; financial institutions for, 78–79; history of, 24–25, 62–63; idealism from, 59–60; leadership in, 146; Muslims for, 158–159; National Socialist Movement and, 48. *See also* fundamentalism

CHS. *See* Confederate Hammerskins

Church of Jesus Christ Christian, 63–64, 150

civilian paramilitary groups, 53–54

civil rights movement, 43–47, 101–105, 105

Civil War, U.S., 35

Clinton, Bill, 92

Cold War, 156–157

Cole, Charles, 143

Colescott, James, 38

collective action, 118–120, 119

Commercial Laws, 23–24

communism, 39

Comparet, Bertrand, 62

competition, 148–150

Confederate Hammerskins (CHS), 51–52

conservatism, 16

conspiracy theories, 22–23, 50–51, 55–58, 135, 146

Constitutional Sheriffs and Peace Officers of America (CSPOA), 142–143

contemporary critical rhetoric, 149–150

contemporary discourse, 128–133

Corporon, William, 9

Covenant, the Sword, and the Arm of the Lord (CSA), 67
criminal backgrounds, 121–122
Criminal Extremist Coalition (CEC), 45
Crusius, Patrick Wood, 129
CSA. *See* Covenant, the Sword, and the Arm of the Lord
CSPOA. *See* Constitutional Sheriffs and Peace Officers of America
culture, 43, 50, 53, 61–62

data: for attacks, 91, 91–92; dataset construction, 163–164; from elections, 90; empirical, 118; from environment, 122–123; on perpetrators, 118–120, 119; theory and, 8
Davis, Chuck, 144
Deep South, 107, 110
Dees, Morris Seligman, 11
Degan, William Francis, 176n108
dehumanization, 125
democracy, 6, 14–17, 94, 160–161
Democratic Party, 58–59, 80, 98, 98–99, 183n18
demographics: of African Americans, 37–38; of minorities, 108–109, 134–135; regressions models for, 165, 165–166; violence and, 111–112; of white supremacy, 36
Dennis, Rutledge M., 30
DePugh, Robert, 63–64, 176n105, 179n153
DHA. *See* discourse-historical approach
discourse: analysis, 131–133, 149–150; of antigovernment sentiments, 141–144; of Christian Identity movement, 145–148; contemporary, 128–133; far right, 135–136, 140–141; of militias, 143–144; politics and, 5–6, 112
discourse-historical approach (DHA), 131–132
discrimination, 132
diversification, 17–18, 28–29, 153–154
Dole, Bob, 92

domestic terrorism: for FBI, 11, 66–67, 151; history of, 7–8; for law enforcement, 118–119; 9/11 attacks, 95; Oklahoma City bombing, 47; scholarship on, 1–4; violence in, 4–7, 57–58
Duke, David, 11, 19–20, 45–46

Eastern Hammerskin (EHS), 52
economics: of KKK, 38; median income, 122–123; recruitment and, 42, 61; religion and, 31–32; status theory, 97, 116
education, 105, 123
EHS. *See* Eastern Hammerskin
elections, 141; activism and, 111; for far right, 90–94, 91; for minorities, 154; scholarship on, 99–100; white supremacy and, 142–143
El Paso Walmart shooting, 3, 129
empirical data, 118
empowerment, 95, 96–98, 98–100
environment, 122–127
Equal Pay Act, 101
Eshelman, M. M., 60
ethnicity, 15, 25, 129
Europe: Euro-American Alliance, 43; far right in, 128–131, 151, 156–157; fascism in, 132; Latin America and, 13, 120; skinhead subculture in, 3–4, 50, 53; "2083: A European Declaration of Independence," 128–130; white supremacy in, 3
Evans, Hiram, 38
exceptionalism, 156
exclusionism, 16
extreme right. *See* far right

Fair Housing Amendments Act, 103
far right: abortion for, 26–28; activism by, 54–55, 95, 130; alt-right and, 157–158; anti-Semitism of, 25–26; attacks, 118–120, 119; contemporary discourse of, 128–131; criminal backgrounds and, 121–122; dehumanization by, 125; democracy for, 16–17; discourse, 135–136, 140–141;

far right (*continued*)
discourse analysis and, 132–133;
diversification for, 153–154; elections for,
90–94, *91*; ethnicity for, 15; in Europe,
128–131, 151, 156–157; for FBI, 46;
geographical distribution of, 154–155;
glocalization of, 156–157; for government,
100, *101–105*, 105–107; history of, 1–4,
30–31, 68–69; ideology of, 11–12, 14–17,
96–97, 163–164, 183n17; jihadism and,
158–159; KKK as, 17–18; lethality from, 81,
82, 83–85, *84*; military culture of, 43;
partnerships within, 48–49; perpetrators
of, 125–127, 128; policies for, 140–141,
151–153, 159–161; in politics, 12, 80–81,
94–95, 148–149; propaganda of, 54;
prototypes of, 34; racism by, 137–138;
recruitment for, 38; religion for, 66–67,
74–76, *75*, 136, 145–146; rhetoric of, 8, 11;
scholarship on, 12–14; sociological
characteristics of, 125–127; tactics of,
70–71, 77–81, *78*; targets for, 72–77,
73, *75*, *77*; theoretical insights from,
87–89; theory of, 28–29; trends of,
30–31; typology of, 17–18; in United
States, 7–8, 68–69; violence by,
4–7, 10, 71, 90, 95, 96–98, 98–100, 111–112,
165, *166*
fascism, 13, 33–34, 39, 132
fatalities, from violence, 81, 82, 83
Federal Bureau of Investigation (FBI):
domestic terrorism for, 11, 66–67, 151; far
right for, 46; hate crimes for, 4–5; KKK
for, 44–45; Marshals Service and,
176n108; Oklahoma City bombing for,
70–71
Federal Reserve system, 146
Ferguson protests, 178n134
financial institutions, 78–79
FOAK. *See* Fraternal Order of Alt-Knights
Ford, Henry, 61
foreign terrorism, 5
Forrest, Nathan Bedford, 35

Fort Bragg, 1–2
Fortier, Lori, 180n3
Fortier, Michael, 180n3
Fort Stewart, 2
FotNG. *See* Friends of the New Germany
Founding Fathers, of United States, 23–24
Fraternal Order of Alt-Knights (FOAK), 129,
136
Friends of the New Germany (FotNG), 40
fundamentalism, 24–26, 59–68, 158–159
Furrow, Buford, 66

Gaard, Conrad, 62
Gale, William Porter, 63
gender, 120
geographical distribution, 107, *108–109*,
110–111, 154–155
Georgia Militia, 59
Germany, 39–42, 120, 132
Global Terrorism Dataset, 164
glocalization, 156–157
GOA. *See* Gun Owners of America
Gonzalez, Armando, 143–144
government: Aryan Nations and, 67; in
conspiracy theories, 50–51; credibility for,
160; far right for, 100, *101–105*, 105–107;
KKK for, 36, 39; militias against, 56–57,
64; politics of, 31; public goods and, 116;
rhetoric against, 74; tyranny, 22; against
white supremacy, 46–47. *See also*
antigovernment sentiments
Great Depression, 38, 61
Greensboro Massacre, 10, 47
Griggs v. Duke Power Co., 102
gun control, 102
Gun Owners of America (GOA), 55
Gurr, Ted, 116

Hamm, Mark, 51
Hammerskin Nations (HSN), 18, 51–53, 79,
134–135, 139, 150
Hanger, Charles J., 70
hate crimes, 4–5, 152–153

Hate Crime Statistics Act, 51
Heick, Robert, 49
Herring, William, 150
Herrington, Clifford, 149–150
hierarchies, 35
Hine, Edward, 60
Hispanics, 48, 111, 154
history: of American nativism, 31–34; of
    Aryan Nations, 63–64; of Christian
    Identity Movement, 24–25, 62–63; DHA,
    131–132; of domestic terrorism, 7–8; of far
    right, 1–4, 30–31, 68–69; of Germany,
    39–40; of KKK, 19, 35–39, 68; of
    neo-Nazis, 40–41; of rhetoric, 23; of
    violence, 26–27; of white supremacy, 10
Hitler, Adolf, 42–43, 48–49, 135
Hitler Youth, 40
Hoosier State Skinheads, 53
HSN. See Hammerskin Nation

iceberg theory, 81, 82, 83–85, 84, 88–89,
    157–158
idealism, 34, 59–60
identity, 25, 116–117, 130
ideology: of Aryan Nations, 65–66; for
    attacks, 93–95; British Israelite, 60–62; of
    conspiracy theories, 22–23; diversification
    of, 28–29; of far right, 11–12, 14–17, 96–97,
    163–164, 183n17; of fascism, 13; of hate
    crimes, 152; idealism and, 34; ideological
    fatigue, 140–141; ideological typology,
    9–12; influence of, 62–63; of Know-
    Nothing Party, 30–34; of militias, 144,
    177n124; against minorities, 18–19;
    narratives for, 7; of nationalism, 14–15;
    organization and, 63–64; partnerships
    from, 59–60; policies and, 114; pro life,
    26–28, 104; of racism, 88; regions and, 36;
    of religion, 24–25; rhetoric and, 92;
    scholarship on, 71; of segregation, 19–20;
    society and, 127; tactics and, 85–87,
    86–87; targets and, 77–81, 78; of
    terrorism, 5; theory and, 7; for violence,

116–117, 159–160; of white supremacy,
    50–51
immigration, 40, 128, 142–144; Border
    Watch, 46; minorities and, 155; politics of,
    20–21, 32–33, 37–38
Imperial Mansion, 38
inclusive approach, 14
Independent, 179n143
initiation fees, 38
integration, 43–44
Internal Revenue Service (IRS), 64
internal rhetoric, 139–141
International Monetary Fund, 22
interpretive rhetoric, 133
interracial couples, 49, 152
intimidation, 84, 86
IRS. See Internal Revenue Service
ISIS, 114
Islam, 75–76, 77, 116–117, 128, 158–159
Israel, 13

Jefferson, Thomas, 70
Jews, 3; African Americans and, 44, 129;
    conspiracy theories about, 135; as
    ethnicity, 25; in Independent, 179n143;
    Jewish Community Center of Greater
    Kansas City, 9–10; Jewish Orthodox
    terrorism, 117; as minorities, 50–51; in
    United States, 154; violence against, 11,
    66–67. See also anti-Semitism
jihadism, 158–159
Johnson, Lyndon B., 183n18
Jones v. Alfred H. Mayer Co., 102

Kaur, Paramjit, 1
Keystone United, 18, 135, 139
King, Martin Luther, Jr., 63, 101
KKK. See Ku Klux Klan
Klean Klan, 43–47, 133
Know-Nothing Party, 30–34
Koehl, Matt, 42, 48
Koop, C. Everett, 27
Koresh, David, 176n108

Kuhn, Fritz, 40
Ku Klux Klan (KKK), 88–89, *101*, 135,
 179n140; Bund compared to, 40; as far
 right, 17–18; history of, 19, 35–39, 68;
 immigration for, 20–21; law enforcement
 for, 93; leadership in, 43–47, 49, 150;
 LGBTQ community for, 79–80; media
 for, 138; neo-Nazis compared to, 10–11;
 paramilitary training for, 176n105;
 partnerships with, 48; UNSKKK, 133–134

LaManno, Terri, 9
Lanza, Adam, 178n130
Latin America, 13, 120
law enforcement, 12, 22, 57–58, 93, 104,
 118–119
leadership: activism for, 45; for ANP, 42–43;
 in Aryan Nations, 67–68; of Butler, 65; in
 Christian Identity movement, 146; of
 Forrest, 35; in KKK, 43–47, 49, 150; of
 Klean Klan, 46; of MOM, 55; for
 neo-Nazis, 41–42; in politics, 58–59; in
 religion, 62; rhetoric of, 19–20; of
 Simmons, 37–38; of Swift, 62–63; in
 terrorism, 120–121; violence and, 68–69
Lee, Harper, 9
lethality, 81, 82, 83–85 84, 119, *119*
LGBTQ community, 72–74, *73*, 76–77, *77*,
 79–80
liberalism, 16, 56, 157–158
Lincoln, Abraham, 70, 137
literature, 43, 69
logic, 131–132
lone wolf theory, 180n3
Long, Huey P., 62
Lynch, James, 150

Madole, James, 41
mainstreaming, 148–150
mainstream media (MSM), 143
marginalization, 117
marital status, 121
Marquis, Mercury, 70

Marshals Service, U.S., 176n108
Martin, Trayvon, 138
mass media, 41
Mathews, Robert, 66–67
maximalist approach, 15
McAdam, Doug, 99
McCarty, John, 18
McDonald v. Chicago, 104
McVeigh, Timothy, 57, 70–71, 119,
 180n3
media, 37, 41, 44–45, 55, 138, 143
Mein Kampf (Hitler), 48–49
Merkel, Angela, 151
methodology, 163–165, *165–166*
Metzger, Thomas, 11, 45–46, 49, 65
Mexico, 46, 143–144
MHS. *See* Midlands Hammerskin
Michigan Militia, 56–57, 119
Midlands Hammerskin (MHS), 53
Miles, Robert, 64
military, 10–11, 43, 51, 58, 69, 179n153
militias, 86; Atomwaffen Division, 3; BLM
 and, 59, 141–142; Border Watch, 46;
 civilian paramilitary groups, 53–54;
 discourse of, 143–144; diversification of,
 17–18; against government, 56–57, 64;
 hierarchies in, 35; ideology of, 144,
 177n124; law enforcement against, 57–58;
 membership in, 121; Militia of Montana,
 22; MOM, 55–56; organization of, 54–55,
 61–62; partnerships between, 56; in
 politics, 142; propaganda for, 160;
 psychology of, 115; Rise Above
 Movement, 3; scholarship of, 21–22;
 Sovereign Citizens, 85; III Percenters,
 58–59; in United States, 21, 53–59;
 violence by, 2, 58–59, 77–81, 78; for white
 supremacy, 11–12
Miller, Frazier Glenn, Jr., 9–11
minimalist approach, 14–15
minorities, 72, *73*, 165, *166*, 181n10;
 demographics of, *108–109*, 134–135;
 elections for, 154; Hispanics as, 48;

ideology against, 18–19; immigration and, 155; Islam as, 75–76, 77; Jews as, 50–51; violence against, 6–7, 44, 110

Moghadam, Assaf, 150

Montana Militia (MOM), 55–56

Mountain Church of Jesus, 64

Mountain Minutemen, 143, 176n105, 179n153

MSM. *See* Mainstream Media

Mudde, Cas, 17

music, 49–50

NAAWP. *See* National Association for the Advancement of White People

narratives, 7, 25, 33, 58

National Alliance, 2, 134, 140

National Association for the Advancement of White People (NAAWP), 45, 134

National Football League (NFL), 142

National Guard, 57

nationalism, 14–15, 33–34, 58–59, 73–74, 97

National Resistance Party (NRP), 41

National Socialist Liberation Front, 47–48

National Socialist Movement (NSM), 39–40, 129, 136, 140, 149–150

National Socialist White People's Party (NSWPP), 42

nativism, 15

nativist agendas, 55

Nazism, 19, 39–43

neo-Nazis, 2–3, 40–43, 89, 149–150; KKK compared to, 10–11; Nazism for, 19; pro life ideology for, 26; propaganda for, 137; religion for, 138; in United States, 10, 47–48

New World Order, 22–23, 55–56, 58, 144

New York Mirror, 33

NFL. *See* National Football League

Nichols, Terry, 180n3

9/11 attacks, 95

North Valley Jewish Community Center, 66

NRP. *See* National Resistance Party

NS Bulletin, 48

NSM. *See* National Socialist Movement

NSWPP. *See* National Socialist White People's Party

Oath Keepers, 59, 141–143

Obama, Barack, 2, 99, 141, 146–147

Obergefell v. Hodges, 105

Oklahoma City bombing, 47, 57, 70–71, 81, 180n3

Oklahoma Constitutional Militia, 57

Old Testament, 25

Order, The, 66–67

Oslo shooting, 128

Our Race (Totten), 61

Outlaw Hammerskin, 53

Pag, Wade Michael, 1–2

Palter, John, 42

paramilitary training, 176n105

Parks, Rosa, 101

partnerships, 48–49, 56, 59–60

PATRIOT Act, 21–22

Patriot Front, 138

patriot movements. *See* militias

Perkins, Jonathan, 62

perpetrators, 113–115, 118–127, *119*, *128*

Peters, Pete, 67–68

planned attacks, 123–125

Planned Parenthood of Central Missouri v. Danforth, 103

POC. *See* political opportunity structure

polarization, 6, 153–154

policies, 56, 114; for far right, 140–141, 151–153, 159–161; for violence, 100, 101–105, 105–107

politically correct terminology, 130

political opportunity structure (POC), 97, 99–100, 105–107

politics: activism and, 12–14; conservatism, 16; discourse and, 5–6, 112; empowerment and, 95, 96–98, 98–100; far right in, 12,

politics (continued)
80–81, 94–95, 148–149; of government, 31; of immigration, 20–21, 32, 37–38; leadership in, 58–59; liberalism, 16; militias in, 142; nationalism in, 33; polarization in, 6, 153–154; political efficacy, 93–94; political science, 131; political violence, 4, 72, 113–114, 117–118, 124, 151–152, 183n17, 183n19; regressions models for, 164–165, 165; society and, 7–8, 111–112; in United States, 90, 100; white supremacy in, 4–5, 42, 58; world, 135; after World War I, 37
populism, 17
Porth, Arthur Julius, 63–64
Posse Comitatus, 63
postmaterial thesis, 96
Pratt, Larry, 55
pro life ideology, 26–28, 104
propaganda, 41; for activism, 66–67; of far right, 54; for militias, 160; for neo-Nazis, 137; for recruitment, 68; for religion, 60–61; rhetoric of, 64; for skinhead subculture, 139; for WAR, 51; on YouTube, 144
protest thesis, 96
psychology, 8, 115, 117–120, 119, 124–126, 151–152
publications, 60–61
public goods, 116
publicity, 51–52
public life, 31
Putin, Vladimir, 145

racism, 87; against African Americans, 48; antigovernment sentiments and, 60; anti-Semitism and, 64–66; in attacks, 123–124, 139; by far right, 137–138; ideology of, 88; impact of, 30; integration and, 43–44; internal rhetoric of, 139–141; against interracial couples, 49, 152; music and, 49–50; in nativist agendas, 55; about Obama, 146–147; rhetoric of, 133–138;

xenophobia and, 15–16. See also segregation
radical activism, 123, 126–127, 155
Rafferty, James, 136
RAM. See Rise Above Movement
Rand, Howard, 61
recruitment, 38, 41–42, 61, 68, 115–118, 125
Red Army Faction, 120
Regents of the University of California v. Bakke, 103
regressions models, 164–165, 165–166, 183n17, 183n19
Rehab Act, 103
religion: attacks on, 181n10; economics and, 31–32; for far right, 66–67, 74–76, 75, 136, 145–146; fundamentalism of, 158–159; Hitler and, 42–43; ideology of, 24–25; immigration and, 33; Islam, 75–76, 77; leadership in, 62; for neo-Nazis, 138; propaganda for, 60–61; in public life, 31; rhetoric for, 145–148; segregation and, 147; Sikh, 1–2; in United States, 60–61; U.S. Catholic Conference, 26–27. See also specific religions
Republican Party, 58, 80, 98, 98–99, 183n18
rhetoric: contemporary critical, 149–150; ethnicity in, 129; of far right, 8, 11; against government, 74; history of, 23; ideology and, 92; about immigration, 143–144; internal, 139–141; interpretive, 133; of Know-Nothing Party, 33; of leadership, 19–20; of propaganda, 64; of racism, 133–138; for religion, 145–148; for violence, 133
Rhodes, Stewart, 59
RHS. See Rocky Mountain Hammerskin
Ricci, Travis, 152
right wing groups. See far right
Rise Above Movement (RAM), 3, 136
Rizvi, Maulana Syed Raza, 146
Robb, Thomas, 135
Rockwell, George Lincoln, 41–43

Rockwell Report, 41
Rocky Mountain Hammerskin (RHS), 52
Roe v. Wade, 26–27, 102
Romantic Violence, 49
Roof, Dylann, 138
Ruby Ridge incident, 54,
    176n108
Russia, 156–157

Sandy Hook Elementary School shooting,
    137, 178n130
Sawyer, Reuben H., 61, 179n140
Schaeffer, Francis, 27
scholarship: authoritarian personality in, 95;
    classification in, 18; discourse in, 131; on
    discrimination, 132; on domestic
    terrorism, 1–4; on elections, 99–100; on
    far right, 12–14; iceberg theory, 88–89; on
    ideology, 71; inclusive approach in, 14;
    methodology for, 163–165, 165–166; of
    militias, 21–22; minimalist approach in,
    14–15; on political violence, 113–114,
    117–118; on terrorism, 114–115
*Schuette v. Coalition to Defend Affirmative
    Action*, 105
Scriptures for America, 68
segregation, 19–20, 39, 65–66, 105, 147
Shelton, Robert, 47
Sikh religion, 1–2
Simmons, William, 37–38
single issue thesis, 96
SKINFEST, 52
skinhead subculture, 1–4, 12, 20, 79; HSN
    and, 150; propaganda for, 139; in United
    States, 18, 47–53
Smith, Gerald K., 62
social breakdown theories, 96, 107, 108–109,
    110–111
social movements, 18–21
Social Nationalist Aryan Peoples' Party, 48
social policies, 56
social science, 131
society, 7–8, 111–112, 127

sociological characteristics, 120–122, 125–127
sophistication, 81, 82, 83–85 84
Southern Poverty Law Center (SPLC), 11,
    47, 57, 90
Southern Publicity Association (SPA), 37
Sovereign Citizens, 23–24, 85
SPA. *See* Southern Publicity Association
SPLC. *See* Southern Poverty Law Center
spontaneous attacks, 123–125
SS Action Group (SSAG), 47
statistical results, 163–165, *165–166*
status theory, 97, 110, 116
Stormfront, 11
Stormtrooper, 41, 43
Suhayda, Rocky J., 43
Supreme Court, 26–27, 39, *101–105, 102*, 106
Swift, Wesley, 62–64
symbolic narratives, 33
symbolic targets, 85–86

tactics: of far right, 70–71, 77–81, 78;
    ideology and, 85–87, 86–87;
    sophistication of, 81, 82, 83–85 84; for
    violence, 72–77, 73, 75, 77, 87–89
Taking Aim, 55
targets, 72–81, 73, 75, 77–78, 164
terrorism, 5–6; Global Terrorism Dataset,
    164; hate crimes as, 153; immigration and,
    142; jihadism, 158–159; leadership in,
    120–121; 9/11 attacks, 95; PATRIOT Act
    against, 21–22; political violence and,
    151–152; recruitment for, 115–118;
    scholarship on, 114–115; symbolic targets
    for, 85–86; targets for, 72; violence in, 81,
    163. *See also* domestic terrorism
Texas Klan, 46
theoretical explanations, 94–95
theoretical insights, 87–89
theory, 7–8, 28–29
Thompson, Linda, 56, 177n124
III Percenters, 58–59, 141–143
Tilly, Charles, 116
To Kill a Mockingbird (Lee), 9

Tutten, C. A. L., 61
training, 10, 176n105, 179n153
Tree of Life synagogue, 3
Trochmann, Jon, 65
Trump, Donald, 93, 135, 145–146
"2083: A European Declaration of
  Independence" (Breivik), 128–130
typology, 9–18
tyranny, 22

UCJ. See United Citizens for Justice
UKA. See United Klan of America
Underwood, Reat Griffin, 9
United Citizens for Justice (UCJ), 55
United Constitutional Patriots, 143–144
United Kingdom, 20
United Klan of America (UKA), 44, 47
United Nations, 22
United North & Southern Knights of the
  KKK (UNSKKK), 133–134
United States: African Americans in, 137;
  American exceptionalism, 156; American
  fundamentalism, 59–68; American
  nativism, 31–34; Anglo-Saxon Federation
  of America, 61; Catholic Conference,
  26–27; Deep South in, 107, 110;
  democracy in, 160–161; ethos of, 4–7; far
  right in, 7–8, 68–69; Federal Reserve
  system in, 146; Founding Fathers of,
  23–24; Germany and, 41–42; Great
  Depression in, 38, 61; Hate Crime
  Statistics Act in, 51; Jews in, 154; law
  enforcement in, 22; Marshals Service,
  176n108; median income in, 122–123;
  Mexico and, 46, 143–144; military, 58;
  militias in, 21, 53–59; nationalism in,
  58–59, 73–74; Nazism in, 39–43;
  neo-Nazis in, 10, 47–48; politics in, 90,
  100; religion in, 60–61; skinhead
  subculture in, 18, 47–53; society of, 29;
  United States v. Paradise, 103; white
  supremacy in, 137, 159–160; world politics
  for, 135; World War II for, 40–41

Unorganized Militia of United States, 56
UNSKKK. See United North & Southern
  Knights of the KKK

vandalism, 84, 86
Vanderboegh, Michael, 58–59
Vinlanders Social Club (VSC), 149
violence, 183n17, 183n19; in activism, 92,
  98–99, 155; against African Americans,
  36, 47; antiabortion, 26–28; from
  anti-Semitism, 63; Brady Handgun
  Violence Prevention Act, 104; crime
  and, 148–149; democracy and, 94;
  demographics and, 111–112; in domestic
  terrorism, 4–7, 57–58; by far right, 4–7,
  10, 71, 90, 95, 96–98, 98–100, 111–112,
  165, 166; fatalities from, 81, 82, 83;
  geographical distribution of, 107, 108–109,
  110–111; at Greensboro Massacre, 10, 47;
  history of, 26–27; ideology for, 116–117,
  159–160; against Jews, 11, 66–67; of KKK,
  39; leadership and, 68–69; lethality of,
  119, 119; by militias, 2, 58–59, 77–81, 78;
  against minorities, 6–7, 44, 110; against
  National Guard, 57; perpetrators of,
  113–115, 125–127; policies for, 100, 101–105,
  105–107; political, 4, 72, 113–114, 117–118,
  124, 151–152, 183n17, 183n19; pro-life,
  27–28; psychology of, 8, 151–152; rhetoric
  for, 133; Romantic Violence, 49; tactics
  for, 72–77, 73, 75, 77, 87–89; in terrorism,
  81, 163; theoretical explanations for,
  94–95; Violent Crime Control and Law
  Enforcement Act, 104; for white
  supremacy, 1–4
Viper Militia, 57
Volksfront, 140
VSC. See Vinlanders Social Club

Waco incident, 54, 176n108
WAR. See White Aryan Resistance
WAR-associated skinhead groups (WAR
  Skin), 51

Warren, Earl, 101

WAR Skin. *See* WAR-associated skinhead groups

Watchman of Israel (Beauchamp), 61

Weaver, Randy, 176n108

Weaver, Samuel, 176n108

Weaver, Vicki, 176n108

Western Hammerskin (WSN), 52

White Aryan Resistance (WAR), 45, 49–52

White Patriot Party, 11

white supremacy: African Americans for, 11; in Deep South, 107, 110; demographics of, 36; elections and, 142–143; in Europe, 3; fundamentalist, 24–26; government against, 46–47; history of, 10; ideology of, 50–51; media promotion for, 37; militias for, 11–12; NSWPP, 42; in politics, 4–5, 42, 58; psychology of, 126; publicity for, 51–52; social movements for, 18–21; UKA for, 44; in United States, 137, 159–160; violence for, 1–4

white supremacy movement, 1–2

Whole Woman's Health v. Hellerstedt, 105

Wild, Joseph, 60

Wilkinson, Bill, 45–46

Wilson, John, 60

World War I, 37

World War II, 40–41, 61–62

Wray, Christopher, 5

WSN. *See* Western Hammerskin

xenophobia, 15–16

YouTube, 144

Zald, Mayer, 18

Zimmerman, George, 138

Zionist Occupation Government (ZOG), 66

Columbia Studies in Terrorism and Irregular Warfare

Bruce Hoffman, Series Editor

CPSIA information can be obtained
at www.ICGtesting.com
Printed in the USA
LVHW011458101220
673827LV00003B/3

9 780231 167116